The
Astrology
Advantage

The Astrology Advantage

Use Your Horoscope for Personal
and Professional Success

OPHIRA AND TALI EDUT

The AstroTwins

SIMON ELEMENT
New York   London   Toronto   Sydney   New Delhi

SIMON
ELEMENT

An Imprint of Simon & Schuster, LLC
1230 Avenue of the Americas
New York, NY 10020

First Simon Element hardcover edition August 2024

SIMON ELEMENT is a trademark of Simon & Schuster, LLC

Simon & Schuster: Celebrating 100 Years of Publishing in 2024

For information about special discounts for bulk purchases,
please contact Simon & Schuster Special Sales at 1-866-506-1949
or business@simonandschuster.com.

The Simon & Schuster Speakers Bureau can bring authors to your live event.
For more information or to book an event, contact the Simon & Schuster Speakers
Bureau at 1-866-248-3049 or visit our website at www.simonspeakers.com.

Interior design by Davina Mock-Maniscalco

Manufactured in the United States of America

1   3   5   7   9   10   8   6   4   2

Library of Congress Cataloging-in-Publication Data has been applied for.

ISBN 978-1-6680-1720-3
ISBN 978-1-6680-1722-7 (ebook)

Contents

Introduction:

The Astrology Advantage

Do you ever wish that the people in your life came with an instruction manual? That you could understand their real motives, find empathy, and settle your differences fast?

Turns out, we *are* all born with a mystical manual of sorts. It's called your astrological chart, and it's a map of the planets overhead at your exact moment of birth.

As the founders of the popular daily horoscope site Astrostyle .com, the astrologers for *ELLE* since 2009, and the authors of over twenty books and counting, we've been sharing its secrets with more than twenty million people a month for nearly three decades. We also co-created the first astrology-based reality dating show, *Cosmic Love*, which streamed on Amazon Prime Video. (Spending six weeks as matchmakers at a Malibu mansion was one of the more interesting parts of this profession!)

When we were first introduced to astrology some thirty years ago, instant curiosity struck. There was a personality test based on our birthdays that could make life less confusing? Sign us up!

Learning about our zodiac sign (Sagittarius, in case you're wondering) was validating in ways that surprised us. It explained so much about who we'd always been—our humor, our eclectic social groups, and our can-do approach to life. And those other eleven zodiac signs? Well, our friends, foes, and family pretty much fit theirs to a tee.

At the time, we were University of Michigan art students on the cusp of graduation. Life was about to fill up with huge decisions we didn't feel equipped to make. Astrology looked like a system that could help with that.

When we dove deeper into our moon and rising signs, and then did a full birth chart of all our planets, we were galactically gobsmacked. The accuracy was astonishing! For the first time, we felt permission to be complex humans. As identical twins, it was even cooler, because we could see the different ways each of us expressed these personality traits.

After starting careers in magazine publishing and web design in the 1990s, we went on to become professional astrologers, launching with our first column in *Teen People* magazine in 2002. To get there, we plowed through a treasure trove of New Age astrology books and first-generation astrology software. We interrogated our friends about their birth times, and looked at thousands of natal charts to understand what all the complicated patterns meant. It was like learning how to code a website, a task that we also mastered simultaneously. (Coincidence?) In short order, we gave a live astrology chart reading to Beyoncé, wrote our first book, and began building a platform at Astrostyle.com. The world, it seemed, really wanted this knowledge too.

As die-hard skeptics who were anything *but* "witchy," we were shocked to find ourselves leaping from curiosity to full-on adoption after seeing our full birth chart. We certainly didn't intend to use our undergraduate degrees to launch an astrology platform. But there was no denying the gut-punch of truth that struck as we read the printed, coil-bound document containing our birth chart. This information was more than mere "confirmation bias." Much more.

For fellow critical thinkers whose first response is to dismiss astrology, or to view it as an affront to common sense, we say this: We hear you. We get you. We *were* you.

Just remember that a skeptic and a cynic are two different things. A *cynic* denies a hypothesis outright, never even testing or trying it for themselves. The mere existence of the unknown threatens them.

A *skeptic* suspends judgment—swims against the mighty current of their own knowledge base (and, dare we say it, human ego)—and tries the damn thing on. If it's not a fit or it doesn't click after you investigate, cool. Onward. Thanks for stopping by.

Consider this: What if a moment of curiosity, of willingness, could open dimensions of yourself you never would have accessed otherwise?

The spirituality of today is a fruitful realm for cynics and skeptics alike. Most believers disguise their connection to the divine, diminish it, dismiss it with words like "woo-woo." The subtext is, *I'm normal. I'm not part of some cult. I'm an intelligent, informed, and science-backed person. But I've also seen some things I can't explain or deny.*

That dissonance can be disorienting for many people, leading us to hide or downplay our interest in astrology, numerology, "signs from the universe," and other wonder-inducing phenomena. But this is changing. A few decades ago, yoga, plant-based diets, and meditation were not yet normalized by the mainstream, and were considered as fringe as some still regard astrology today.

Here's hoping that the cultural acceptance of spiritually supportive tools continues to grow.

Shortly after our first birth chart experience, we started to think of astrology as the "source code" that programs every human. Naturally, we wanted everyone to have access to it. But we soon learned that astrology has a marketing problem. Like JavaScript or CSS, it's not simple to master. It's also stigmatized, thanks to fluffy tabloid horoscopes that could apply to anyone ("you'll bump into an intriguing person today . . .") and snake oil practitioners who've populated the public face of the "brand." Don't worry, our eyes are rolling right along with yours.

Done right, astrology is a spiritual science, a personality test on steroids (star-oids?), and a helpful inner guidance system. It can tell you uncannily accurate things about yourself that can't just be dismissed as random coincidence. After looking at thousands of charts, we feel confident in astrology's people-hacking and problem-solving powers. We've seen it change perspectives with the speed and simplicity that personal breakthroughs sometimes demand.

Luckily, a crisis isn't required to benefit from astrology. It's remarkably effective for navigating the day-to-day choices that can paralyze us with uncertainty. Did you know that the average adult makes over thirty-five thousand decisions a day? There's a reason experts have coined the term "decision fatigue." With the Astrology Advantage, we hope to dramatically reduce yours!

While it's amazing to interpret all those symbols and squiggles on a birth chart, most people don't have the mental bandwidth to learn this new lexicon. That can be too steep a price of admission for astrology's real benefits.

We knew there had to be a better way! This book is our dedication to making one.

INTRODUCING: THE I*AM ARCHETYPES (INNOVATOR, AUTHORITY, MAVEN)

With the Astrology Advantage, you no longer have to master astrology—or even know it—to tap into its power and advantage.

We distilled key parts of astrology into an archetype system, I*AM, that anyone can put into practice. It's designed for the person who wants to *use* astrology as a helpful guidance system for timing, planning, or navigating difficult dynamics—without having to *learn* it.

And we've got you covered. I*AM shorthands your full astrological chart into one of three archetypes: I (Innovator), A (Authority), or M (Maven). It's the cosmic version of your favorite personality test: Myers-Briggs, the Enneagram, CliftonStrengths . . . the list goes on. Behold: this book is your cosmic CliffsNotes!

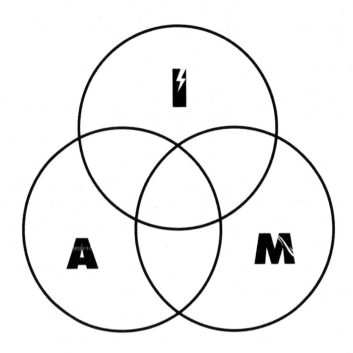

The I*AM algorithm we created encapsulates the full magic of your chart—thirteen points of it, to be exact. Then, it shows you exactly how to use your unique cosmic code to gain the Astrology Advantage. The beautiful part is that you don't have to remember where Venus was when you were born (or Saturn or Mars or any other planet).

We've tested this system to great success with thousands of clients, students, and business owners. We've given workshops to CEOs and C-suite execs at some of the biggest and most successful companies to help their team building, performance, and management. We even created a yearlong membership program for spiritual entrepreneurs and experts, who designed businesses with a complete I*AM curriculum.

As the unofficial "plug-in oracles" for our friend groups, women's circles, professional organizations, and almost any community or team we join, we know the I*AM System works because the people we've shared it with actually retain it and adopt it. You probably remember your Enneagram type or your Myers-Briggs profile, right? Or at least, whether you're an introvert or an extrovert? Like these tools, the I*AM System can be put into practice right away. This book will show you how.

Once you understand *your* primary archetype—Innovator, Authority, or Maven—you'll be excited to learn about the other two profiles. We recommend that! After all, we don't live on this planet alone. Differences are too often the source of friction and conflict. But it's not the differences that are the problem, it's our lack of understanding about them. Most of us erroneously expect others to see the world exactly as we do, and to behave accordingly. Big mistake. Understanding the I*AM archetype of your colleague, partner, children, or parents can give you the grace and space to truly experience "I'm okay, you're okay." Even your adversaries can become your allies when you both start playing to your natural strengths!

When you're ready to dig deeper into the I*AM System, you'll discover that the thirteen points in your chart add up to a specific I*AM score, which incorporates all three archetypes. Almost everyone we know is a blend of Innovator, Authority, and Maven placements in a unique mix. (We *have* seen a couple cases where someone has zero of one of the archetypes, but it's rare!)

In our case, we have six Innovator points, four Authority, and three Maven. Technically that makes us "low on Maven," so we know that's an energy that we need to either consciously cultivate for the sake of balance—or bring Mavens onto our team so we can play to our natural Innovator strengths. We've seen people who have ten Authority points and no Innovator, and others who have an equal hybrid, such as five Innovator, five Authority, and three Maven. Don't worry, we cover the hybrid profiles here too! Those folks have amazing range.

The best part about an astrological personality test? There's no quiz, no assessment to leave you wondering if you answered right. All you need is your birth date, place, and time to calculate your I*AM archetype. (If you don't know the time, there are workarounds, too, which we cover on page 18.)

WHY YOU NEED THE ASTROLOGY ADVANTAGE

A system is best when you can immediately apply it. It should be practical and serve a day-to-day purpose. It should also help you make better decisions, optimize your time, and figure out how to invest your energy into the competing demands of work, family, and relationships. In short, a good system helps you better understand the psyche of yourself and of those around you, and use that knowledge to be more successful, personally and professionally.

In *The Astrology Advantage*, we'll show you how to use your cosmic blueprint—your I*AM archetype—to optimize countless parts of your life. For our astro-geeks, there's an optional section on the astrology of I*AM.

And you'll get a clear, easy map—written in plain English and not astro-jargon—with sections on topics as diverse as relationships, parenting, personal style, home design, and career. Dig in and discover how to use the I*AM System for:

Satisfying work. Craft a career path and daily routine that's productive and set to your natural rhythms.

Thriving relationships. Finally make peace with the different ways you and your loved ones are wired, and create compromises that don't feel like you're settling.

Impactful communication. Learn what each archetype needs to feel heard, and how you can express yourself most effectively.

Supportive environments. From your ideal workspace to your home layout, figure out what you need to thrive.

Personal style. How can you outwardly adorn yourself to bring out your most compelling traits?

Functioning families. How to navigate daily dynamics with parents, kids, and relatives using the I*AM System.

It's not an accident that we chose the declaration "I am" for this system. It's a phrase that holds the power to unlock your magic and your soul's purpose.

Think about it: How much time do we spend saying "I'm not" or "I don't" or "I can't" or "I wish"? Our conversations, at least our internal ones, are steeped in scarcity and latched on to lack.

Or, we misuse the term "I am" to present a false image to the world so nobody sees us struggle ("I'm a lawyer" or "I'm a mom of three"). This supposed advantage actually puts us at a *disadvantage*, because we trap ourselves in a narrow box and are never free to be our full, multidimensional selves. It becomes performative, contrived, and based on "who I want you to *think* I am." Being fake is exhausting (just ask anyone who's ever had an Instagram account). It limits us. How can we discover our soul's purpose if we're always trying to convince the world that we've got it all figured out? There's no space left for the experiments and struggles that help us grow.

What astrology taught us is that every human being contains not only multitudes but a pastiche of paradoxes and contradictions. We're messy, complex, and our own biggest blind spots. By virtue of this, we have some automatic disadvantages—and astrology can help offset those.

That's why knowing your birth chart—your cosmic code—is the gift we want every human to have. Suddenly, you're able to see yourself with objective distance. You're no longer a victim of the judgments, thoughts, and prejudices people may have about you. You can see others through more tolerant eyes, too. It's like having a superpower.

Finally, you can say "I am THIS *and* I am also THAT." You can own your paradoxes and humanity. "I am an accomplished business-person *and* I am also someone who typically procrastinates." Or, "I'm in a loving marriage *and* I love spending time by myself."

The next question this system answers is: Why? The Astrology Advantage allows you to learn, for example, *why* you might procrastinate . . . and to do something about it besides beating yourself up or trying to be someone you aren't. It's a planetary permission slip to be more of who you already are, to work with your natural rhythms.

As you learn about your cosmic wiring in this book, you may discover that you procrastinate because you're an Authority who doesn't have a sense of security and you can't focus on the task in front of you until you do. Or you're an Innovator feeling unproductive in an open-plan office because you really need to hole up at a quiet park bench to do your best thinking. Or you're a Maven trying to pigeonhole yourself into a nine-to-five job when you're meant to be a multi-hyphenate creative!

As business owners for over thirty years, we've often heard the advice that "What got you here won't get you to the next level." And it's true. We need an advantage beyond the ones that come from the ever-shifting external world. Imagine if *your* advantage wasn't limited by the job market, the economy, your relationship status, and so on—because it came from within you! *That's* the birthright that lies in your birth chart.

J. P. Morgan is famously quoted as saying that "millionaires don't use astrology, but billionaires do." While this might be an urban legend, the sentiment resonates: *the people who listen to the universe receive its bounty.*

It's no secret that many US Founding Fathers, including Benjamin Franklin and Thomas Jefferson, were Freemasons who tapped the power of the stars. Franklin's wildly popular almanacs contained *ephemerides*—day-by-day charts of where the known planets would appear in the sky, which was divided by zodiac signs, along with new and full moons and eclipses. Good old Ben, aided by the new technology of the printing press, understood the power of having the Astrology Advantage.

Ben Franklin never openly claimed to be an astrologer. But consider this: For centuries, astronomy and astrology were not viewed as separate. Scientists didn't rule out spirituality or mystery when they discovered a mathematical equation or a miracle of physics. Instead, it brought everyone closer to the divine.

Today, people say things to us like, "I'm a scientist, so I don't believe in astrology." Guess what: there's nothing to believe in! Astrology is a tool and a system, a cosmic calculator and a measurement of where the known planets are from our vantage point on Earth.

This binary, *either/or, do/don't* mindset is a newer development, catalyzed by twentieth-century industrial and technological progress. As humans began to rely on the machine, we forgot that *we* aren't machines ourselves!

Astrology is an attempt to recover and reclaim our "pre-mechanical" selves. After all, what good is it to gain technological advantages and squander our spiritual ones? We've lost touch with that original celestial source code that's already scripted in us, the very spark that makes us unique. Cutting off connection to mystery and consciousness has left us isolated, divided, and adrift from purpose.

We want you to reconnect to what evolutionary astrologer Steven Forrest calls "the poetry of the sky." In it, you will find your own verse and song, your uniqueness. You'll find your Astrology Advantage.

HOW THIS BOOK IS STRUCTURED FOR YOU

In the first part of *The Astrology Advantage*, you'll learn about the I*AM archetypes and, if you're curious, the astrology behind this methodology (it's completely optional, but we know that astrology can be a captivating rabbit hole, and we're here to satisfy your curiosity if it strikes!). Get ready to exhale a huge sigh of relief as you find permission to be your complex yet perfectly designed self.

Next, we'll give you the Astrology Advantage to professional success—from effective communication, to productivity and time management, to designing the ideal workspace, to building a successful team that brings out everyone's best. Imagine each member of your organization working in a role, schedule, and flow completely suited to their nature. That's how we run our twenty-year-strong company, Astrostyle, and have a joyful team where everyone is in their zone, growing and learning at the pace that's right for them. We want your workplace, community, and organization to have this Astrology Advantage too!

Lastly, we'll show you how to use your I*AM archetype in your personal life and relationships. You'll unlock your Astrology Advantage with relationships, family, home decor, style, parenting, and more. Not only can we all benefit from an instruction manual to *ourselves*, but we could certainly use one for the people we love most—no matter how well we think we know them.

Enough talking about I*AM. Let's start using it—together!

Calculate your I*AM Type at
https:// astrostyle.com/ iam

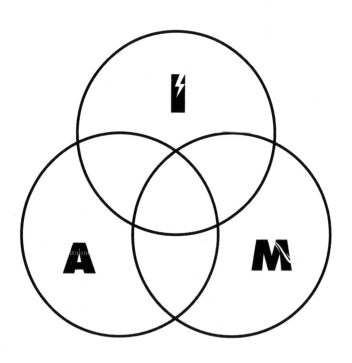

The I*AM System

WHAT EXACTLY IS THE I*AM SYSTEM?

The I*AM System is a new personality test, created by us, that uses astrology to identify your personal success archetype by calculating data from thirteen planetary points in your astrological birth chart.

There are three distinct I*AM archetypes, determined by your time, date, and place of birth:

I = **Innovator**
A = **Authority**
M = **Maven**

Innovators come up with big ideas that push us out of our comfort zones and thrust us into the future. Their lives are laboratories, an endless stream of experiments (some better than others). Drivers of progress, these disruptors and visionaries defy categorization. Their astrological charts contain mostly cardinal signs: Aries, Cancer, Libra, Capricorn.

Authorities are the trustworthy types who like responsibility and structure. They can take an Innovator's ideas and map them to a schedule or plan. Authorities skew conventional, even mainstream, in their tastes—no matter how refined. They are the safe harbor that many people count on. Their astrological charts contain mostly fixed signs: Taurus, Leo, Scorpio, Aquarius.

Mavens are the info sponges and entertainers, the hosts with the most. Once the Authority has made the plan, they're the marketing and PR department. Mavens embrace change and keep us from getting stagnant. Their role is to spread ideas to the masses and help them gain adoption. Their astrological charts contain mostly mutable signs: Gemini, Virgo, Sagittarius, Pisces.

WHICH I*AM ARCHETYPE AM I?

So, what exactly determines whether you're an Innovator, Authority, or Maven? We used a method in astrology called the modalities (or qualities) to distill the essence of your chart into an I*AM archetype.

Your I*AM score is determined by how many of the thirteen main planets and placements in your birth chart are in each of the qualities. These thirteen points include the Sun, Moon, ascendant (rising sign), lunar nodes, plus Mercury, Venus, Mars, Jupiter, Saturn, Uranus, Neptune, and Pluto.

The astrological chart is a map of the sky overhead based on your exact time, date, and location of birth, a blueprint of your personality, strengths, and challenges. Later in the book, we'll explain more about the astrology behind I*AM—which you are free to read or skip if you'd rather *not* delve that far into the "system behind this system." But we know many of you will want to learn more and more as you go! We also add in the four elements to give you a deeper cut on your I*AM archetype after you learn more about it.

HOW TO CALCULATE YOUR I*AM PROFILE

Finding your archetype is easy with our free I*AM Calculator: https://astrostyle.com/iam

To find your I*AM archetype, you'll need the same three pieces of information that you do for a traditional astrological birth chart:

- Your date of birth (month, day, year)

- Your place of birth (city, state, country)

- Your time of birth

Don't know your exact birth time? If you're eager to discover your I*AM archetype right now, enter 12:00 noon as a placeholder. (More on how to find your birth time or work around not having it a little later in this section.)

Your Primary I*AM Archetype

When you calculate your I*AM, you will be given your primary archetype. There are three primary archetypes possible:

1. Innovator

2. Authority

3. Maven

Just as you would read a horoscope for your sun sign ("I'm a total Scorpio, loyal to the end!" or "Proud Aries here."), you'll read this book for your primary archetype. For example, if you're a Maven, focus on the Maven sections of every chapter to unpack the information about yourself.

In rarer cases, people have a hybrid of two primary archetypes. If that's you, read for both archetypes in the chapters to follow. Yes, it's more to take in, but lucky you! Hybrid I*AM folks have amazing range and can be some of the most versatile people on the planet. The three hybrid archetypes are:

1. Innovator-Authority Hybrid

2. Innovator-Maven Hybrid

3. Authority-Maven Hybrid

How Do I Interpret the Numbers in My I*AM Score?

When you read your I*AM results, you will see numbers corresponding to each of the three archetypes, shortened to **I**, **A**, and **M**.

This represents how the thirteen astrological placements used in the I*AM algorithm assemble themselves based on *your* unique moment of birth. Seeing this, you can get an idea of how balanced you are between the energies.

The I, A, and M split varies between people. We've seen some evenly balanced with 4 Innovator, 4 Authority, and 5 Maven. That would make one a Maven who has a good deal of facility with the traits of the Innovator and Authority.

Other I*AM results are wildly skewed in one direction: 0 Innovator, 9 Authority, and 4 Maven. That's a clear-cut Authority there!

YOUR IAM SCORE		
3	**6**	**4**
Innovator	Authority	Maven

While you're bound to relate strongly to your primary archetype, don't stop there. Understanding the traits of all three archetypes is the key to living a truly balanced life.

We recommend borrowing another archetype's habits, especially if you score low in one of the three I*AM categories. Or maybe you bring in a team to "fill in the blanks" so you can excel where *your* primary archetype is strong.

Our I*AM calculation (as twins we have the same one, but not all twins do) gives us this split: 6 Innovator, 4 Authority, and 3 Maven. Innovator is our primary archetype while our chart is low on Maven, an energy we often have to balance for through conscious effort.

As you learn the I*AM System, you'll gain access to the full range of energies across the three I*AM archetypes. We'll show you how!

What Astrology Is Used to Calculate My I*AM Archetype?

If you want to learn more about the astrology of I*AM, we've got you covered in this book. In the next section, we explain the planets, zodiac signs, and other starry stuff we used to derive your I*AM profile.

Do I Need to Understand Astrology to Use I*AM?

Not at all! You're welcome to skim that section, bookmark it for later, or skip it altogether. You don't have to become an astrologer to get maximum benefits from this book.

In fact, that's exactly *why* we created I*AM! This system is a bridge to fill the knowledge gap for the many people who desire astrology's benefits but don't want to retain or learn its mechanics.

Is I*AM the Same Thing as My Birth Chart or Natal Chart?

Essentially, yes. It's calculated using all the same planets and points we'd look at in a traditional birth chart reading. The I*AM System allows you to use your astrological birth chart as a guiding tool without having to learn the complex craft of chart interpretation or to know any astrology at all.

I Don't Know My Birth Time. What Should I Do?

Many people don't know their birth time, which is especially important for determining the ascendant (rising sign). You can still use the calculator, but know that at least one of the points won't be accurate. If you were born in the US and your birth certificate doesn't list your birth time, there's one more place to check! The Office of Vital Records in your state of birth may have full records that include the documented time.

THE 6 I*AM ARCHETYPES AND HYBRID ARCHETYPES

Meet the I*AM Archetypes: Innovator, Authority, and Maven

By now, you've calculated your I*AM and have found your primary archetype, which is either Innovator, Authority, Maven, or one of the three hybrids: Innovator-Authority, Innovator-Maven, or Authority-Maven. You'll learn how to flex your archetype to gain the Astrology Advantage in every area of life.

First, the basics. Let's get into what these archetypes mean!

Innovator (I)

Innovators are the fire-starters and the "first responders" of the I*AM System. Their birth charts are mostly comprised of cardinal signs (Aries, Cancer, Libra, Capricorn), the zodiac signs that start each season (spring, summer, fall, winter). Not only do Innovators embrace the new, but they also embody it! Tireless trailblazers, their visionary powers help them see possibilities where others only see roadblocks—if they see anything at all.

The downside of being so ahead of the curve? Well, Innovators can risk the pitfalls of wrong timing, or they could be typecast as eccentric rebels without a cause. Their bold ideas may not be embraced by the mainstream until years later, and in some cases, they may never even get credit for them. But when they *do* set a trend that catches on, get ready for an adoring fan club! Their ultimate role is as thought leaders and trailblazers. People count on them to spark a winning idea or plan. Then, Innovators leverage their impressive networks or fanbases to make their novel concepts part of the zeitgeist.

What motivates them: Being first, connecting dots, birthing movements

Superpowers: Style, self-assuredness, ability to make something out of nothing

Path to success: Having the "It Factor"

Pitfalls: Being elitist, exclusionary, too "out-there" or far ahead of the curve

Keywords: Leader, pioneer, futurist, tastemaker, trendsetter, trailblazer, idea machine

Astrology Advantage: Innovators are willing to take a risk when nobody else will

Cosmic profile: Charts are mostly cardinal signs (Aries, Cancer, Libra, Capricorn)

Authority (A)

Systematic and sensible, Authorities are often the voice of mindfulness and moderation, the diplomats who can stand the heat because they know how to play it cool. Their charts are primarily composed of fixed signs (Taurus, Leo, Scorpio, Aquarius), the mid-season zodiac signs that keep us consistent and stable. For Authorities, the secret to success is simple: following instructions! Authorities are the "how-to" types who love a proven, step-by-step method for success. And once they master those moves, they might just create a winning system of their own.

While Authorities can be talented performers and artists (all those long hours of practice), many are content staying out of the spotlight— at least, when they're not on duty. When it comes to their life's work or a message they believe in, recognition matters to the Authority. These hard workers toil through hours of study, research, labor, and certification programs. After paying these dues, they want the respect and acknowledgment they deserve!

What motivates them: Stability, recognition, mastery

Superpowers: Patience, persistence, determination, integrity

Path to success: Paying dues and earning their place at the top

Pitfalls: Being rigid, following instructions to the letter, timidness, need for praise, people pleasing

Keywords: Expert, public figure, project manager, do-er, award-winner, achiever

Astrology Advantage: Authorities can cut through chaos and identify what really matters

Cosmic profile: Charts are mostly fixed signs (Taurus, Leo, Scorpio, Aquarius)

Maven (M)

Curious, collaborative Mavens are the messengers of the world! Their birth charts are primarily composed of mutable signs (Gemini, Virgo, Sagittarius, Pisces), which fall at the end of each season. They are the editors, the ones who come in and add the finishing touch that makes the whole project sing. Since Mavens are more flexible and comfortable with change than the other two archetypes, they can "chameleon" to fit into a variety of situations and social groups.

While they've got plenty of original material, the Maven's true superpower is taking someone's lofty or lesser-known concepts and making them utterly viral. Mavens are the editors and publicists of the zodiac—the ones who complete the package with a winning touch and are gifted at making almost any topic sound irresistible. Their role is to be the change agents, evangelists, conversation-starters, and spreaders of ideas. They need to find a path that allows them to express a wide range of their talents. A social role that involves teams, interactivity, and communication, and harnesses their natural people skills is where Mavens shine.

> **What motivates them:** Novelty (fun! shiny! new!), community, making connections
>
> **Superpowers:** Cleverness, charisma, inclusivity, the gift of gab, witty wordplays
>
> **Path to success:** Making everything go viral
>
> **Pitfalls:** Coming across as a BS artist, all talk/no action
>
> **Keywords:** Messenger, hype machine, cultural celebrity, trend spreader, cheerleader

Astrology Advantage: Mavens are community and team builders who bring people together

Cosmic profile: Charts are mostly mutable signs (Gemini, Virgo, Sagittarius, Pisces)

Meet the Hybrids: Innovator-Authority, Innovator-Maven, Authority-Maven

Because there are thirteen data points in I*AM, some people's spread will be an even split between two of the archetypes (6, 6, and 1). If you're a hybrid, lucky you! You have twice as much of an Astrology Advantage than others, with easy access to the energies of not just three, but *six* signs. That's half the zodiac! Read the sections for both of your primary archetypes as you move through this book.

Innovator-Authority (IA)

The Innovator-Authority has trailblazing ideas aplenty, thanks to their Innovator DNA. But the systematic Authority walks that talk and needs to translate any lofty concepts into a form that's ready for mass adoption. The Innovator-Authority hybrid is able to see the future *and* live in the present, making this hybrid type quite the super-producer. (Imagine the gifted musician who also remixes their own album.) They fashion original concepts into tangible form, and they're not afraid to put in the hard work to do it. The IA may be struck by "eureka" moments out of the blue and will need to disappear for a block of time to get the idea on paper. They may even emerge from the "laboratory" with a full-fledged product ready to launch.

What motivates them: Complex concepts, building something new, producing something epic

Superpowers: Stamina, strategic thinking, determination, persistence, vision, foresight

Path to success: Changing "business as usual"

Pitfalls: Workaholism, single-mindedness, elitism, ego

Keywords: Producer-director, wunderkind, fearless leader, visionary

Astrology Advantage: Innovator-Authorities don't just dream up big ideas, they bring them to life

Cosmic profile: Charts are mostly cardinal signs (Aries, Cancer, Libra, Capricorn) and fixed signs (Taurus, Leo, Scorpio, Aquarius)

Innovator-Maven (IM)

Innovator-Mavens have lots of ideas and a million more for how to share them. But without the grounded, systematic Authority in their profiles, they can get scattered in their execution, and risk falling into the "jack-of-all-trades" category. This type thrives in a role that lets them wear many hats, bouncing between wildly different tasks. Flexible hours and deadlines work best for Innovator-Mavens, as anything too rigid will cramp their childlike spirits. They're happiest when allowed to be their creative, multi-passionate selves, guided by their curiosity and pioneering souls. This can be the archetype of the artist who succeeds after being "discovered" and managed by a savvy agent, or the genius coder whose idea goes viral with a venture capitalist's backing.

What motivates them: Disrupting the status quo, exploring and sharing new ideas, a creative challenge

Superpowers: Spontaneity, courage, ingenuity, insatiable curiosity, willingness to try new things

Path to success: Proving that the "impossible" is possible

Pitfalls: Impracticality, destructiveness, chaos, burning through resources, lack of discipline

Keywords: Magicians, entertainment directors, scientists, philosophers

Astrology Advantage: Innovator-Mavens are versatile shape-shifters who have serious range!

Cosmic profile: Charts are mostly cardinal signs (Aries, Cancer, Libra, Capricorn) and mutable signs (Gemini, Virgo, Sagittarius, Pisces)

Authority-Maven (AM)

The Authority-Maven is the original "edu-tainer," a natural teacher (Authority) who makes learning fun (Maven). Whether a credentialed or self-made expert, these super-producers won't hide out in any ivory tower or dish out dry, academic fodder for elite eyes only. Authority-Maven hybrids have a flair for bringing complex concepts to the everyday person, empowering them with savvy shortcuts and hacks. This archetype can thrive by sharing "how I did it" stories, especially presented in a media-savvy and fun style (think: the thirty-second TikTok expert). They can talk about the same topic fifty different ways, and somehow, it never sounds boring.

What motivates them: Studying new and old ideas, passing on wisdom, telling stories

Superpowers: Style, self-assuredness, resourcefulness, engaging presence

Path to success: Being the "savvy sage"

Pitfalls: Analysis paralysis, performance anxiety, getting lost in the weeds

Keywords: Expert, teacher, way-shower, impresario

Astrology Advantage: Authority-Mavens excel at distilling complex data into a fun, teachable format

Cosmic profile: Charts are mostly fixed signs (Taurus, Leo, Scorpio, Aquarius) and mutable signs (Gemini, Virgo, Sagittarius, Pisces)

Innovator Cheat Sheet

Core Driver: Creativity

Core Value: Freedom

Anchored In: The Future

Ingenious, independent, irreverent, and all about "I," the Innovator is a pioneer and a paradox rolled into one ever-changing being. Freedom is everything and Innovators won't trade theirs for the security of a steady job or relationship—at least, not without some serious cosmic claustrophobia. Having a future that excites them is what gets the Innovator leaping out of bed every day.

In life. Innovators are visionaries who live in the future tense. They hate small talk, narrow minds, and anything they view as provincial. The world worth being in is "out there" in the distant, aspirational realm, among people who are "up to things" in life. Innovators are mostly confident in their opinions, but they may not vocalize them because others often don't understand their futuristic concepts and may shoot their ideas down. Their discerning ways can come across as elitist, snobbish, or entitled without them realizing it.

In love and relationships. Independent and eclectic, Innovators don't always have a type—at least, not a physical one. Their partners had better be smart, savvy, and willing to put up with their sometimes outrageous demands for freedom. Innovators can frustrate their mates because they can't be pinned down or forced to follow convention. (Planning a regular date night? Good luck!) Anything *but* old-fashioned, Innovators need autonomy. They could have their own pied-à-terre, or they might hole up in the spare room while their sweetie is aching to canoodle on the couch. Does it feel like everything's on *their* terms? Um, yes. But their fascinating and fearless approach to life makes it worth the trouble. Dating an Innovator feels like always being on the cusp of something big happening, a steady and heady dopamine rush from their absolute addiction to novelty. Even Innovators who follow convention will have a rebellious streak, delivering the sexy mystery that keeps everyone on the edge of their seat. Hot!

At home. Since Innovators are constantly immersed in projects, it can be hard for family to hold their attention. It's not that they don't care about others, but Innovators prioritize chemistry over biology. They get easily swept up in a charismatic new connection or passion project, which can breed resentment among "neglected" relatives. In fact, their loved ones tend to get the leftovers. Can't beat the Innovator's wandering spirit? Join 'em on their adventures! A family creative project, like building a hydroponic vegetable garden or starting an Etsy shop, allows the Innovator's creativity to be rolled into quality time with their clan.

At work. Innovators are independent. They need lots of breathing room and no micromanaging. Natural leaders, they do well with their own turf. But they run into issues when they have to follow someone else's hierarchy, plan, or timeline. Innovators work best when inspiration strikes, whether that's at 3:00 p.m. or 3:00 a.m. Deadlines are subject to interpretation. Innovators may be best suited as entrepreneurs, business owners, or "intrapreneurs" running their own department according to their blueprint. Even then, they are likely to shift roles and have an eclectic career path immersed in cutting-edge developments that combine culture, tech, society, or arts.

Off duty. Is there such a thing? Life, work, and adventure constantly overlap and bleed into each other for the Innovator. Whatever sparks a sense of expansiveness and discovery will pull the Innovator into the next spontaneous adventure (which might just turn into a business or brand-new lifestyle).

Best role. Initiating new ideas, working on a project or role with a lot of independence, being the visionary

Worst role. Anything that requires them to answer to too many other people or follow someone else's master agenda

Authority Cheat Sheet

Core Driver: Clarity

Core Value: Longevity

Anchored In: The Past

The stable, able Authority sets the pace and keeps the rest of the world steady. Linear and structured, these hardworking builders prefer to go deep rather than wide. They're also quite nostalgic, at times ruminating on the past. Brick by brick, they construct their domains and rack up achievements through hard work and practice. That's how they earn their rank as Authority, after all. By investing in their own proficiency and working hard toward mastery, they become the eventual experts. Authorities take pride in their work and like to achieve. They are best served by finding their "lane" in life and getting better and better at it each day.

In Life. Authorities are achievers who strive for "a life well-lived." Moderate and even stoic at times, they take their commitments seriously. Financial and emotional stability is their aim in life, and they approach risk with great caution. Since they are often building a legacy or striving toward a goal (such as a master's degree or winning a competition), Authorities always need to build on a firm foundation. While they're interested in trends, they're not prone to mindlessly following or setting them—at least, not on purpose. These natural experts are the "how-to" people, here to break systems into simplified steps that can be mastered through dedication and practice. Authorities can be hard on themselves (and others) for mistakes. They need permission to experiment and not be perfect.

In love and relationships. Authorities want long-term stability from their love lives. They don't enter or exit relationships lightly. The conventional romance script is probably at least 90 percent fine by them. After all, they'd rather build a satisfying life with their "person" than waste time getting no return on their emotional investments. Devoted partners, Authorities love making memories. Their stiff upper lips will quiver looking through photo albums and mementos. The past is either demonized or glorified. While their typically secure "attachment style" makes Authorities model citizens at monogamy, they may stay in an unsatisfying situation because of their devotion or discomfort with rocking the boat. Breakups take them a long time to process. If and when they *do* finally leave, the Authority's habit of learning from experience serves them well. They can apply what they've discovered to their next relationship.

At home. Welcome to the relaxation station. The Authority home is often the favorite hub for friends and family to commune, an oasis from the chaos of the outside world. That's because Authorities innately understand how to create a comfortable, welcoming space where everything (and everyone) has a place. While they might have one of those traditional dining rooms that only gets used once a year or a couple of "do not touch" art pieces, in general, the Authority likes to fill their home with comfort and ease—leaving work and stress far behind.

At work. Without a plan and priorities, Authorities can't function. They like to manage and delegate, and work best in an organization where everyone has a clear-cut role, including them. Natural inspectors and auditors, they can see flaws in the plan that everyone else misses. While this might earn them a reputation as buzzkills, their eagle eyes ensure longevity, not just a splashy launch. Our nine-to-five workday suits Authorities best. They'll roll up their sleeves to get a project past the finish line but prefer consistent hours so they can make the most of their time off, too.

Off duty. This archetype wants clear boundaries between personal and professional time. Don't call them on the weekend and don't disturb them when they're on break. They're the reason "out of office" autoreplies still exist. Call them old-fashioned, but this is how to get the best out of an Authority when they do come back online! Consummate event planners, Authorities can put together an epic party or plan an elaborate, packed vacation itinerary. Curating these plans is their specialty. Authorities also cherish their own downtime and will use it fully to shop, read, cook, or enjoy their hobbies.

Best role. Making plans, managing projects and people, being the experts or knowledge-bearers on a topic, coaching

Worst role. Following a shoddy plan, disrupting the status quo, multitasking

Maven Cheat Sheet

Core Driver: Connection

Core Value: Experience

Anchored In: The Present

Magical, mischievous, and multifaceted, the Maven is a study in dynamic energy. These "always on" people love wearing many hats and might just don them all at once. Restless and dynamic, they live for a peak experience and are the life of the party, full of personality, and down for whatever. But don't let their spirited style fool you: Mavens aren't simply looking for a good time. They are the connectors, community builders, and central communicators of the I*AM archetypes.

Mavens are masterful marketers and talented teachers. They make information digestible and give surprisingly astute feedback. (Thought they couldn't listen and talk at the same time? Guess again!) Their contagious enthusiasm and keen observations help bring great ideas to the masses.

In life. *Carpe diem!* Life was meant to be lived, at least according to Mavens. Experience junkies and information sponges, these crowd-pleasers don't want to miss a moment of the action. If there's a way to squeeze in an extra coffee date or snag concert tickets, Mavens will find a way to RSVP "yes." And these popular people won't be short on invites. Mavens are the superconnectors and community builders who love to share, interact, teach, and learn. While some Mavens sport multiple degrees, most of them prefer to matriculate in the school of life, supplemented with the wisdom of their favorite TED-talking guru. Need a hug? Feel like a dance party? Maven emotions are big, colorful, and immediate. They are empathic mirrors who can be great listeners, offering wise counsel and practically reading other people's minds. They can be excellent mimics because they're so tuned in to everyone, never missing or skipping a detail.

In love and relationships. Forget about long *walks* on the beach. Mavens want long *talks* . . . on the beach, in bed, or just about anywhere. Conversation is the key to the Maven heart, and they love to brainstorm, gossip, and kick around ideas. Mirror, mirror: it's important for a partner to match the Maven's mood and intensity in order to bond with them. They're excited? The other person had better turn up the dial! They're crying? Their significant other needs to get misty-eyed instead of going stony and cold. Common friends (and enemies) are required. Mavens need empathic and nonjudgmental listening from their mates. While they'll give everyone else advice for days, it's much rarer for them to open up and receive it. They tend to mask their most intimate feelings with humor, intellect, or outright avoidance. When a Maven actually shows vulnerability, their heart is in another's hands. But Maven lovers be warned: they could change the emotional channel just as quickly!

At home. Who wants to play? From game night to movie screenings to group dinner parties where everyone prepares part of the meal, Mavens are always ready for fun. Dropping by for a coffee and chat? Door's unlocked. You can join the watch party or craft-making or whatever the Maven's in the middle of when you do. Mavens' experimental style spills into their homes, where their colorful and eclectic personalities are just as bold. To ensure that their many projects don't crowd every corner, Mavens should implement a great organization system to keep clutter at bay. At their best, Mavens can curate the most fascinating spaces. You'll never get bored browsing their bookshelves and curiosities, each one having a special story to go with it.

At work. Unafraid to experiment, Mavens are consummate jugglers who'd rather be busy than bored. The can-do Maven is an asset to any team, capable of doing three people's jobs in one-third of the time. And yet, they still keep the break room, watercooler, and Slack channels alive with the latest buzz and office humor. These super-fast processors would rather have a job done than perfect. They'll speed through tasks, bringing a playful energy to all they do. Get this Maven a workshop! The ultimate tinkerers, Mavens are hands-on types who have piles of projects in various stages of completion. Colleagues and family members may be intimately acquainted with what we call the "Maven Mess." One Maven we know has become a clutter coach after devising ingenious ways to keep her zillion undertakings organized and out of sight. Think: strategically systematized bins, boxes, and binders.

Off duty. Is there a library book to devour? A series to binge? An all-day convention or festival? No second of free time shall be wasted by the Maven. These pop culture vultures and media junkies want to do it all. Natural communicators and social architects, Mavens are all about their friendships. While they fancy themselves inclusive (and will present as such), their radar is always up for like-minded people, and they do tend to run with a crowd, even if they're not as exclusive as Innovators.

Best role. Connecting dots and people, crunching through large amounts of information quickly

Worst role. Having only one main job or role, anything where they feel isolated, repetitive tasks

HOW THE I*AM ARCHETYPES WORK TOGETHER

There's a beautiful interchange between the three I*AM archetypes. When each is playing to their natural strengths, they complete the picture of any project or plan.

Innovators come up with big ideas that push us out of our comfort zones and thrust us into the future. Their lives are laboratories, an endless stream of experiments (some better than others). Drivers of progress, these disruptors and visionaries are here to shake things up!

Authorities are the trustworthy types who like responsibility and structure. They can take an Innovator's ideas and map them to a schedule or plan. When everyone else freaks out, Authorities stay calm and in control. They are the safe harbor that many people count on.

Mavens are the info sponges and entertainers, the hosts with the most. Once the Authority has made the plan, Mavens are the marketing and PR department. They embrace change and keep the rest of us from getting stagnant. Their role is to spread ideas to the masses and help them gain adoption.

And put it all together? If the Innovator says, "Let's start a business!" they'll lay out the initial concept and get everyone inspired: This enterprise will rock people's worlds and disrupt a stagnant market—and the Innovator knows exactly how to swing the hammer for maximum impact. The Authority will get to work with filing LLC paperwork, getting everyone outfitted with the right tools, software, orientation packets, and benefits. Hey, if this company's gonna succeed, the Authority knows that it needs a solid foundation. The Maven will tackle social media and sales, spreading the word through viral posts, company merch or general team-building camaraderie, and at networking events, where the Maven will tell everyone within earshot about their amazing new brand, starting a buzz even before the business officially goes live.

SCORING THE I*AM CHART

When you look at the overall score of your I*AM chart, you may notice that you're high in some areas and low in others. Or perhaps as you read through the descriptions of the archetypes, you'd like to pump up the volume on your plucky Innovator vibe or dial back some of that stern Authority energy. It's always a balancing act!

The I*AM System can help you find your optimal state. We like to call it "Astro-Ayurveda," in the spirit of the Indian and Nepalese practice of tuning the body's energies for optimal health.

When you have five or more planets in one of the I*AM types, you skew high in that area and will strongly express its traits. This can be a natural strength, but at times it can also be too much of a good thing. Three or less of any I*AM archetype is considered low, and you may need to consciously work to bring more of that energy into your life. Some people are a fairly even balance (5-4-4), and while they may have one main archetype, they can easily access the gifts of the other two.

Whatever your breakdown is, you can tap into the principles of Astro-Ayurveda to balance what you have a whole lot or not very much of in your I*AM chart. Here's how to make those adjustments to gain the Astrology Advantage.

High Innovator (5 or more): Natural Leader

You're an excitable, courageous, and motivating leader who's never at a loss for groundbreaking ideas. When you're lit up about a plan, you dive right into action. Trouble is, your "fire, ready, aim" strategy can lead to expensive mistakes, wasted time, and burnout as you hustle around the clock to meet your goals. Adopting a mantra of "go slow to go fast" can be a game-changer, giving you a chance to evaluate decisions before you've set a major mission in motion.

Low Innovator (3 or less): Reluctant Leader

Where did the passion go? No matter how many brilliant ideas you dream up, you're quick to talk yourself out of them, citing a laundry list of all the (completely *unproven*) reasons they won't catch on. Underneath it all, you're afraid to be rejected, criticized, or mocked—to risk being a trailblazer. Details bog you down and you may avoid taking chances on anything that doesn't come with a guarantee. While you'll certainly play it safe, life can feel small and uninspiring. Work to develop a greater risk tolerance, perhaps with outside support from a coach or team that keeps your focus on the end goal and cheers you on when you start to lose your nerve.

High Authority (5 or more): Stickler for Structure

In your well-ordered world, everything is done "just so," creating an impressive outcome that commands respect. Yet, when do you get to let your hair down and relax? Focusing on how things look (including, ahem, your hair) may prevent you from fully engaging with the things you work so hard to create. Moreover, your adherence to rules and procedures can create a tense atmosphere at work and home. The truth is, you're only trying to make people happy! Unfortunately, your focus on results can turn you into a people pleaser. This diverts attention away from the genuinely caring connections that you excel at creating . . . once you take the pressure off yourself!

Low Authority (3 or less): Resistant to Structure

Your eternally youthful spirit is refreshing, but when someone needs to be the adult in the room, you're the last to raise your hand. You may resent anyone who comes across as an "authority figure" and rebel against structures—even if they'd make your life one thousand times easier. As a result, you often run out of money, miss appointments, and frustrate people who are depending on you. Commitments that require a good deal of responsibility can feel frightening, but don't run away! Resilience is a muscle worth building, in the name of having a richer life, deeper relationships, and more meaningful experiences—the things that simply take more time to build.

High Maven (5 or more): Loves to Experiment

Is it recess yet? Your life is organized around playtime; in fact, you'll turn the most mundane task into a game. A true jack-of-all-trades, you enjoy juggling many projects, but it's easy for you to get scattered and overwhelmed. Chaos may follow you, creating rifts with colleagues and anyone who you share space with. Learn to prioritize so you actually finish the brilliant plans that you start. A social butterfly, you easily attract and collect friends. Storytelling is one of your gifts, but you also love gossip. Your loose-lipped style can come back to haunt you, though—and might even burn some important bridges.

Low Maven (3 or less): Afraid to Experiment

You're a creature of habit who's more interested in finding what you love and sticking with it than experimenting with new options. Nothing wrong with having clear desires, but this change-averse attitude can leave you out of the loop, and behind the times. Break out of your well-worn groove periodically and see "what the kids are doing." When it's time to make important decisions, you may freeze or panic. Get a diverse range of opinions before rushing ahead, but don't wait forever! Sometimes you have to take the first step in order to see the whole trail.

START HERE

Calculate your I*AM Type at
https:// astrostyle.com / iam

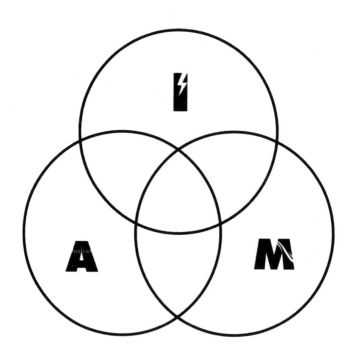

The Astrology Behind I*AM

So what exactly determines whether you're an Innovator, Authority, or Maven? As mentioned earlier, we used a method in astrology called the modalities (or qualities) to distill the essence of your star chart into an I*AM archetype.

Your I*AM score is determined by how many of the thirteen main points in your birth chart are in each of the qualities. These thirteen points include the sun, moon, ascendant (rising sign), lunar nodes, and all the planets from Mercury through Pluto.

THE ASTROLOGY CHART VS. THE I*AM CHART

Since astrological charts contain their own alphabet of symbols and visual markers, learning to interpret them can take time. Viewing your chart as a "chart" (in the modern spreadsheet sense of the word) can make it easy for the layperson to scan and quickly see where they may have a lot of planets in certain qualities.

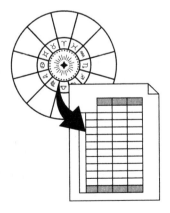

The 3 Modalities

The I*AM System employs one of astrology's two main subclassifications of the twelve zodiac signs, called the modalities or qualities. (The other subset, which we'll touch on later, is the elements: fire, earth, air, and water.)

The modalities divide the zodiac into three distinct groups called cardinal, fixed, and mutable. These groupings are based on the seasons and each contain four zodiac signs.

Cardinal signs: Aries, Cancer, Libra, Capricorn

Fixed signs: Taurus, Leo, Scorpio, Aquarius

Mutable signs: Gemini, Virgo, Sagittarius, Pisces

Here's how it breaks down for the three I*AM archetypes:

Innovators: Mostly Cardinal Signs

Cardinal signs begin every season and have qualities of initiating, leadership, and trailblazing. Thus, they are the signs that drive the Innovator archetype.

Authorities: Mostly Fixed Signs

Fixed signs fall in the middle of each season and are the workhorses and producers, contributing to the Authority score.

Mavens: Mostly Mutable Signs

Mutable signs fall at the end of every season. They are the adapters and communicators that inform the Maven archetype.

The 13 Points of the I*AM Algorithm

The I*AM algorithm looks at thirteen specific data points in your chart, calculating the zodiac sign that each was in at your exact time of birth. The thirteen points are:

1. Sun ☉
2. Moon ☽
3. Rising/Ascendant **A**ˢᶜ
4. Mercury ☿
5. Venus ♀
6. Mars ♂
7. Jupiter ♃
8. Saturn ♄
9. Uranus ♅
10. Neptune ♆
11. Pluto ♇
12. Lunar South Node ☋
13. Lunar North Node ☊

Most people only know their sun sign, which is commonly referred to as "my zodiac sign" or just "my sign." But there's a reason why all the Libras out there are created differently, and thus will generate different I*AM results. (Same for the other eleven signs.)

At your exact time of birth, every single planet in the sky—plus the sun and moon—was aligned with one of the twelve zodiac signs. Each heavenly body becomes part of your cosmic makeup, working together to create the blueprint of your soul.

So you aren't just a Libra (or an Aries . . . or a Virgo). You might be a Libra sun with a Scorpio moon, Mercury in Virgo, and Uranus in Capricorn, and so on. This is what astrologers call the birth chart, or natal chart, and it's how we interpret "the story of you."

Fascinating fact: only someone born at your exact time and geographical location will share your birth chart. There are practically as many cosmic combinations as there are humans on the planet. Even as identical twins, born four minutes apart, we have subtle variations in our birth charts.

If this information feels like a lot to take in, well, it is! Astrology is an ages-old divination system that's evolved from ancient Babylon into modern times. It's a study and a practice. And that's exactly why we created the I*AM System. We want you to get all the juice you can out of your chart—to get the Astrology Advantage—without having to remember all the detailed nuances that go into it.

What the 13 Points of the I*AM Algorithm Mean

Your Big Three: Sun, Moon, and Rising Signs

Your sun sign represents the essence of your personality and reveals how you shine. This is the fuel you burn and the way you light up the world. Its companion, the moon, is in charge of your inner life and emotions. Your moon sign shows what you need to feel safe and nurtured. The zodiac sign on the eastern horizon at your birth reveals your rising sign, also called the ascendant. Your rising sign reveals the first impression you'll make on others and how you like to be seen in the world.

The Personal Planets: Mercury, Venus, and Mars

The planets closest to the sun are called the inner planets, or personal planets, and direct our day-to-day, interactive affairs. Your Mercury sign influences the way you communicate and socialize, and also governs how you learn, problem-solve, and digest information. Venus and Mars are the celestial lovebirds! Your Venus sign directs the way you seduce, how you style yourself, and your aesthetic sensibility. Mars is pure passion and drive; where it lands in the zodiac at your birth directs your turn-ons and what you'll fight for, too.

The Outer Planets: Jupiter, Saturn, Uranus, Neptune, and Pluto

The slower-moving outer planets, spanning from Jupiter to Pluto, direct your bigger decisions and shape generations. Bountiful Jupiter is your lucky charm. Your Jupiter sign shows where things come quickly and easily to you. Stern, disciplined Saturn is Jupiter's cautious, curmudgeon-y counterpart. Where your Saturn sign lands can be a challenging area of life; where you'll struggle but grow stronger.

The final three planets move us through an interesting journey: Uranus (higher consciousness), Neptune (subconscious), Pluto (unconscious). Want to disrupt the status quo? Look to your Uranus sign for clues about your activism and ideals—and where you can't be fenced in! Neptune is in charge of your spirituality, fantasy, and the dream realm. Your Neptune sign is the creative director of your chart. Pluto governs the unconscious realm, and its position in your chart reveals your "blind spots"—places where you may project your own traits onto others, grapple with addictions, or go into denial. This is where you'll need to do what Carl Jung called "shadow work"—the act of assimilating parts of yourself that you consider undesirable into the rest of your personality—in order to evolve.

These powerful points in the sky connect to where eclipses were taking place when you were born. Astrologers look to the lunar nodes to understand your life path and karmic purpose. These mystical points help us answer the big questions like "Why am I here?" and "What's my destiny?" Beyond the day-to-day, the nodes reveal your soul's journey, from past lives to your ultimate destiny.

While we won't go in-depth on these planets and points in *The Astrology Advantage*, you can calculate a free birth chart on our website at **https://astrostyle.com/birthchart** and read our many resources on astrology. There's no need to do so in order to get the most out of this book! However, as your interest in astrology grows, learning your full astrological birth chart adds a powerful dimension to working with the I*AM System.

THE I*AM SCORE: PUTTING IT ALL TOGETHER

To get your final I*AM score, the algorithm calculates the modalities of each of the thirteen data points. Here's an example, using our own birth chart:

- Sun Sign: Sagittarius (M)

- Moon Sign: Scorpio (A)

- Rising Sign: Capricorn (I)

- Mercury Sign: Scorpio (A)

- Venus Sign: Scorpio (A)

- Mars Sign: Scorpio (A)

- Jupiter Sign: Capricorn (I)

- Saturn Sign: Gemini (M)

- Uranus Sign: Libra (I)

- Neptune Sign: Sagittarius (M)

- Pluto Sign: Libra (I)

- Lunar South Node: Cancer (I)

- Lunar North Node: Capricorn (I)

	MODALITIES		
	Cardinal (I) Aries Cancer Libra Capricorn	**Fixed (A)** Taurus Leo Scorpio Aquarius	**Mutable (M)** Gemini Virgo Sagittarius Pisces
Sun			X
Moon		X	
Mercury		X	
Venus		X	
Mars		X	
Jupiter	X		
Saturn			X
Uranus	X		
Neptune			X
Pluto	X		
North Node	X		
South Node	X		
Rising/ Ascendant	X		
SUM	6	4	3

PLANETS

Add them all up and here's our final I*AM score: 6 Innovator, 4 Authority, 3 Maven

ADD THE 4 ELEMENTS: FIRE, EARTH, AIR, AND WATER

In astrology, there's an additional way that every chart is "scored" or "weighted." It uses the four elements of the zodiac, another subgrouping of the twelve signs. These elements are fire, earth, air, and water, and each one encompasses a trio of zodiac signs.

Fire signs: Aries, Leo, Sagittarius

Earth signs: Taurus, Virgo, Capricorn

Air signs: Gemini, Libra, Aquarius

Water signs: Cancer, Scorpio, Pisces

The number of planets you have in these zodiac signs and their element adds another layer of nuance to your I*AM type. Like a tint of a color ("navy blue" or "light blue"), finding your dominant element makes your I*AM archetype even more personalized. This will help you further clarify how to use your I*AM gifts in a practical way!

How Do the Elements Work with I*AM?

When you add the zodiac element into your I*AM score, you get an even more complete and unique portrait of your personality. Like a "tint" of a color, the elements add nuance to how you'll express your I*AM modality. Knowing if you're high in earth, for example, or low in air, can help you balance that energy in your life.

A Maven whose chart is high in fire signs may have a talent for spreading the hottest ideas, like a celebrity publicist. But this "Fire Maven" may also need to dial down the heat of their intensity so as not to burn people out.

An Authority whose I*AM score contains a pool of sensitive water signs could be an expert leader in a healing field. But the empathic "Water Authority" is equally susceptible to becoming an emotional sponge who carries the weight of the world's problems on their shoulders. You know that person who always seems to be helping a friend during a crisis or hosting the family for the holidays? A good chance they're a Water Authority.

An Innovator whose chart is heavy on earth planets is in luck! They know how to stay grounded even though they're big, bold dreamers—and can probably monetize some of their wilder ideas faster than Innovators strong in the other three elements.

The goal of adding the elements is to help you focus. Instead of ruminating over the "perfect" path, you can get out of your head and into action. You've got gifts that the world needs now—and it's time to stop swerving and start serving!

How the 4 Elements Shape Your Personality

Fire

Makes you direct, forthright, action-driven, energizing, motivating, bold, and attention-grabbing. You're here to get the party started and get everybody active! You may best serve the world by championing a cause you're passionate about or through a public and spotlight-grabbing forum.

Earth

Makes you grounded, sensible, wise, time-tested, service-driven, and focused on security. You're here to establish something that's built to last or to carry on a tradition. You may best serve your mission by rolling out your ideas one careful step at a time or giving people a structured system to follow.

Air

Makes you heady, thoughtful, communicative, friendly, and breezy. You're here to spread a message to a wider audience, exchange ideas, and to be among "the people." You may best serve your mission by going wide instead of deep and creating something that's lighthearted and inclusive.

Water

Makes you caring, empathic, intuitive, reflective, introspective, and intimate. You're here to connect with people emotionally and express your ideas through art, music, and creativity. You may best serve your mission by going deep instead of wide or working in a private or exclusive forum.

Once you know your element, you can start to map possible ways to share your unique I*AM light. For instance, an intimate Water Innovator might feel best contributing their trailblazing ideas in a private coaching group, since water is empathic and nurturing. An Air Innovator, on the other hand, might have a podcast or video series, since air is all about spreading a message far and wide.

SCORE YOUR CHART WITH THE 4 ELEMENTS

Use our cosmic calculator to find your dominant element at https://astrostyle.com/iam. Your chart may have two or even three dominant elements. Again, it's all about the Astro-Ayurveda! Look at where you're high (five or more planets in one element) and where you're low (two or less planets in one element), then use our tips below to bring balance.

High Fire

You can be impatient, impulsive, domineering, and burn out or lose interest fast. Work on finishing what you start, not taking on too much at once. Be a compassionate listener instead of preaching or trying to save the day.

Low Fire

You can be fearful or self-doubting. Work on taking more risks and going with your gut. Allow yourself to express anger in the moment, rather than stuffing it down.

High Earth

You can be overly fixated on safety and security, and you can be judgmental. Work on increasing your risk tolerance by taking small and calculated chances. Step out of the echo chamber and surround yourself with people who challenge you.

Low Earth

You can be ungrounded and have trouble managing or holding on to money. Work on following simple systems and cultivating habits that keep your feet on the ground (and money in the bank). A financial planner or advisor could be your saving grace.

High Air

You can be scattered and "all talk, no action." Work on being on time, keeping your word, waiting to share about your ideas until you have real results.

Low Air

Change and movement are hard for you. Work on proactively trying new things, opening your mind, and exposing yourself to new experiences to avoid getting stagnant. Ask more questions instead of assuming.

High Water

You can be fearful, insecure, or hide behind others. Work on establishing trust and widening your comfort zone, sharing even when you're scared. When you feel out of place, nurture or volunteer and you'll feel more at ease.

Low Water

Compassion is not your strong suit; you may turn to your head instead of your heart for answers. Work on tuning into your body and intuition and stepping into people's shoes before judging.

THE I*AM DIAGRAM: PUT IT ALL TOGETHER

The I*AM Diagram is our visual table showing your entire breakdown of Innovator, Authority, Maven, as well as fire, earth, air, and water

PLANETS	ELEMENTS				MODALITIES		
	Fire Aries Leo Sagittarius	**Earth** Taurus Virgo Capricorn	**Air** Gemini Libra Aquarius	**Water** Cancer Scorpio Pisces	**Cardinal (I)** Aries Cancer Libra Capricorn	**Fixed (A)** Taurus Leo Scorpio Aquarius	**Mutable (M)** Gemini Virgo Sagittarius Pisces
Sun	X						X
Moon				X		X	
Mercury				X		X	
Venus				X		X	
Mars				X		X	
Jupiter		X			X		
Saturn			X				X
Uranus			X		X		
Neptune	X						X
Pluto			X		X		
North Node		X			X		
South Node				X	X		
Rising/Ascendant		X			X		
SUM	**2**	**3**	**3**	**5**	**6**	**4**	**3**

placements. If you're more advanced in your astrology understanding, you may want to work with the I*AM Diagram to tap into the strengths of both your modalities and your elements. It converts your natal chart, which is typically shown as a wheel with various symbols denoting the planets and zodiac signs, into a spreadsheet-style chart.

Which I*AM Are You?

Calculate your I*AM Type at
https:// astrostyle.com/ iam

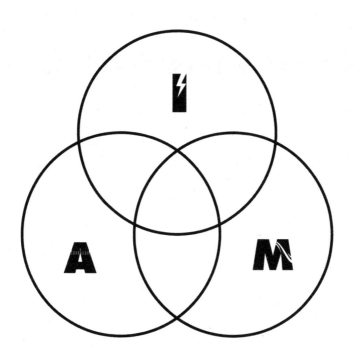

COMMUNICATION

The Astrology Advantage
in Communication

"Nothing brings down walls as surely as acceptance."
—*Deepak Chopra*

C oexisting ain't easy! The palpable differences between the three
personality types can make for needless conflict and power struggles. Yet, the bone of contention often stems from one major source,
which is the way the three I*AM archetypes communicate.

It's not simply the way each type articulates thoughts, but also the
manner in which they hear each other. Interactivity means something
totally different to the I*AMs.

Innovators prefer parallel play, where two or more people immerse
themselves in individual projects, enjoying the collective hum of creative productivity. Authorities live for schedules and plans: everyone
on the team has a role and they check in regularly and overlap to work
together as needed. Mavens love to engage: co-creating, brainstorming,
and getting in the sandbox together.

Trouble comes in when the I*AM personalities fail to understand
the other's preferred method of communication. The best intentions
are misinterpreted, and suddenly everyone's blaming, shaming, and
projecting all over the place.

One Innovator we know has described her Authority partner's

most enraging quality as when he speaks to her in what she's dubbed "command voice." The slightest hint of this tone can set her off like a pipe bomb.

"He begins talking to me in this clipped, formal way. He tells me rather than asks me what I should be doing, how and when I should be doing it . . . which is usually right now and just like this," she fumes. "And it doesn't matter what project I'm in the middle of. What he needs suddenly becomes mission critical. It makes me feel like an errant child being put in the time-out chair by her stern daddy. It's enraging!"

Her Authority partner, of course, tells a different tale. "What she describes as command voice," he explains, "is me trying not to lose my temper because she's lost track of time again." He goes on to explain that his Innovator has "blown me off for hours while she works on one of her projects for 'fifteen more minutes' and leaves me waiting around or makes us late for a plan that's been on our calendars for weeks."

But what if they learned to translate the tone and read each other's subtexts with greater facility? Sure, in an ideal world, partners would have direct communication 24/7. But most humans don't operate that way.

For example, what if the Innovator's "fifteen more minutes" was not a sign of disrespect but more of an SOS that they were overwhelmed by the project, needed help transitioning out of their focused work mode or even talking through a battle plan. Of course, the Innovator needs to build a stronger muscle here, too! Understanding that the Authority lives by the clock, the Innovator should make clear appointments with them and consider those times sacrosanct. That includes a start time *and* an end time. "We have one hour together" or "I have to get back to my desk by two p.m."

To be sure, creating effective communication among the I*AM archetypes can be a lifelong process and not a linear path to success. But understanding what each type needs will arm everyone with an Astrology Advantage. Rather than feeling misunderstood and disrespected, each archetype can find a way to communicate that works for them and gets the real message through.

I*AM Communication At-a-Glance

	RESPOND TO	**DISLIKE**
INNOVATORS	Opportunity	Small Talk
AUTHORITIES	Certainty	Flakiness
MAVENS	Urgency	Stuffiness

INNOVATOR COMMUNICATION

The Innovator responds to *Opportunity*
The Innovator dislikes *Small Talk*

Most people never know what will come out of an Innovator's mouth, which makes this type both fascinating and a little bit intimidating! At times these visionaries are as sharp as machetes, their message potent and awe-inspiring. But when Innovators are preoccupied (which is often) or midway through putting the whole puzzle together, they can be as foggy as a Northern California morning.

Innovator Communication Superpowers

Problem-Solving. Natural problem-solvers, Innovators have a genius way of connecting the dots and delivering inspiring solutions. They'll pull from a vast database of resources that span a surprising range of references. How (and why) is the Innovator referencing neoclassical architecture *and* '90s hip-hop in the same sentence? Nobody knows, not even the Innovator, until they reach the end of the thought. They're "building the plane in the air," as the saying goes.

Disruptors. True originals, Innovators march to their own unapologetic beat and tend to have strong opinions. Their friends and coworkers may get an unexpected stream of blunt commentary from these rebellious provocateurs. Innovators are not afraid to say something totally different that disrupts the status quo. ("I know we talked about reducing the marketing budget, but I'm going to propose that we double it! Here's why...")

Long-range vision. At times, it might seem like the Innovator is playing devil's advocate or being purposely difficult. Most of the time they're not. Innovators have a sixth sense that picks up nanodetails and nuances, like a slightly out-of-tune note in a symphony or a word that just needs a synonym to make the whole sentence sing. While it might seem fussy, once that detail is added, everything comes together. Note to people who cling to the past or insist on doing things "the way they've always been done": the Innovator loves pushing people out of their comfort zones and challenging conventional ideas.

Sharp memories. Often, it may seem that Innovators aren't paying attention, and a lot of that has to do with their body language (limited eye contact, fidgeting, organizing their desks while people talk to them). But surprise: Innovators have sharp memories! They'll shock everyone by recalling some of the most "random" details: a friend's great-grandmother's maiden name, the zodiac sign of a roommate's high school crush, or that a colleague grew up just outside Santa Fe.

Breaking the Ice with an Innovator

Stand out from the herd

Create FOMO

Surprise them

Want to move past the superficial and get to know an Innovator better? Folks who are interested in a friendship, working together, or testing a romantic spark with the Innovator will need to differentiate themselves. How to do that in sixty seconds or less? Grab an Innovator's ever-moving attention by sharing something cutting-edge and exclusive—a juicy tidbit of gossip, a witty line that catches them off guard, an invite to a big event where the Innovator can make new connections. Say something a little shocking, in a declarative tone, to disrupt their distracted daze.

Dangle the carrot and (gently) push an Innovator's FOMO buttons. This I*AM type hates feeling like they're behind the curve! Just don't make the Innovator feel uncool with questions like, "Have you heard of [insert band, film title, buzzy indie celebrity]?" They might fake it by saying, "Yeah, I think so," nodding along, then planning the first moment to get away from you so they can google this impresario. To avoid that break in the conversation, simply start sharing about "This cool new performer I discovered," and pull up the artist's social media to show the Innovator on the spot.

Delivery is everything with the Innovator. A touch of snark or a wry insider tone will make the Innovator giggle appreciatively. If the aim is a romantic connection, it also helps to be a bit of a moving target. Scarcity works well for anyone who's selling themselves to the Innovator—and clinging is the ultimate turnoff. Avoid lingering for too long, but don't ghost them! Keep floating back to chat with the Innovator, to show continued interest while building intrigue. When the Innovator starts pursuing, that's the green light. Our Innovator friend Peri literally ran down the beach to tap an attractive guy on the shoulder. "Tell me your name in case I never see you again," was her line. They've been married nearly thirty years.

What Innovators Like to Talk About: Big, Novel Ideas

Future-focused Innovators are curious and irreverent, interested in what's possible rather than what's been done before. Just learned about a groundbreaking study that could reshape the future of women and work? Tried a raw food reset that produced glowing skin and balanced microbiome? Do tell! The Innovator isn't just all ears; they'll engage with memorable opinions that make everyone think.

Warning: the Innovator's sly humor and "in the know" references can seem exclusionary. Is anything ever cool enough for them? Perfectionism can haunt these impatient types, who are often forced to wait for the world to catch up with the utopian or cutting-edge visions that seem so obvious to the Innovator.

What Innovators Hate to Talk About: Small Talk

Want to lose an Innovator in ten nanoseconds? Lead with small talk about mundane topics like the weather or your last doctor's appointment. Start gossiping about people in the room or lobbing superficial, small-minded judgments. ("Her brows are a mess!" or "What was he thinking, leaving the house in that shirt?") Innovators have sublime taste, but they aren't snobs. Mad scientists at heart, Innovators understand that people's gifts aren't always apparent on the surface. Plus, they wouldn't want to be judged for their own daring moves (or off-duty outfits), and have set plenty of tongues wagging with their unconventional choices. While Innovators appreciate a touch of highbrow snark, pettiness brings them down. They'd much rather talk about big ideas—and are at their best when they do.

Conversational Style: All Over the Map

In conversation, Innovators may interrupt people, finish their sentences, or drift into daydreaming, especially when someone's giving them instructions. Their fix-it filter is naturally set a little too high, which at times causes them to seem rude and abrupt. "What problem needs to be solved here?" the Innovator wants to know—and fast. But that doesn't stop Innovators from rambling on about *their* process or vision. Too often, Innovators aren't able to deliver what they demand: a clear, cohesive explanation. "You know, it's like a solar-powered micropanel that also gets energy from moonlight so you can keep it in your purse. And I got the idea while I was driving through the desert with my friend Alex, who I met when I was in grad school in the craziest way . . ."

Why can't the Innovator seem to get to the point—much less make one? These "vague visionary" moments happen when Innovators are dreaming up something new, and their ideas are only half downloaded from the cosmic cloud. Explaining their lofty concepts is an Achilles' heel, if not an epic feat, for Innovators. Like engineers, they want to examine things like a puzzle, looking at all sides of a situation or pontificating like chin-stroking philosophers.

Observe them in the wild: many Innovators will gaze skyward while talking, as if an invisible movie screen is playing over their heads. This is how Innovators access their intuition and speedily process information at the same time. In pursuit of such divine inspiration, Innovators might not make eye contact (it's too distracting for them), which can be off-putting to their conversation partner. Then, when the fire of inspiration is lit, the Innovator stares so deeply into your eyes, you feel utterly engulfed by their fervor!

How to Talk with an Innovator

Since Innovators are often deep in thought about the future, coming back to the present can be a transitional process, and that shows up in their communication habits. The Innovator's focus is often like an old-school Polaroid picture. The photo exists, but it's being brought in from the darkness and needs a moment before it's fully developed. Colleagues and friends who have something important to say should warm the Innovator up first. Ask them a few questions about a latest project or fascination so they can ease back into connection.

More than any other archetype, the Innovator needs a bridge to come out of their focused flow state and get back in sync with the rest of the world. Before launching into a discussion, it's best to give the Innovator a few minutes to focus and ground themselves. Otherwise, the checked-out Innovator will miss half the conversation.

While Innovators hate small talk, they love to hear funny stories or "exciting news!" and updates on whatever a friend is working on. Start by sharing about a recent event or a cute shop that just opened up. At a restaurant, give the Innovator a few minutes to take in the decor, scan the QR code for the menu, peruse the specialty cocktails the house is serving. Allow the Innovator to sink back into the moment and it won't be long before they're fully engaged in the dialogue.

Where to Have a Discussion with an Innovator

Innovators are at their conversational best when they're away from the distractions of home base or their workspace. It allows them to unhook from their current mental fixation and move their attention elsewhere. Still, these busy folks usually have to be caught on the fly. Word to the wise: unless you want to wait around while the Innovator sends "one more email" or loads the dishwasher, suggest meeting at an outside location that's not their home or workplace.

Our recommendation? Scout out nearby coffee shops or places the

Innovator could pop out for a meal. Research has proven that chewing helps to relieve anxiety and boost attention—two things Innovators could use help with when communicating with others.

Meet the Innovator at the venue rather than swinging by to pick them up. Even if the Innovator arrives a few minutes late (which is likely), their journey to your designated spot helps them transition out of the clouds and back into their bodies so they can be present.

Innovators are discerning and settle right into locations that are aesthetically pleasing. They love a curated cafe done up in vintage wallpaper or a restaurant styled by an award-winning interiors team. Make sure the menu is as captivating as the decor, so the foodie Innovator has something to crow about as they get comfortable in conversation.

To have a productive discussion with an Innovator, avoid spaces that are *too* buzzy, with loud music or people swooshing in and out the door. Grab a table in the back, preferably in a quiet corner. Otherwise, the Innovator will be busier people-watching than concentrating on the conversation. Venues where it's easy to overhear conversations are also a no-no. Innovators want to speak freely, and their forward-thinking ideas and lifestyles aren't always appropriate for a "general audience."

Giving Feedback to an Innovator

Perfectionists who can be exceedingly hard on themselves, Innovators tend to take any critiques to heart. Too often, they become defensive or cover up their sensitivity with a self-deprecating or guarded persona.

Most Innovators would benefit from developing a thicker skin. However, this pioneering type is often begging forgiveness because they "forgot" to ask permission. Innovators know that most people won't understand their ideas until they see them in action, so they have to cleverly devise ways to push through the approval process so they can show the world their genius.

"The words 'performance review' immediately make every hair on my body stand on end," Ilene, an Innovator, says, clenching her jaw. "For me, that usually translates into 'you've pushed things too far outside the box again.' So I come to the meeting feeling like the bad kid in class, ready to be scolded by the teacher."

The best way to give feedback to an Innovator is to try what activist Loretta J. Ross coined "calling them in" (as opposed to calling them out). Through this technique, the Innovator feels respected rather than scolded or shamed. The Innovator wants to feel like two equals are sitting down together, not like they're facing a punitive parent correcting a misbehaving child. Any whiff of the latter may instantly provoke a bratty, defensive response from the Innovator.

Calling in is intended to invite reflection, which the philosophical Innovator likes. Rather than harping on the problem, it's best to position the circumstances as a "misunderstanding" or a "communication breakdown." Then, engage the Innovator in designing a solution together.

For example, when dealing with a chronically late Innovator, don't begin by ranting about their disrespect for other people's time. That might provide temporary relief, but it won't change the Innovator's errant conduct. Instead, bring up the issue in a neutral way, offering room for the Innovator to problem-solve.

"I noticed that it's been hard for you to make our noon meeting work lately. Is there a better time in your schedule for this?" Empathy also dissolves the Innovator's knee-jerk defensiveness. "I've observed that we haven't been able to consistently meet every week. It's important that we connect so I can keep my part of the project moving along. Is there something I can do to support you?"

Frequently, an Innovator will try to accommodate the group rather than speaking up for their needs. This archetype aims to please, often at the expense of a realistic solution. Maybe there's something that can be taken off the Innovator's plate, as this perfectionistic type struggles to delegate.

Of course, there will be times when Innovators need to be called out. In such cases, their critic should brace themselves for a barrage of defenses, and should not (we repeat *should not*) get sucked into a debate.

Instead, it's best to calmly and lovingly reschedule time to talk about this further when cooler heads prevail. Fortunately, the Innovator will step back and process the feedback, likely returning to the conversation with a renewed (and appreciative) POV, owning their mistakes and vowing to do better. Hold them to it and ask them how they plan to follow through! There's a good chance they've devised an innovative solution that will exceed expectations.

How an Innovator Deals with Conflict

Conflict is tricky terrain with Innovators. They love to brainstorm and gather information to make their ideas better. But being told "no" or "you can't" or "it won't work" will typically infuriate the Innovator and make them dig in their heels.

Innovators are not afraid to be challenged in a friendly, transparent way. In fact, they relish a spirited discussion where everyone shares their unique perspective. For these forward-thinkers, every conversation might as well be taking place in a Parisian salon.

Once the Innovator has made a decision, their willpower and determination kick into overdrive. Innovators' astrological charts are primarily made up of strong-willed cardinal signs. When they get an idea in their heads, they're downright bullish about carrying it out, whether that's learning to make mole sauce from scratch or sanding their own floors. They'd rather everyone just get out of their way and let them do it. For the Innovator, the joy is as much in the learning process as it is in the final result. They don't mind making mistakes along the way. They love to "throw spaghetti on the wall," as the saying goes, to see which "noodles" stick.

Loved ones who are brave enough to step in and try to stop an Innovator once they're in motion might want to armor up. The Innovator's first response may be angry; aggressive, even. They're speeding along at 100 mph and any advice (or basic questions!) can feel to them as if someone pulled the emergency brake.

Truth is, the Innovator probably *does* need to stop . . . before things get any messier or more expensive. But for anyone who hopes to attempt an Innovator Intervention, we recommend hopping on the Innovator's speeding train *first*. Get interested in what they're doing and the "why" behind it. The Innovator has a method to their madness. They don't take kindly to anyone trying to change their mind. But they are instantly warm to ideas that are presented as an enhancement to what the Innovator is already doing. Innovators *will* change course if you can point out clear benefits to your plan B.

We can think of many times that, in hindsight, we would have benefited from a strong soul helping us press pause before we started an epic Innovator undertaking. Case in point: when Tali moved to Fort Greene, Brooklyn, in the late 1990s, she scored the top floor of a brownstone overlooking a park. The square footage was roomy enough for two, which made her space the perfect landing pad for friends who, like Tali, migrated from Detroit to NYC. The only problem? The apartment was a railroad-style unit, so the two bedrooms opened into each other.

Inspiration struck and Tali decided to build a wall that would enclose the second bedroom and give everyone more privacy. Without *really* thinking things through (or asking her landlord for permission), she raced to Home Depot and talked to the guys in the drywall department. A few days later, Sheetrock, metal studs, insulation, and a framed inside door were dropped on the landing of the brownstone. Since they arrived midday while friends were at work, Tali lugged all the pieces up to the third floor one by one—an arduous and dangerous task. It took her a full six weeks to complete the room because, why? She didn't ask anyone for help.

Looking back at her twentysomething self, she's perplexed by her own stubbornness. "I guess I wanted to show everyone that I *could* do it myself," she admits. "Plus, when I told people I was using metal studs for the framing, they started telling me I should have used wood; it would have been easier. I wasn't going to tear down all that work! They were harshing my buzz."

When Tali's friend Mike, a carpenter, came over months later, he admired her handiwork and grit. He also let her know that he could have done the job for her in a weekend. Swallowing her pride, Tali swore she'd never push herself through a solo build again—at least not without checking in with her people first!

When an Innovator Should Take a Time-Out

Innovators aren't always aware of when they need to take a break from conversation. They may carry on chatting, only half listening or drifting in and out of attentiveness. When an Innovator's vague and disjointed commentary becomes hard to follow, that's a sign that they need to stop, drop into their bodies, and roll—or shall we say, move—for a few minutes of physical activity. A walk around the block can be a sanity-saving reset for this I*AM archetype.

Another moment to call a time-out is when the Innovator becomes defensive. These high-achievers don't take kindly to anyone poking holes in their plan and may bring out the sharp knives when they feel like they're being judged. For folks who think the Innovator didn't notice all their personal slip-ups or less-than-obvious "flaws," surprise! Suddenly, the Innovator is using those vulnerable parts of their foe's life as ammunition to wage their counterattack. They feel justified. After all, someone is bashing the very things Innovators hold dear: their visionary ideas. However, these battles can get ugly and hurtful. It's best for both people to step away and de-escalate before torching all the remaining goodwill.

Communication Challenges: Impatience

Innovators are *interesting* . . . but not always *interested*. Self-referential (and on a bad day, self-centered), Innovators perk up once they understand how the subject matter pertains to them and their core mission. Instead of letting their minds trail off to the next thing they have to do, Innovators need to build rapport and consciously meet people on a mutual wavelength. This will establish the trust and solid connection the Innovator craves.

Their seeming disinterest can be especially frustrating to people who have spent hours generously playing sounding board as the Innovator pontificates about their latest world-changing business idea. When Innovators make a conscious effort to care about things that have nothing to do with them, it will go a long way in creating fair, reciprocal communication in their relationships.

At the very least, Innovators can use body language cues to signal that they're engaged. They can do this by making eye contact a little more and give an affirmative like "you're so right" or "that makes sense" or "do you mind clarifying one thing?" Asking questions instead of just rushing into their own stories ("that reminds me of a time when I...") will also help show the Innovator's conversation partner that they're not competing for the mic, but rather, are genuinely interested in what the other person has to say!

Friends and colleagues hopefully can learn not to take an Innovator's meandering attention to heart. But there are ways that Innovators can help that—particularly when making a first impression.

Especially salient are techniques like mirroring (reflecting back what someone said à la "I hear you saying X—is that correct?") and matching (subtly repeating a person's body language, e.g., if they cross their arms, you can do the same a minute later). Some experts even suggest syncing with the other person's rate of breathing!

As Innovator sisters and business partners, we've learned the wisdom of having a neutral third party to help us navigate sensitive discussions. Our (Maven) life coach Lois has stopped us midway during polarizing discussions, asking us to use the above-mentioned mirroring technique. Lois is a brave soul, because stopping an Innovator before they "make their point" is dicey territory. Turns out, *not* making the point was actually the point. As Innovators, we needed to *hear* what the other was actually saying instead of spinning out into emotional reactivity.

Sure it felt weird to say things to each other like, "What I hear you saying is that you need more support with our social media posts." But invariably, mirroring turned the dialogue down from boiling hot to a gentle simmer, allowing us to empathize with the other's experience instead of battling for domination. (Yes, even identical twins can go there some days. . . .)

AUTHORITY COMMUNICATION

The Authority responds to *Certainty*

The Authority dislikes *Flakiness*

Authorities are linear and goal-driven communicators. Firm believers in "word economy," they construct their sentences with exquisite care. While they've got plenty of interesting things to say, most Authorities would prefer if others talk first. These efficient souls are careful investors with their time and attention. Before an Authority opens up, they want to know the other person's values and whether a connection might stand the test of time. Conversations are the Authority's opportunity to discover: *Who is this person and what's important to them?* To these ethical souls, few things matter more than a person's values.

Authority Communication Superpowers

Acknowledgment. While Authorities may not gush (at least, not in a phony way), nobody gives a genuine compliment quite like they do. This is the person who should deliver the toast at a wedding or birthday party. Authorities know how to eloquently acknowledge people with a touching tribute or thoughtful feedback. They're the friends who send a birthday card, bring a hostess gift, or have a floral arrangement delivered. Even as kids, many Authorities come across as older and wise beyond their years, even parental. Although it can feel smothering, in the right doses, the Authority makes people feel safe.

Sound advice and opinions. Asking an Authority's opinion elicits a sensible answer, guided by time-tested wisdom and proven concepts that they've mastered. This type will often quote an "authority" from their own archives: a Stoic philosopher, a favorite thought leader, their high school track coach. Authorities can come across as formal or stuffy, even if they roar with appreciative laughter at a joke. Getting an Authority to relax and have fun (without them being in charge) is a high compliment, as they rarely trust anyone enough to fully follow their lead.

Accountability. Calm, sensible, and self-assured, Authorities are the world's accountability partners. Got goals? Authorities are great at keeping teams, projects, and families on track. They earn people's trust quickly, bolstering their competence with solid experience and consistency. Authorities know what works because it's been proven time and again! And they'll gladly share their "been there, done that" wisdom to spare others the struggles that they went through.

Sentimentality. Communication sweetens over time with the Authority, who may begin with a formal tone only to reveal a total mushball underneath the stern exterior. Count on the Authority to recall your wisest and wittiest remarks or to re-presence the most meaningful exchanges you've had over the years.

Breaking the Ice with an Authority

Breaking the ice with an Authority can feel like a formal dance— or at the very least an incredibly polite exchange that makes the other person walk away thinking, "Wow, there still are some kind people in the world."

But a word to the wise: don't probe too deeply into the Authority's life in the initial dialogue. That's not to suggest they want conversation to be superficial or boring—just impersonal enough so that the Authority feels a sense of control over the pacing. Boundaries are a big deal to the Authority and nosy questions set off their alarm bells—even if these queries come from a genuinely curious, open-book sort of person.

Authorities love to share their expertise and opinions. Anyone who meets an Authority in line at the ice cream shop might ask them if they've tried any of the featured monthly flavors and if so, what they thought of them. Little things matter to these fastidious folks, so any chance to share their catalog of knowledge is a surefire way to warm them up.

Take a look at what the Authority is wearing. If they're the stylish type, you can bet that they put some careful thought into curating the look. Serve up a compliment and the Authority might, unprompted, share the backstory of the little vintage shop in Woodstock where they found the frames for their cat-eye glasses. One Authority we know has full sleeve tattoos on both arms. Each piece of ink reveals a connection to her interests, including a major arcana tarot card and ball of yarn and knitting needles. We've watched her come to life when people ask her the meaning behind a certain piece.

What Authorities Like to Talk About: Their Discerning Taste

For starters . . . you! Most Authorities are such polite, patient listeners that people will naturally open up and reveal much more than they expected. A typical Authority will sit patiently through many monologues and soul-baring secrets, even if they cringe inwardly. As long as their principles and values aren't violated, the Authority is glad to provide that safe space. If you're an Authority, you've probably been told, "I feel like I've known you my whole life!" when you just met an hour ago, simply because you put the other person at ease.

While this superpower can get Authorities stuck in one-sided relationships, it can also establish their advantage. The Authority's spacious silence buys them time to read body language and to discern people's true character and motives. Through their interested yet appropriate questions, Authorities learn: What kind of upbringing did this person have? Where did they go to school? What traditions matter to them? (Noted. Filed. Cataloged.)

As the Authority begins to systematically lower their guard, they reveal their wealth of knowledge on a broad range of topics. Authorities love to teach what they've learned, to share wisdom, and dissect problems detail by detail. They don't mind flaunting their refined tastes, either, which gives them a chance to display their thoughtful natures. There's nothing superficial about interactions with Authorities *after* their loyalty tests have been passed.

However, friends shouldn't expect mutual transparency from the Authority too soon. These folks tend to be private, especially when they run into an issue they don't know how to problem-solve on their own. Authorities need a judgment-free zone when they want to get personal. It's the only type of space that feels safe enough for most Authorities to even *think* about opening up! Even then, it's useful to approach the Authority with questions and statements like, "What do you think you should do about that?" or "Tell me about the solutions you're considering."

What Authorities Hate to Talk About: Superficial Fluff

Want to fall out of an Authority's favor? A lack of sophistication and lowbrow values may elicit instant eviction from their friend list. While Authorities appreciate a history-making disrupter, they have zero patience for a rebel without a clue. Don't tell the Authority "I forgot to vote in the last presidential election" or pepper them with trivial data about a D-list reality star. This person will be subjected to a lifetime of the Authority's sneering and may never be given a second chance.

Authorities like to be the experts on most subjects, but if they aren't, they become visibly uncomfortable. That doesn't mean they *won't* entertain new topics. But it's important that they feel invited to learn and engage in the conversation. It's best to pause between revelations so the Authority can ask intelligent questions and draw parallels to things that they *do* understand.

Our friend Derek is a caring, affable guy who's regularly invited to hang out with "the girls." A sentimental Authority, he genuinely enjoys dissecting emotions, which is something he doesn't always get to do with the dudes in his life. However, Derek regularly finds himself seething inside during protracted discussions about topics he deems "shallow," like makeup tips or celebrity gossip. "What am I even doing here?" he's wondered in moments where he just couldn't contribute to the conversation. Derek even admits to huffing around and getting up noisily in an attempt to break the energy—and ideally, change the subject to something more in his wheelhouse. Passive-aggressive? Some might say so, but Derek considers these indirect cues his Authority-esque way of "dropping a polite hint."

Conversational Style: Formal and Engaged

Once people have spilled their souls and shown their hands, the Authority is ready to take charge! They've established themselves as the wise "adult in the room," and now it's time for the Authority to claim their turf and direct the agenda—to bring their conversational A-game.

Authorities have a treasure trove of topics to talk about, ones meant to spark intellectual discourse. Much Authority pontificating would be fodder for a fascinating podcast, if only they'd think to hit record. Authorities want to engage people on a profound level. Even their humor is highbrow, dripping with dry wit and clever turns of phrase that have the legs to become lasting inside jokes.

In conversation, rule-bound Authorities like to establish policy, process, and protocol so that everyone has a chance to be heard. Polite Authorities take longer to make their point and hate to be interrupted—especially when they're midway through a keen line of questioning. The Authority's insistence on ground rules might annoy more free-flowing types who want to snark freely, talk over each other, or make off-color jokes. But there won't be any slander suits under the Authority's watch.

Most people will ultimately be glad to take the Authority's lead, creating a climate of civility and mutual respect. However, there can be times when communicating with an Authority feels strained; phony, even. Getting the Authority to "let their hair down" could be as arduous a task as removing hundreds of bobby pins from a Carnival queen's feather-headdress updo.

The good news? Cracking the Authority's veneer is not required for people to feel safe opening up to them. Authorities are surprisingly deft with personal topics, even if they're more likely to quote current mental health statistics or hand a friend a book than they are to drop a vulnerable anecdote from their own lives into the thread.

Until the Authority begins to process the life lessons of their "teachable moments" (never say "mistake"!), they're unlikely to utter a word about their struggles. Unfortunately, this masking can block the Authority from forming rewardingly reciprocal connections with their friends. In some cases, it's only when the Authority faces a challenge like a loss or an illness that they wave the white flag and surrender to support.

How to Talk with an Authority

Open that calendar app. The Authority lives by the ticking clock, preferring to schedule everything. Planning in advance brings out the best in the Authority. This is not someone who is afraid of a "Hey, we need to talk" text. However, we recommend reframing it as, "Let's set up a time to talk, I have some things I'm eager to discuss with you." Knowing it isn't a 911 emergency can help set up a softer runway for the Authority.

Note to the impatient people out there: rarely are Authorities ready to dive into an impromptu meeting or hangout. Since the Authority's time zone is the past, they're often ruminating on the many things that they need to get done. Asking the Authority to switch gears without ample warning can throw this archetype into an anxiety tailspin.

Even if they have nothing else going on, Authorities like to set themselves up for maximum connection. Give them fifteen minutes (minimum) to close out all their distractions, get camera-ready, and set up with a mug of coffee in their optimal seating area. Authorities give their best when they feel grounded and secure.

Where to Have a Discussion with an Authority

Authorities are sensitive to their environments. For an Authority to open up, allow them to choose the meeting location. Don't be fooled by their casual tone. As laid-back as they may *want* to be, location matters. Send a link to the Authority so they can check out the menu and determine if it meets their price point, tastes, and aesthetic standards. Better yet, send them a few options—and expect to whittle down that list for a while.

Often, the Authority invites friends to drop by their place, which has been carefully designed (and redesigned) to their socializing specs.

Take heart: Their desire to host is not just about control or comfort. The Authority's home is their "command center." They want to be able to serve guests their special selection of imported teas or reach for a helpful book that's relevant to the conversation. Being in the Authority's sanctuary is generally a win-win.

Giving Feedback to an Authority

Authorities are perfectionists, exceedingly hard on themselves, and prone to ruminating about their missteps. For that reason, feedback should be delivered delicately and *never, ever* in a public forum that may "tarnish" the Authority's good standing in the eyes of society. Those who embarrass the Authority may become a mortal enemy whom they resent for eternity.

It's okay to bring things to the Authority's attention and give them clear directions. But for conversations that are a correction or call-out, critique should be buffered in a "praise sandwich." As much as Authorities despise feeling wrong, they light up like the Rockefeller Center Christmas tree when acknowledged and validated. Start by telling them what they've done *right* and use it as a lead-in to the feedback. Then, end the appraisal of the Authority with glowing words of confidence. "I know you're the perfect person to nail this new strategy!" or "I'm so excited to see what you come up with. You're so brilliant and this is right in your wheelhouse."

It can also help to deliver the feedback in "we" language rather than "you," so that the Authority doesn't feel singled out. "Hey, we need to make a pivot in our strategy" or, "circumstances have changed and we need to rethink our plan of action." In other words, turn this into a collaborative brainstorming process. Ask the Authority questions like, "If you could go back in time, what do you think we could have done differently?"

Or, if it gets personal, turn them into the advisor. "You're such a pro at this stuff—you don't need me to tell you anything. What advice would you give yourself here?" The Authority's answers are certain to impress!

Does this seem high-maintenance? Well, yes. This is the "delicate area" for Authorities, and the cost of doing business with them may feel like pandering to a fragile ego at times. But trust us, the Authority's internal dialogue is a thousand times harsher than anything an outsider could say. They hate to disappoint or let anyone down, to "fail" to meet a promise. By taking this gentler approach, the Authority isn't getting off the hook, but rather, feels safe to move past their mistake with dignity intact.

How an Authority Deals with Conflict

Ready for a protracted game of mental chess? Authorities are skilled negotiators who masterfully bend disagreements in their favor— all while making their "opponent" feel like the resulting outcome is a win-win. It's not that the Authority wants the other person to lose or is trying to gaslight anyone. They simply don't want to admit that they were wrong. And if we get technical about it, they're probably in the right. Because Authorities are so exacting with their words and actions, they error-proof their communications in advance. Calling them to the carpet will elicit a swift reply of intelligent reasons *why* the Authority made their move. It might even be followed up with a letter from their attorney or a link to a legal website.

It's hard to argue with that kind of logic! So . . . don't. To resolve conflicts with Authorities, we recommend reframing the issue as something along the lines of brainstorming, masterminding, assessing, or examining. Authorities *love* to problem-solve as long as *they* are not deemed "the problem."

Nevertheless, there will be times when the Authority does something a friend, colleague, or partner deems problematic. (Again, this should be positioned as "an area that has room for improvement" unless it's an actual violation of the law or boundaries.) For best results, address the matter as an inquiry rather than a complaint. "Hey, I was thinking we might try a different approach to managing our finances. I'd love to run a few ideas by you and hear your thoughts."

When an Authority Should Take a Time-Out

TMI! Authorities get overwhelmed when presented with too many options. Although they've been known to scour for a needle in a haystack, they do so at a measured pace. When it comes to daily communications, Authorities hate to be peppered with endless choices. "We could pick up fried chicken and have a picnic on the beach or rent bikes and head to the oyster shack . . . or maybe just drive and see what we find along the way?" Overload!

What Authorities often fail to see, however, is that it's their own fussiness that causes others to fear choosing the wrong thing and displeasing them. When they start to get frustrated at people who are simply trying to make them happy, it's time for the Authority to take five . . . minutes *or* hours. Otherwise, a condescending tone—or temperamental rant—can hit people below the belt in a damaging way.

Communication Challenges: Can't Loosen Up

Need advice? Authorities are sympathetic, but only to a point. When they go into problem-solving mode, Authorities want to identify the core issue and find the best answer. Once that's done, they don't want to dwell. It's time to move on and take action!

Authorities will coach, but coddling is not their style. If the person they're advising drags out their "process" for too long, the Authority can grow impatient and even harsh, like a teacher scolding a misbehaving student. Our financial advisor, a stern but loving Authority, has been known to preach at us that "The numbers don't lie." True indeed, but not what one wants to hear during a slow revenue month!

Truth is, none of us has all the answers. And for the typical

Authority, being the go-to solution center can make relationships feel burdensome and unrewarding. It's not healthy for anyone to feel like the constant caregiver surrounded by slacking, immature adults—even if the Authority has enabled this behavior by being so reliable. Instead, Authorities should use their capabilities to teach people self-sufficiency skills, even if that means letting them struggle and find their own way.

Serving too much tough love, however, can brand the Authority as uncompassionate, even tone-deaf. Life is not always linear, and healing is a process. Not everyone can just "get over it" on a designated timeline, including the Authority. Reminder to the "A Team": a day will come when you need that grace yourself.

A rigid or fixed stance can actually hurt the Authority, because it stops them from evolving and taking risks. Friends of the Authority should encourage them to follow their curiosity when they're playing it too safe. They grow so much when they open themselves up to new experiences and perspectives. The best way to support an Authority is to make a safe entryway into new vistas—especially ones they would never try on their own!

MAVEN COMMUNICATION

The Maven responds to *Urgency*
The Maven dislikes *Stuffiness*

Mavens are gifted communicators who understand that the best things in life aren't actually "things," but rather the richness that arises when people are engaged in deep connection and conversation. Naturally philosophical, Mavens love to explore the "why" behind everything. But they're just as keen to partake in witty banter. These friendly souls find common ground quickly. People fascinate the Maven. Whether they love 'em or hate 'em, they'll spend hours unpacking social dynamics. Gossip is the Maven's guilty pleasure (and their own undoing). Mavens' loose lips have been known to sink some ships until they learn the power of discretion.

Maven Communication Superpowers

Acceptance. These gregarious souls can be among the most accepting people on the planet. It doesn't take long for the Maven to welcome someone into their fold and dub them a friend. When the Maven's connected with someone, they couldn't care less about what they did yesterday, or even an hour ago. As Oscar Wilde said, "Every saint has a past, and every sinner has a future."

Curiosity. Mavens thrive on novelty and tend to get bored easily if they're not stimulated. As a result, they may pepper people with questions, almost as if they're interviewing them for a talk show—or in some cases, interrogating them for an investigation. But make no mistake: Mavens aren't simply trying to pry into everyone's business. They're seeking meaningful exchanges that help them grow and learn.

Mirroring. Mavens are mirrors. This interactive archetype is gifted at reflecting back to people what they need to hear and has a way of making others feel seen and understood. They may "become" the person they're talking to, unconsciously mimicking their accent and adopting their body language without even realizing it! This trait is highly effective at creating a fast subconscious bond with the other person. Imitation is truly a form of flattery when communicating with a Maven.

Active Listening. Not only are Mavens consummate conversationalists, they're also highly active listeners who pick up nuances of tone, body language, and other signals. Mavens know how to make other people feel heard and might even finish their sentences to prove it. When they use superpowers to elevate the energy, all boats will rise.

Sometimes Mavens are a little *too* good at this, reading into a cough or a twitch and taking it personally. Mavens can lose chasms of time worrying and overthinking this: *"What did they mean by that?"* Meanwhile, the other person has totally moved on—if they even noticed this "breach" at all—but they've been living rent-free in the Maven's head since it happened. Mavens can gain hours back into their lives by curbing the ruminating habit and learning to clear up misunderstandings in the moment. Better for the Maven to ask, "Did I say something to offend you?" or "Did that not make sense?" than to assume anything.

Breaking the Ice with a Maven

Mavens are hands-down the easiest people to break the ice with, whether you're looking to form a friendship or an emotional attachment. But it's best not to catch them in the middle of their "tinker time" (i.e., when they're wrapped up in a passion project). Outside of that, Mavens are ready to drop everything and engage in conversation. The harder part? Getting the Maven to *stop* talking once they rev up. These folks thaw quickly, even if they seem frosty at first.

Mavens admire intelligent wit, and love when people say something silly, funny, or sarcastic. Their sparkling eyes will quickly turn in the jokester's direction and they'll banter back and forth until the other person quits. Bonus points to those who can impersonate a celebrity or supply some corny humor—even a self-effacing dad joke—into the mix. Goofy, lighthearted fun is a huge plus with Mavens.

This archetype is equally philosophical. They're just as eager to engage with people who say something profound about the state of the world, or reveal a high EQ with a comment about attachment styles or data from a recent study. Trivia and facts are the Maven's jam.

Social intelligence also ranks high with Mavens. Cultural critics at heart, Mavens love to people-watch and dissect human dynamics. Without being *too* mean, a person hoping to engage the Maven could muse aloud within their earshot. "Wow, this isn't exactly what I'd call a diverse crowd . . ." Mavens *do* love to gossip and may form a bond around a mutual enemy or distaste for the way things are being done.

What Mavens Like to Talk About: Anything and Everything

There's almost nothing the Maven won't talk about! With their conversational dexterity and wide range of interests, Mavens are the most fascinating people to be seated next to at a dinner party. It's not just because they can flow from discussing the evolution of trap music to French cooking techniques without missing a beat. Mavens get excited about what *others* have to say, too.

Bring up a topic that's unfamiliar to the Maven and they'll find a way in. They'll ask their conversation partner to "say a little more about that," then surprise them with insightful questions. A talk with a Maven can transport someone from familiar terrain to a completely new perspective. Mavens love to spark people's curiosity and get the wheels turning in everyone's minds. It's little wonder that so many Mavens wind up working as therapists and coaches.

Beware the endless tangent when talking to this I*AM type! Mavens often go wider than deeper, dancing through a range of topics in a breathtakingly short amount of time. But every Maven has a couple of key obsessions, subjects that they're so impassioned about they could deliver a TED talk on demand.

Maven Brittany is a talented interiors photographer whose portraits regularly grace the covers of glossy magazines. While she easily jumps into whatever conversation is happening at the party, she comes to life when talking about discovering her love of composition in an eighth-grade photography class. As her friends, we delight in hearing about the ways she gets subjects to relax and not give the camera what she hilariously calls "picture face," or her "no hydrangea" policy when styling sets.

The Maven's Achilles' heel, however, is a love of gossip—often paired with a vicious talent for smack-talking. While studies show that bonding over a mutual enemy can cement friendships faster than many other things, this is a slippery slope for Mavens. Even when attempting to empathize, they can deliver a harsh opinion or slip up and tell someone's personal business. Those indiscretions may come back to haunt the loose-lipped Maven!

What Mavens Hate to Talk About: Responsibility

Boring people, step to the left. There's nothing more torturous to a Maven than listening to pedestrian conversations where no one is challenging convention. A suburban mom droning on about her kid's soccer practice or a wealthy one-percenter ranting about a clueless political candidate they're voting for because "tax breaks"? These folks had better check their privilege or the Maven might do it for them. Socially intelligent Mavens are ambassadors who understand the interplay between groups. High snobbery will get anyone canceled with the Maven and fast!

Every Maven has clear-cut buzzkill topics, subjects they'd rather eat glass than talk about. These are areas of life where the Maven may feel messy and not totally on top of things, even like they're "in trouble," as one Maven puts it when his wife brings up the verboten subject of improving his income. Why so touchy? Mavens put a lot of effort into convincing the world that they've got it all together. But a deep inner restlessness is always simmering below their polished presentation. This archetype can struggle with serious imposter syndrome. Like jugglers, they live with the fear that they'll drop one of the balls and the whole act will fall apart.

Mavens live in the present, but many of them have unfinished business from their past that they are working hard to forget. Guilt can be a pervasive emotion for Mavens, one that dogs them until they finally deal with the cleanup process and restore integrity to their lives. They'll usually wonder why they didn't give themselves that inner peace sooner! Yet, until the Maven is ready to go there, woe betide the person who pokes the metaphoric bear by suggesting the Maven take a deeper look at the issue they're trying desperately to keep in the shadows.

Conversational Style: Wildly Expressive

Conversations with expressive Mavens crank up to a high pitch fast. The topic doesn't matter. Whether they're talking about narrowly escaping disaster or lamenting that their favorite waterproof mascara was discontinued, there's an urgency and immediacy to Maven expression. Their eyes gleam. Their voices boom. They wring their hands and wave their arms. Mavens use hyperboles like "You're killing me" or "It will change your life" or "I swear on my firstborn child." Even the less demonstrative Mavens can simmer with intensity or righteous indignation. They cannot—and will not—be ignored!

For the most part, the Maven's palpable aura is unintentional. To this I*AM type, everything feels like it's happening *now* and all at once. Their communication style reflects this immediacy. It may be playful, dramatic, tearful, angry . . . but it's never lukewarm.

Many a Maven is guilty of being a "close talker," standing inches away and staring deeply into people's eyes. To Mavens, the body is the conductor for their symphony of self-expression. They scream with delight when they run into an old friend on the street, high-five co-workers so hard their palms tingle, and crush their favorite person in a bear hug. Mavens will storm through the house when they're angry, pace when they're on a phone call—and the best thing anyone can do is stay out of their way!

Storytelling is the Maven's superpower. These raconteurs know how to bring their words to life, so friends should make sure they have more than a few minutes to spare before asking the Maven to fill them in on anything. Then, they should allow the Maven to paint a vivid picture: the scenery, mood, people, and play-by-plays of the actions.

Listeners might grow irritated by the deluge of details were it not for the Maven's Oscar-worthy reenactment of the scene. These "mirrors" will literally go into character, mimicking body language, speech, and even accents with stunning accuracy. They know how to draw out suspense, build excitement, and leave listeners on the edge of their seats waiting to hear how the story ends. Humor is another gift many Mavens are blessed with, so get ready to roll on the floor with laughter!

How to Talk with a Maven

A rich text thread or comments section on social media counts as a full conversation for a Maven. As long as they're engaged, they feel connected, which is important to these relationship-focused types. Send a Maven a link to an article, an emoji-laced love note, or a quick "Are you free to talk?" text. They'll pick up their phone in a nanosecond.

To coax the Maven off their devices, we suggest doing something interactive—but not distracting—together. They love to wander through a farmer's market and talk while checking out the booths. Or rent a kayak or grab coffees and walk the trails at a city park. Mavens focus best when in motion. Best of all, activities like these will force the Maven to detach from their phones and actually concentrate on the conversation without checking their new app and social media accounts every few seconds.

Where to Have a Discussion with a Maven

Mavens are communal creatures who thrive when they share experiences with a like-minded group. Drop them in any party and they'll work the room, collecting data and fascinating details about the most interesting folks in the mix. The trouble is, the Maven can be so enamored of all the strangers (soon to be friends) they meet, they lose track of the friends they came with. The same can be true at family gatherings. Mavens are drawn to shiny new people—or the ones they haven't seen in a while.

It's not that the Maven is trying to ignore anyone. But to get a daily allotment of one-on-one time with the Maven, it's best to ask for it! State a clear and specific desire for the Maven's undivided attention. If they know someone wants that, they will gladly supply it. Mavens won't likely freak out if they get a "we need to talk" text. (Although we recommend a more playful, nuanced way to deliver that request, like, "I'm eager to share a few things with you, can you meet me out tonight?") The Maven probably knows the perfect twenty-four-hour diner or dive bar where they can sink into conversation and break things up with a game of pinball if the mood gets heavy.

Giving Feedback to a Maven

Mavens love feedback as long as they don't feel personally insulted or chastised. As mischievous seekers who tend to beg forgiveness rather than ask permission, Mavens are no strangers to getting in a little bit of trouble. But as lovers of personal growth, these curious souls are also eager to learn. If they've asked for someone's tutelage, they genuinely want to kneel at their throne and make this person their guru. These are the people who will pore over directions, memorize the manual, and obsessively watch videos to learn technique.

Some Mavens may request a performance review. They don't want smoke blown up their behinds—at least, not if they respect the person reviewing them! Mavens genuinely want to hear a mentor's thoughts and feedback with plenty of adjectives.

That said, this feedback should be rooted in the Maven's development and growth. Critics should point out what they're doing well, then position any commentary as "the next phase of development" for the Maven. Correcting the Maven should be done in a neutral, nonpunitive tone of voice. More than any other archetype, Mavens have a "bad kid" complex. When they feel they've messed up, they may begin acting out and rebelling in a childish way.

To prevent any parent-child dynamics from snowballing, it's best to acknowledge their progress and achievements up front. Mavens can clap back with force when they sense that their contributions have been overlooked. They may not realize how their tone and words come across, especially when backed by an intense swell of emotion. Mavens can be reactive and defensive, quick to eviscerate others. Their sharp verbal skills can cut deeper than they realize.

How a Maven Deals with Conflict

More than the other I*AM archetypes, Mavens love to be mirrored. When a Maven goes high, they want the other person to match their over-the-top energy. Mavens often speak in "we" and "us" statements and respond eagerly to conversational hooks that have an invitation ("What if we tried...").

Given this, it can be a struggle for anyone who finds themselves on a different page than the Maven. No matter how cool they play it, they are highly sensitive to any type of separation. Some Mavens may even interpret a divergent perspective as a sign of abandonment, especially if that's one of their childhood wounds. Out come the knives! The Maven's sharp tongue can slash anyone's ego to shreds.

People close to the Maven may have to develop a thicker skin in order to not take their heat-of-the-moment reactivity to heart. Yet, people in the Maven's inner circle may also need to hold the Maven accountable to practicing more mature methods of communication when they feel threatened. Emotional regulation is a skill many Mavens must learn as adults. The pause between thought and response can be the saving grace for Mavens when negotiating differences.

If at all possible, conversations with Mavens should be expressed in "we" language, even when the Maven has a completely opposite stance. "Let's see if we can find some common ground" or "How can we create space for both of us to get what we need?" Words of affirmation can work wonders to keep the Maven from freaking out. What they want to know more than anything—but probably won't find the serenity to ask—is that they are still loved and accepted.

When a Maven Should Take a Time-Out

There's a surefire way to know when a Maven needs a time-out and it's all about their tone of voice. They go from being bubbly and encouraging to mean-spirited, critical, and sarcastic. Mavens can come across as confrontational, as if they're purposely playing devil's advocate or looking for a fight. Carrying on the conversation is the worst thing anyone can do in moments like these. Instead, the first order for Mavens is to physically move!

Emotional energy builds quickly in their bodies, and Mavens should release it before it peaks. They may need to shed some of their frenetic electricity in order to get present with people and remember to be nice again.

A spontaneous dance party or a quick cardio session can take Mavens from rage monster to endorphin-filled bliss. We know Mavens who keep a meditation app, a journal, and an online therapist within reach at all times. Since Mavens are *not* good at self-suppression, these outlets can spare both their sanity and their reputations.

Communication Challenges: Lack of Filters, Mood Swings

Blurt alert! Mercurial Mavens do best when they practice mindful communication. Rather than just say whatever comes to mind and clean it up later, they can redeem themselves by practicing the power of the pause.

Mavens' gut-spilling transparency can be awesome at a yoga retreat or in a tearjerker toast. But in business and social settings, Mavens can quickly land in hot water if they go #NoFilter too fast. "Should I have shared about my complicated breakup at the board financial meeting?" they wonder, as the shame hangover kicks in.

The Maven's loose lips can also sink other people's ships, too. Because of their desire to bond and connect, they may thoughtlessly use their friends' personal intel as social currency. If a Maven is at odds with a frenemy, they may slip into a vengeful mindset, raking the person over the coals and in extreme cases, revealing a deep, dark secret that they swore they would never tell. Mavens may also break confidence out of "concern," which can torch the trust between them and their people.

When the Maven's mood crashes, their bad vibe can swallow a room whole. The glass isn't just half empty, it's shattered into a million pieces. Daring to offer the Maven a pep talk or advice in those moments is as dicey as picking up the shards from that broken glass. It's best to treat the Maven with kid gloves at times like these! The mood will pass soon enough, and it's better not to fuel the Maven's inner fire.

Sure, those Maven charms redeem them most times. But do they want to be branded as the loose cannon? Unlikely. Mavens can use their honesty to become an asset, not a liability. These dynamic types need to learn to read the room, or at least do a temperature check before they open the floodgates. A pinch of Maven magic goes further than they think.

WORK

The Astrology Advantage
at Work

What does each I*AM archetype need to succeed in the workplace? By now, you won't be surprised to hear that each personality comes with a strikingly different productivity model. Repetitive routines and clear-cut systems may be optimal conditions for the Authority to thrive, but feel stultifying to the Maven, who needs to float between tasks throughout the day. Meanwhile, the Innovator inspires awe by spinning up groundbreaking methodologies—then drives everyone crazy by forgetting to orient the team to their novel approach.

As we've studied the types, we discovered something fascinating: each one has a favorite "time zone," a state they live in most comfortably. For Innovators it's the future, where anything is possible. Authorities feel grounded when mastering time-tested techniques from the past. Au courant Mavens know how to pull magic from the present moment by simply tuning in.

What we believe all three archetypes share is this: a desire to live a life of purpose and meaning. Using the Astrology Advantage, they can connect the dots between their soul urges and the external, business-oriented world. And they can create a space (or spaces) that help them be their best, guided by their unique I*AM temperament.

We've even created a workspace design floor plan for each I*AM archetype to maximize productivity according to *their* specific flow. We've outlined where each I*AM thrives, along with stumbling blocks to avoid. Energy creates more energy, so when you're ready to get into motion, what you'll read in this section is a springboard to help you dive into the game of life.

THE I*AM TYPES AND TIME

Innovator: The Future

Authority: The Past

Maven: The Present

The Innovator lives in THE FUTURE

They are here to create something wholly unique and disrupt the status quo. Careers that allow them to ideate and be visionaries are much more satisfying than repetitive, overly structured jobs. Their definition of workspace is flexible, and can range from the cafe table to their favorite sofa to an oversized dining table—anywhere that allows them to dream without distraction, free from the constraints of the clock.

The Authority lives in THE PAST

They are here to achieve mastery through practice and safeguard traditions. They feel best in a stable career with a body of work that builds incrementally on each accomplishment. Authorities like a more traditional workspace that supplies and supports a sense of achievement, in a place that's separate from their private life.

The Maven lives in THE PRESENT

They are here to create connection and community through a shared peak experience. Careers where they can wear many hats, experience variety, and interact with people will be most satisfying. Their workspaces can quickly turn into museums (or messes!), as these collector-curators always have a million projects percolating.

INNOVATOR CAREER PROFILE

What motivates them?: Status, connecting dots, birthing movements

Superpowers: Style, self-assuredness, ability to make something out of nothing

Paths to success: Creating something wholly unique

Pitfalls: Being elitist, exclusionary, too "out-there" or far ahead of the curve

Innovators are here to write new rules—for life, work, anything that matters to them. Don't bother telling them that "this is the way it's always been done." Rather than follow a well-worn path, Innovators want to spin up something unique that disrupts the norms. To fulfill their mission, they need to look far ahead of the present moment and time travel to the future.

Other times, their ideas come years too soon, and very few people are ready to adopt what the Innovator is evangelizing. Being "ahead of their time" can be a compliment or a curse!

The competitive Innovator is often the MVP superstar, a member of the special people's club. Take Innovator Tom Brady, who was an NFL champion until the unheard-of age of forty-five. Innovators thrill at the opportunity to smash right through any ceilings you set over their heads.

Still, much of the Innovator's professional success is made up as they go. They're building the plane while flying it, scripting the movie while filming it. Eventually, like a picture coming into focus, the Innovator can explain the concept that's seized their imagination.

When their bold brushstrokes work, Innovators can be powerful thought leaders who change their communities, if not society overall. Steve Jobs, the creator of Apple, who invited us all to "think different," had seven Innovator placements. Because of their ability to "hold space" for a future vision, Innovators excel as company founders and CEOs—although they may need to bring in a process-driven team to keep their enterprises on track with timelines and revenue goals.

INNOVATOR TIME MANAGEMENT

Innovator Time Zone: The Future

The visionary Innovator has sights set on the future. They don't care what's been done already. They're rewriting the rules, inventing something unique, and changing the course of events for all of us. To fulfill their soul's purpose, Innovators need to look far, far ahead of the present moment. Like a picture slowly emerging, their desired outcome gradually comes into focus. However, the Innovator needs ample time to dream before they can articulate this exciting future vision that tingles in their bones.

When Innovators are in the zone, time is elastic. Think of Keanu Reeves's character in *The Matrix*, who could slow down and speed up time with his mind (Innovator #goals). Good news: many Innovators can and do learn how to do a version of this, no special-effects studio necessary! An Innovator who wants something can will it into being, like the Law of Attraction at 10x speed. Their phones ping, they have a serendipitous run-in with someone who's got a direct connection to exactly the thing they need.

The ancient Greeks believed in two types of time: kronos and kairos. Kronos is linear and measurable. Kairos is quantum, dreamy, limitless—the space where we commune with the gods and muses. Ideally, Innovators would follow the 80/20 principle, hanging in kairos for 80 percent of the time then sitting down to "focus" the other 20 percent of the day. After a proper dip into divine inspiration, Innovators can download their inspired material from the "cloud drive" over their heads. (Suggested bumper sticker for Innovators: *I'm not procrastinating, I'm downloading.*)

Last thing: Innovators need a few minutes to transition as they move between states. Often, this means making sure they take care of some bodily needs! As they shift from being inspired ("in spirit") to being embodied, they're hungry, foggy, stiff, and a little grumpy. Innovators can offset this by making sure they have easy access to water, food, fresh air, and amenities to help them ease back into the mundane side of life: checking emails, picking up the kids, grocery shopping. It can be jarring to go from their "high" to this. Playing music or listening to a great podcast is one way that Innovators can keep that tingle while they go through the motions of day-to-day life.

INNOVATOR PRODUCTIVITY

Innovators Thrive on:

- A self-created schedule with minimal micromanagement

- Autonomy and decision-making power

- Projects that have limitless possibility and potential

- Flexible priorities that can shift as needed

- A loose hierarchy, with roles and accountabilities designed to suit the project at hand

- One-on-one mentorship at various project phases

- Creating rituals that make the hard or "boring" parts of a project (especially planning) into a creative and enjoyable experience

- Breaking overwhelming tasks into micro steps with rewards along the way

- No micromanaging or looking over their shoulders—the Innovator's muse can't be rushed!

Innovators Stumble with:

- Too loose of a structure and going fully free-range

- DIY overload: trying to handle things that require experts

- Articulating their vision or innovation, then resisting asking for directions or support

- Doing things "last minute" without a template

- Ditching instead of delegating: getting bored and abandoning projects when novelty plateaus

- Remembering that they live in a body! Not having enough food, exercise, or free time because they've said "yes" to too many things

WHAT INNOVATORS NEED TO SUCCEED

A blank canvas. Innovators love "start-up energy"—the dopamine rush of a new project, the early stages where the canvas is still mostly blank. That's when they feel that spaciousness, and their imagination unfolds like a gorgeous silk fan. Want to excite an Innovator? Give them permission to play the role of changemaker. Whether they're moving your furniture into a new configuration, rebranding your business, or reinventing the corporate cafeteria, these imagineers will find a better, more future-forward way to do it. "If at first the idea is not absurd, then there is no hope for it," said Albert Einstein. Words to live by for the Innovator, whose concepts may sound outright preposterous to listeners at first.

Opportunities to iterate. Innovators love to ideate, and thrive when they work according to the principles of "design thinking." If Thomas Edison had ten thousand experiments that didn't work, the iterating Innovator has ten thousand drafts of their master plan.

Ample dreamtime. Losing track of the clock is the Innovator's favorite luxury. Alas, this habit is not supported by our culture, which is still oxidizing from the nine-to-five Industrial Age workday. And that's a dilemma because Innovators need true spaciousness to create their best work. They never know when the muse will swoop in; it could be 2:00 p.m. or 2:00 a.m.!

Flexible schedules. A self-created schedule with flexible priorities and deadlines suits the Innovator best. The Innovator's experience of time can feel either harried or limitless, depending on what they're doing. When they have spaciousness to dream, download, and channel new ideas, time stretches like a rubber band and feels infinitely expansive.

Often, you'll meet an Innovator with a rather mundane day job, one that doesn't consume much cognitive capital, and a growing empire on the side. The paycheck gig gives the Innovator a steady income and the calm space to dream.

Danielle is an Innovator with a master's degree in early childhood development. By day she drives a school bus; after hours, she's writing a book to help educators work better with empathic and highly sensitive children.

Innovator Monique is a gifted intuitive who supplements her ghostwriting practice with dog walking stints (she's got a five-star rating on all the apps). "Some of my best ideas come on those long strolls!" Monique laughs.

Free rein. Micromanagers begone! Self-directed Innovators want to be in charge of their own productivity. Novelty and variety keep this archetype inspired. To get the best from Innovators, they need space to set their own agenda. Keep the doubters and naysayers far away when Innovators are crafting their masterpieces. They need to be encouraged at this stage, not interrogated.

Project management systems. Learning to delegate, ask for help, and work with a team are Innovator weak spots—and important skills for this type to cultivate. Since many Innovators are self-taught, they may lack some of the necessary training that gets their work to industry standards. Private lessons with a patient pro can be a game-changer for Innovators—and their attention span is much better in a one-on-one setting.

For Sandra, things shifted dramatically when a colleague who was assigned to personally mentor her, trained her on a prototyping software called Figma. "I used to spend hours designing a nearly finished product before presenting it to my clients," recalls Sandra. "I would get so frustrated when they didn't like it or gave me a ton of changes, I'd want to fire *them*!

"Now, I draft a rough sketch and have my clients give feedback first," Sandra shares. "I don't start designing or pouring my best creative energy into anything until they approve the colors, layout, fonts, and everything else." Her once-adversarial relationship with bosses and clients has transformed into a pleasurable partnership.

What used to seem like a lot of extra fuss to Sandra ("Sign-offs and wireframes? I didn't 'do bureaucracy'!") now saves her tons of agonizing do-over hours. When Innovators learn to "work smarter, not harder," they can enjoy the steady buzz of an endorphin rush instead of being haunted by a looming deadline and endless revisions. A little project management on the front end will pay dividends when the Innovator reclaims their cherished hours of spaciousness and free time later.

Mentorship. Since Innovators blaze new trails, they may struggle to find people who have walked a similar path before them. Still, these futurists thrive with people who can help them create systems and checkpoints that support their growth and emergence. Mentors and managers might have to regularly remind the Innovator to come back down to earth and run their ideas through a reality filter.

Ideal mentors for the Innovator know how to make structure fun and creative. One of the most famous historical examples of an Innovator who thrived with a mentor is that of Helen Keller, who had six Innovator placements in her chart. At nineteen months old, Keller contracted an illness that left her both permanently blind and deaf. She became one of the world's most pioneering advocates for disabled people's rights and inclusion. In the famous movie about her life, *The Miracle Worker*, Keller is shown as a wildly undisciplined child, able to communicate only through gesturing.

At age seven, Helen Keller met her lifelong teacher, Anne Sullivan (an Innovator with *seven* placements!), and learned to read braille, write, and talk. Keller attended Harvard, became a world-famous public speaker and author, and could even "hear" people by placing her hand over their lips as they spoke. In addition to advocating for disabled rights, Keller was a suffragist who campaigned for women's right to vote.

This is the kind of limitless potential that Innovators can actualize—in the face of any so-called adversity—when they gain the tools and training to support them.

INNOVATOR CAREER CHALLENGES

The ticking clock. It doesn't help that most Innovators want to accomplish the work of ten lifetimes in a single journey through this mortal coil. They're often overbooked and overextended, which can be hard on their spirits and rough on their relationships. But still they prevail!

Albert Einstein's theory of time dilation might support the Innovator's productivity with a simple tip: take the express elevator to the top floor—literally and figuratively. After observing a clock on a mountain and another on a beach, Einstein found that clocks appear to move slower when they're closer to earth, due to differing gravitational forces. To break through a creative block, Innovators should simply start defying gravity! When it's time to get things done, Innovators can head to a higher elevation, like a rooftop cafe or a top-floor workspace, where time moves as quickly as their minds do.

Impatience. Once an Innovator is ready to unleash their creations, they move at 3x speed, minimum. (Anyone have chronic whiplash yet?) Small talk and mundane matters irritate this type to the point of exploding. They have zero patience for stray chitchat, especially when it's "go time."

This restlessness can also give Innovators an incomplete set of skills. Unless they're outright obsessed with a topic, sitting through rote lectures and tedious instructions is maddening to them. Innovators want the bullet points, the CliffsNotes, the highlight reel.

Since Innovators live in the future, their ideas are often ahead of the curve. How often has an Innovator wailed, "I thought of that ten years ago!" when someone else becomes an overnight millionaire launching the same failed concept they touted a decade back? The Innovator got blank stares when they mentioned a now-popular idea—their nemesis is getting blank checks and going viral. So unfair!

Project planning. When Innovators feel constrained by outside demands and deadlines, their anxiety can rear up, zapping their boundless creativity. Often, they'll push their work until the last minute and ride over the deadline on a surge of eleventh-hour adrenaline. Few people, if anyone, witness the internal chaos that haunts the Innovator near a due date, but those who live with them have experienced the emotional maelstrom!

How can Innovators support themselves with solid project

management but not lose that beautiful feeling of freedom? It's a matter of mindset. Rather than simulate a fight-or-flight response, the Innovator needs to build project planning time into the beginning of an assignment. When they make it part of a ritual, Innovators learn to love planning—and with their engineering brains, can become quite good at it!

Olive, a fashion merchandiser in her early thirties, learned to make this transition by ritualizing her process with art supplies and a beautiful atmosphere. "I began to hand-draw my calendar and schedule, making cute little doodles and having fun with it," shares Olive. "I make myself an amazing latte, light a scented candle, and play music. If I'm really daunted about starting, I buy flowers! Most important, I give myself ample time. I might start by journaling, drawing, or mind-mapping. I've come up with some of my best creative solutions during this phase by doing it this way."

With the luxury of added time for her projects, Olive's been able to obtain a sorely needed missing Innovator ingredient: a sense of spaciousness!

DIY-ing. Innovators, desperate to do it "their way," often cheat themselves out of valuable mentorship. They can even end up in a parent-child role, where they play the misbehaving and rebellious child and treat their more regimented teammates like iron-fisted dictators.

Sound like needless drama? Yes, especially since it's actually the Innovator who's being a passive dictator by missing deadlines or thwarting teammates' ability to plan their own work. Innovators' colleagues can experience them as difficult, even bratty, when they do this.

In their misguided way, Innovators are trying to protect their most precious natural resource: their imaginations.

Unless they commit to a process with their team, though, Innovators can never scale their ideas to full potential. This DIY habit can also be self-defeating. Ultimately, Innovators will hit a part of the project that they can't do themselves. But since they've alienated coworkers or simply left them out of the process, asking for help at this stage creates breakdowns and burdens.

Innovator Productivity Hacks

- **Manage your projects.** Make a template for project planning to easily plug into before hitting the gas.

- **Leave time to dream.** Plot a nonlinear process with enough time to ideate, iterate, and explore. Then, have a framework to get the work done when a deadline approaches.

- **Pit stop or distraction?** Innovators should mark key checkpoints, like a traveler getting off the highway exit. They should explore, but they shouldn't keep driving if they're lost! The farther the Innovator goes, the more off course they get unless they stop and adjust often! Innovators would be wise to practice the power of the pause for this reason alone. Barreling ahead with blinders on, as Innovators are known to do, can be counterproductive.

- **Do something embodied daily.** Innovators should walk, exercise, cook, get a meal or groceries delivered, keep lotions and oils and candles around. Time indulging the senses attracts the muse, and boosts the Innovator's creativity.

THE IDEAL INNOVATOR WORKSPACE

The Satellite

Innovator Floor Plan

A central drop-off space for project paraphernalia, often a pretty or well-appointed desk where they rarely sit to work. Then, they amass an ever-multiplying list of spaces where they go for inspiration: a favorite cafe, a corner of the couch, an outdoor spot, a just-right chair, the whole dining room table.

Workspace Design for the Innovator

A non-office office. The Innovator's office may be a mere just-passing-through space where all work-related accoutrements live when they're not in use. What you're least likely to find at the Innovator's desk is . . . the Innovator! One way that Innovators can "trick" themselves into staying put is to make their office or workspace feel like anything but an office. Since novelty keeps them inspired, they should turn up the personality by flaunting their taste (art, fashion, books, crystals) and adding lots of plants and other symbols of growth.

Wide desk or table. Achievement-hungry Innovators love a challenge! Growth is what this pioneering archetype is all about. So when it comes to setting up a workspace, the Innovator needs lots of freedom to spread out and explore.

A desk that's a minimum of six feet wide—perhaps even a repurposed dining table—can encourage the Innovator to spend more time in one place. They need that extra elbow room since they're often spreading out various materials to pull together a proposal or pitch. Innovators shouldn't skimp on depth, either. If possible, they should spare a few inches for a chic tablescape of their favorite treasures.

Clever office furniture. Innovators love to break out of traditional office furniture. File cabinets are a rare sight! Rather, they should think of their workspace like a chic hotel lobby, with inviting seating and maybe an oversized lamp or chandelier. Repurposed vintage objects like a library card catalog or mid-century coat rack add to the aesthetic.

As for things like paper and binders? Innovators want work out of sight, but not out of mind. They should put all their clips in pretty baskets or display-worthy containers. Then, it feels like they're opening a treasure box every time they pick up a project.

Privacy screens. Innovators hate when people look over their shoulders, especially when they're developing an idea. The last thing they need is a doubter or naysayer sticking pins in their still-inflating balloons! Even an innocent "What are you working on?" inquiry can frustrate the Innovator, who probably doesn't have the words to explain it. They'd rather share the finished concept and let it speak for itself.

Satellite locations. Being restricted to a single workspace can crush an Innovator's spirit. They never know when the muse will grab them by the collar and pull them into another dimension! And when this happens, it's their duty to follow the creative flow—to whatever location suits best. Often that's *not* at a desk!

Outlining the chapters of their future Pulitzer Prize–winning manuscript, for example, might be best done in the window booth of a noodle shop overlooking a garden. Important messages *can* be returned from a pool lounger. Business deals are more fun over breakfast than in a stuffy boardroom, as far as the Innovator's concerned.

Setting up in new spaces brings a burst of novelty, which tunes the Innovator in to a more inspired frequency. From there, work just flows. The short travel time to their "satellite offices" gives the Innovator a beat to process the noise in their head. Ashley, an Innovator who writes a popular weekly column, swears the right words always come to her when "I finally leave my apartment to go pick up a coffee. Why was I staring at the screen for so long?" Ashley now sets an alarm on her phone every ninety minutes and takes a walk or a stretch break, which has helped her writing tremendously.

AUTHORITY CAREER PROFILE

What motivates them?: Setting big goals and meeting them with excellence

Superpowers: Being the real deal who earned their stripes through hard work, loyalty, and dedication

Paths to success: Creating a system or "proprietary process"

Pitfalls: Getting stuck in a rut, being too rigid about rules and systems

Measure twice, cut once! Authorities are masters at systems and strategies. They believe in working smarter, not harder—if only because they love to relax with a book and a lovely glass of their favorite drink at the end of the workday. Often, Authorities are the linchpin employee or consultant who gets credited for "totally revolutionizing" a company's practices and bringing everyone there a sense of relief.

Natural project managers, Authorities understand that structure and security are the pillars of any successful endeavor. When they have a solid framework to operate within, Authorities make miracles happen—and they'll have the numbers to prove it. These are the people who will "10x sales" or raise a Series A round of financing for the development budget. With their unruffled demeanors, Authorities make it all look so easy.

The truth is, Authorities hate to waste anything, be it time, money, or creative capital. Working efficiently is the name of their game. Authorities have a "knack for a hack," and could make a business out of training other people in their time-saving, results-driven techniques. Make no mistakes, the Authority *won't* show you how to cut corners or game the system. Integrity is a cherished value for these folks. They've just simplified and clarified the process to light a streamlined path to your victory.

AUTHORITY TIME MANAGEMENT

Authority Time Zone: The Past

The Authority is most connected to the past. This clock-watching type has a sense of time as fleeting, a resource to capture and commodify by making the most of every minute. Time is valuable to—and valued by—the Authority because life is a series of steps, the path to progress, the vehicle to their destination.

So why, if Authorities are so goal-driven, is the past so important to this archetype? For the Authority, who traffics in grit and persistence, time is a measure of the sweat equity and the sacrifices they make. When they reflect on their choices, do they feel proud? Do they have a history of accomplishments worth eulogizing, a life well-lived? Were they role models who inspired others and made a difference? Character, which is so important to the Authority, is about actions and not words. So the sum total of the Authority's life, documented by their past achievements, is how they judge their quality of life.

The Authority's ultimate asset is experience. True leadership, as they see it, can only be accomplished with enough time. This mastery comes from the years of study the Authority puts in for a degree or certification. The title or trophy they earned by showing up, pushing themselves, failing, and returning to bat. The two thousand hours of yoga teacher training. The ten thousand hours of Malcolm Gladwell's "tipping point" into true mastery.

The Authority is a builder and their respect for the past makes them a quiet source of comfort for many. Their relationship to time helps them plan the vacations and parties that become cherished memories. It holds communities together and quite often, makes the Authority a proud provider. Authorities are a "proven commodity" who earn their reputations through steady acts of loyalty and service.

In many ways, the Authority has a current advantage over the other types—at least, until the AI robots fully take over the planet. We all live in a type A world, where time is quantified in linear progression and measurable increments. Minutes, hours, days, years, seasons. Births, deaths, weddings, graduations. The Authority tracks time in the way of the Western world, starting and ending the day with the sun.

AUTHORITY PRODUCTIVITY

Authorities Thrive on:

- Plans and routines that repeat cyclically

- Structure and security

- Defined work and break times that don't overlap

- Consistency

- Clear goals and priorities

- Hierarchies and defined roles

Authorities Stumble with:

- Having an overly "stick to the plan" attitude and hitting a plateau

- Working harder not smarter: doing what's comfortable instead of what will move the needle on their goals

- Teacher's pet syndrome—being afraid to challenge authority and risk their security

- Clinging to certainty—loss aversion (avoiding loss, then creating even more loss by doing do)

- Not having enough work-life balance, getting addicted to being "busy" or reliant on praise and validation

- Being scared to ask for advice or guidance because they don't want to look incompetent

- Parentalizing leaders and being afraid of "getting in trouble"

- Comparing their work to others'

WHAT AUTHORITIES NEED TO SUCCEED

Linear processes. It's not just about the destination for Authorities. These "journeymen" want to map out the route in advance, to minimize any risk of wheel-spinning distractions and costly detours. What's the smartest way to get from Point A to Point Z? Authorities like to start with the end in mind, then reverse engineer their way back from there. (Here's where they become time travelers, heading back to their preferred time zone of the past before "the past" has technically occurred!)

And it's not just pie in the sky daydreaming to the tune of, "Someday, I'll be a star!" No. The Authority wants to visualize quantifiable results before beginning their efforts. "My book will be a *New York Times* bestseller," or "My restaurant will be profitable, with all initial investment repaid within five years." Once the Authority knows where they're going, they can identify the road map to success.

KPIs and milestones. Authorities want to accomplish a tangible outcome—success, like everything, is measured! Even when toggling between multiple projects, Authorities know: juggle too many balls at once, and you're sure to drop some. Prioritizing is key. Natural project managers, Authorities like timelines, due dates, and projects broken into steps. At some point in their careers, they may become masterful at a productivity system like James Clear's *Atomic Habits* or the Eisenhower Matrix to determine what's urgent versus important.

Clarity is essential. When is it due? What are the expectations? Authorities work best with plans, priorities, and repeatable routines, as each milestone is an achievement that builds on the prior one and informs the next.

Hierarchy. "Who's in charge around here?" The Authority also wants to know! First and foremost, Authorities recognize that to get things done, they have to talk to people who have access to the necessary levers and dials. They won't waste time on middlemen, unless, of course, that's what it takes to gain access to the executives.

Authorities don't mind hierarchies as long as no one's

power tripping. They understand the weight of responsibility that comes with each rung of the ladder. They're happy to work with experienced people in a chain of command if there's goodwill among all; in fact, they love being groomed for leadership by the pros!

Authorities love to tell tales from the trenches—days as "lowly interns" or prep cooks in the bustling kitchen of a Michelin-rated restaurant. They'll regale you with their "how-I-did-its," as if to prove the point that hard work and dedication give everyone access to growth. Podcaster Amy Porterfield, an Authority, built a "multiple-seven-figure business" with her *Online Marketing Made Easy* podcast. Episodes center around her own experiences with things like launching digital courses, creating winning email campaigns, and personal branding. In addition to sharing golden lessons, Porterfield opens up about early mistakes, making her a natural, relatable teacher for her global network of listeners. A true Authority.

ROI. Authorities are investors, and they want a "return" on all they've poured into their missions. For this reason, many prefer to be salaried employees with the security of a steady income rather than risk the uncertainty of independent contractor life. But even when the Authority opts to write their own paycheck, they'll look for clients who will hire them on a six-month minimum retainer or commit to a long-term package of sessions.

Commission structures appeal to Authorities as long as there's adequate base pay involved. Disciplined Authorities may start saving *and* investing early, flowing funds into growing assets, then impressing all their friends by purchasing their own apartment or retiring early.

Regular breaks. While some people like to overlap business and pleasure, the Authority prefers to keep them separate. They need work-free break times and uninterrupted stretches of productivity to be their best. Get the Authority a door and a "do not disturb" sign please!

At their best, Authorities will do a block of focused work, then get up and take the dog to the park, make a nice meal, or meet a friend for coffee. They like to know when their workday will begin and when it will end. As consummate planners, they love having a reward that replenishes them at the end of the day, or something (and hopefully someone) special waiting at the finish line to celebrate.

California Congresswoman and Authority Maxine Waters popularized the phrase "reclaiming my time," which is exactly what this archetype wants to do at the end of the day!

Benefits and bonus structures. Shiny gold star for the Authority, please! This archetype aims to please. Modest as they may be on the surface, they want their efforts to be recognized, but moreover rewarded. The Authority knows they'll put in the hours and serve up high-quality work. But they'll *really* go the extra mile when performance-based bonuses are involved. Health benefits are always a plus, along with other perks like extra vacation time and free membership to a fitness club. Awards, diplomas, and plaques connoting their service will be displayed on the Authority's wall of fame, the way other archetypes might hang a painting. They take pride in their hard work!

AUTHORITY CAREER CHALLENGES

Rigidity. The Authority can stumble when they become overly inflexible and "stick to the plan" without considering potential detours. This rigidity can lead them to hit a plateau, as they resist exploring new avenues that could ignite growth and innovation. Sometimes, Authorities fall into the trap of working harder rather than smarter, prioritizing comfort over taking calculated risks that could push them closer to their goals. It can also put the Authority at odds with coworkers who have a different productivity style. When the Authority insists these things should be done *their* way, they may wind up picking up everyone else's slack.

Dependence on praise. Reputation is everything to the Authority, who wants to be seen as the highly capable linchpin on the team. "Failure is not an option" is a motto we've heard many an Authority state as if it were their guiding mantra. But this approach is one the Authority might want to rethink. When Authorities feel out of their depth, they might become addicted to "busywork," doing easy tasks that win them validation and praise, while resisting anything that could come with a stumble. They might even shy away from seeking advice or guidance, worrying that it will make them appear incompetent. Unfortunately, this fear hampers their growth and prevents them from tapping into the wisdom and insights of others.

Fear of rocking the boat. Another stumbling point for Authorities is the fear of challenging leaders and risking their sense of security. As a result, they may suffer from the notorious "teacher's pet syndrome." Authorities may also fall into the trap of parentalizing leaders, perceiving them as intimidating figures rather than valuable allies in their professional journey.

When Hashim, a global brand consultant, decided to open up his own practice, he found himself with a client list of "cold, commanding men who think the world revolves around their every whim." He'd regularly exceed his contracted hours, offering up iteration after iteration to these difficult-to-please executives. Protracted Zoom calls made Hashim late for family dinners while he essentially bolstered his clients' egos during the nail-biting process of product launches.

One day, a lightbulb went off. "I'm playing out the dynamic I had with my stern, demanding dad!" It was palm-to-forehead obvious for Hashim once he saw it, allowing him to consider a whole new approach to his professional interactions. (A few sessions of therapy helped too.)

Although Hashim still works with the "high-net-worth dude" client profile, as he calls it, he has finessed his processes. Hashim now begins with a kickoff call that outlines his terms, including overage charges for billable hours and a clear-cut schedule of his availability throughout the week.

Not taking enough risks. The Authority's aversion to uncertainty and loss can keep them from taking necessary leaps forward, inadvertently creating more losses by missing out on valuable opportunities. As a result, they may stay at a going-nowhere job far longer than is beneficial for them.

While persistence can pay off under the right circumstances, Authorities can get stuck in regret and rumination, blocking new opportunities. A reminder to Authorities that growth and evolution are also signs of progress, an achievement in their own right. Sometimes, it's only natural that we outgrow situations as a result of the time we put in. It can be helpful for Authorities to reframe endings as signs of success, rather than a failure or loss.

Authority Productivity Hacks

- Schedule regular check-ins with the "authorities" in their lives to make sure they're fully on track

- Use metrics (goals trackers, spreadsheets, project checklists, dashboards) to ensure that they're performing to expectations and producing results

- Get leadership and project management training so they're comfortable being assertive as an authority and keeping their progress moving along

- Check in at regular intervals: Is this working for *every* part of their life? What might be suffering or out of balance?

- Vocalize worries (don't internalize everything)

- Join an accountability or support group, form a mastermind with others working toward similar goals, hire a coach, and make sure they have someone helping to keep them feeling calm and structured

THE IDEAL AUTHORITY WORKSPACE

The Fortress

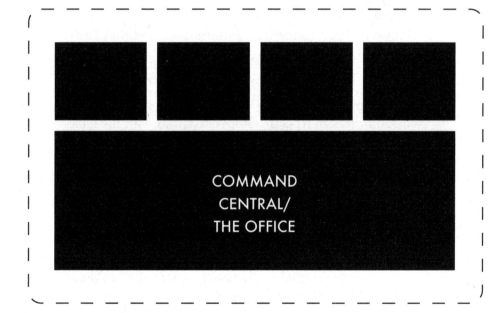

BREAK
Food

BREAK
Family

BREAK
Crafts

BREAK
Fitness

COMMAND
CENTRAL/
THE OFFICE

Authority Floor Plan

The Authority workspace is a command center. Like a pilot settled in front of their navigation panel, the Authority comes to work each day to tackle a serious mission. This no-nonsense archetype wants to accomplish each goal with consistent quality and punctual delivery. The Authority requires a distinctly defined workspace with a clear organizational system that allows them to work on one thing at a time.

Workspace Design for the Authority

A solid desk as the centerpiece. Less is more when it comes to the Authority's workspace style. They should anchor the room with a solid desk that conveys their power, then build around this centerpiece. Bookshelves and filing cabinets keep distractions out of sight—but only as many as are needed. The Authority office is a clutter-free zone!

A clearly defined workspace. Once they beam their laser focus on a task, Authorities are in the zone and they don't take kindly to interruptions. If they work in an open-plan space, Authorities need to find an office-friendly version of the "do not disturb" sign. Regardless, one steely look from an Authority can repel the office chatterbox with the force of an electric fence.

Reliable Authorities need an unintegrated separation of professional and personal space. *Here is where I work. There is where I relax.* Whenever possible, they should install a door or makeshift walls to filter out distractions and create a secure productivity pod.

If they work from home and don't have a door to close, they might want to tuck papers into a cabinet and put their computer behind a screen after hours.

File cabinets and closed shelving. Because the Authority's time zone is the past, they are particularly susceptible to ruminating. They should be highly discerning about which objects they place in their line of vision at their own peril. Even framed photos can cause the Authority to drift down a sentimental rabbit hole, as these relics will pull their focus away from their work. The same is true for paperwork. If the Authority is juggling multiple projects, they should not keep them all on their desk at the same time! This is sure to disrupt the Authority's ability to concentrate on any one mission, as they'll be busy worrying about the other twelve things they need to work on. Out of sight, out of mind!

Closed shelving is a great solution for the single-tasking Authority's office. The Authority might create a bin system for their current projects, placing the assets for each in an individual box or tub, then pulling those out from behind the cabinet doors when they work on them.

On that note, a file cabinet is a must for any Authority working with paper documents. Few things frustrate an Authority more than wasting time, particularly if they're searching all over the place for a contract or brief they need to bring their mission to the finish line. Digital file management is equally important. The Authority needs to easily pull up any PDF or archived email. These are the people who might actually achieve the idealistic "inbox zero!"

Minimal decor that conveys status. To keep their space from becoming too bare-bones, Authorities should accessorize with plants and art and framed quotes. They might stack a few coffee-table books on the shelf or paint the walls a rich hue. Beautiful lamps double as design pieces and help them through those long hours. A solid wall should be claimed to hang framed diplomas and display the awards they worked so hard to achieve.

Whiteboards and Post-it Notes. As data-driven builders, Authorities want to know exactly where they are on the journey toward a goal. A large "year-at-a-glance" wall calendar (preferably dry erase) can help Authorities create a timeline with past, present, and future steps of a project, and be flexible as needed.

Whiteboards and Post-its may not have much visual interest, but they help the Authority measure progress, making them office essentials. Drew Barrymore, an Authority-Maven, wins the award for the most unexpected use of Post-its, which line the walls of a closet-turned–meditation room in her Manhattan apartment. Pressed over the pink flamingo wallpaper is what Barrymore calls her "mosaic of sticky notes." The handwritten affirmations, like *Today Is the Day You Start Trusting Yourself* and *Spiritual Superhero*, seem oddly basic alongside her altar of crystals and candles. But for Barrymore, they turn the small space into what she calls "a room of revelations."

A few luxe paper products. The old-fashioned Authority loves paper (especially a gorgeous yearly planner) and three-ring binders. But having a smart digital asset management system will also help their productivity. A mix of virtual and physical organization ensures that everything has a place and can be easily found when they need it. Keep it simple!

MAVEN CAREER PROFILE

What motivates them?: Connecting people to resources and creating communities

Superpowers: People skills, curating, editing, organizing teams, researching data

Paths to success: Turning an idea into a viral sensation, getting people excited and engaged

Pitfalls: Overselling projects, getting distracted midstream or lost in minutiae

Multi-hyphenate. Multi-passionate. Multitalented. Dynamic Mavens cannot be confined to a single path. With their charts lit up by mutable signs, these "jacks-of-all-trades" have amazing range. But to avoid becoming "masters of none," Mavens will need to sharpen their skills in a few specific arenas. While Mavens don't love silo-ing their lives, it can be hard to know where to place them when they present themselves with an array of traits like: Singer-Songwriter. Inventor. Software Designer. As hard as it is for Mavens to do, picking a focus—at least for the moment—can help them connect with the right people to help their mission. Pro tip for Mavens: it's okay (within reason) to have different business cards or social media accounts for wildly divergent projects.

Social creatures, Mavens have an easier time staying on track when they're working as part of a team—or at the very least, checking in regularly with an accountability buddy. As the superconnectors of the I*AM System, Mavens' work often revolves around helping people, uniting communities, or spreading ideas through the masses.

Natural ambassadors, Mavens flow easily from one group of people to the next. That ability, along with their gift of gab, can make the Maven a natural salesperson. When they believe in a mission, they'll throw their heart and soul behind it, becoming the ultimate promoters and spokespeople. Mavens are also the messengers of the world. PR and marketing are their absolute wheelhouse since they know how to grab public attention with a compelling hook.

As coworkers, Mavens are the ultimate hype people. They'll organize the office softball game and picnic, make playlists for casual Friday, bring coffee and artisanal donuts, and convince HR to make a budget for weekly chair massages for the team. There's no question about it—Mavens can make work feel like play!

MAVEN TIME MANAGEMENT

Maven Time Zone: The Present

For the multi-passionate Maven, time is a vehicle for connection. A moment unshared is a moment wasted. The Maven time zone is the present—right here, right now—and they'll pack as much peak energy as possible into every nanosecond. No resources? No problem! Mavens are masters at creating on the fly and making something out of what seems to be "nothing." It's their hyper-rootedness in the here-and-now that allows the Maven to see what everyone else is overlooking: an opportunity staring them right in the face.

Mavens experience time as synchronous—an "everything every-where all at once" effect. Why have less when you can have more? Maven companionship is like a festival with multiple stages and bands performing at the same time. They love a riveting conversation or an all-consuming project, preferably one that uses their hands. And oh, the things they can make when they start to tinker! Whether hobbyists or gifted artists, Mavens are makers who live for a DIY project that they can lose themselves in.

A helpful image of how Mavens experience time is a radio tuner or an adapter with multiple dials that they can turn up or down at will. Picture the soundboard in a music studio that adjusts the treble, bass, and echo. Mavens are mixmasters who are keenly synced to these nuances—they *need* to have control of those dials to perfect their formulas!

MAVEN PRODUCTIVITY

Mavens Thrive on:

- Human connection and collaboration

- Creative problem-solving

- Hands-on, sensory, and DIY work that engages both brain hemispheres

- Lots of feedback, encouragement, and input

- A sense of fun, friendship, and camaraderie

- Roles that are based around small groups and task forces

Mavens Stumble with:

- High capability, but struggle to prioritize

- The dreaded Maven Mess! When creativity becomes chaos.

- Too many cooks: they're naturally democratic and communal, but without some hierarchy, things can fall apart

- Not asking for help or support, trying to DIY everything

- Watercooler drift—when the social parts of the job become an excuse to procrastinate

- Working on something that they don't believe in

- Talking without walking—do they have actual life experience on the topic that they're giving advice on?

WHAT MAVENS NEED TO SUCCEED

Simultasking. Mavens "simultask," a form of multitasking where they simultaneously pull unrelated information fields together into a genius solution. The Maven is a vector where multiple downloads happen all at once. Life is layered for Mavens, overlapping, one experience bleeding into another. Whether writing a novel, inventing a new musical genre, or engineering a solar-powered lighting system, it's precisely *because* of their astrological short attention spans that Mavens can devise the perfect and original solution that nobody else could have dreamed up. Their work is interconnected and disjointed all at once! It's crucial that Mavens feel free to move between their varying projects, rather than get pigeonholed into one track, which is a recipe for unhappiness.

Spreadsheets, lists, reminder alarms. Mavens are easily swept up in the moment, riding the exciting wave of conversation with a coworker who "popped their head in" or talking to a barista about the benefits of a pour-over versus a French press on their "quick coffee run." Needless to say, the Maven's embrace of "the power of now" can create chronic issues with time management. Sharp as their memories may be, Maven attention scatters easily. More than any other I*AM archetype, these people need to plug appointments into a calendar and set reminder alarms. Otherwise, they'll perpetually piss off their coworkers, showing up twenty minutes late for Zoom meetings, napping through dinner plans, and rushing around like headless chickens.

Task management can also slip into chaos for Mavens until they create an accountability system for themselves. Project management software—even a basic list or spreadsheet—can do wonders to ensure that the Maven checks off every one of their duties. Fortunately, Mavens are masterful with data. They catch on quickly to organizational systems and learn to appreciate the ease a tracking app can bring to their lives.

A platform. Communal and communicative, Mavens have a message, and they need to express it now! Perhaps that's why a good number of these raconteurs are so popular on social media. Mavens become so consumed by sharing their thoughts that they tend to worry less about having every hair and lash in place. When the spirit moves them, they'll turn on the camera and go! (But yes, some Mavens do also wear a full face of makeup to the gym just in case they are inspired to shoot a video while doing leg presses.)

We know just as many Mavens who boycott social platforms in order to protect their privacy and data. A lot of them still have *some* way of reaching their desired audience, be it a podcast, an email list, or a WhatsApp group chat. Whenever Mavens decide to share their wisdom, people sit up and listen. We once watched a reserved Maven who professed to be "a man of few words" move an entire room to tears giving a speech at his father's memorial. No one would have guessed he had it in him, but once the cat was out of the bag, he didn't have a moment to himself for the rest of the gathering.

Variety. Ask any Maven what their favorite spice is and you'll probably get a list of five savory herbs, proving that indeed the Maven's answer should be "variety." Perpetually experimental, Mavens want to check out every font combination and background theme before making a presentation. They love to get their hands in the metaphoric clay! But this can definitely turn into "too much of a good thing," especially if the Maven ever wants to create a consistent brand . . . or actually generate a finished product.

Back in our freelance web design days, we consulted on a website overhaul for a 120-year-old family-owned diner. It had a massive menu—Greek, Asian, American, and Italian dishes were offered along with a full spread of diner classics for breakfast, lunch, and dinner.

Amazed, we asked the owner how the kitchen staff handled so many recipes without melting down. Her answer? "Almost everything on the menu uses the same five ingredients. The only variety is the meat and spices." A-ha!

This lightbulb moment is one we want to pass along to the Mavens. Their "recipe catalogs" may be massive, but they can still be managed! The Maven who knows their five main ingredients will be able to live multiple lifetimes in one. #MavenGoals

Tinker time. Call it a distraction, a diversion, or plain old procrastination—but Mavens get deep satisfaction (and stress relief) when they slide down the latest rabbit hole. Sometimes they're processing a problem, and only when they divert themselves from it does the a-ha solution strike. But good luck to the Maven trying to explain why they just disappeared on a five-hour excursion instead of grocery shopping or finishing that marketing report . . . oops!

It's no surprise to us that Albert Einstein and Thomas

Edison were both Mavens. The mad scientist inventor arche-type is oh so Maven because they don't know 'til they know. They need to build what we call "tinker time" into any proj-ect so they can try their ideas out every which way. (Pity the lab assistant who had to clean up Edison's "ten thousand ex-periments that didn't work" before his first lightbulb finally went on.)

Co-pilots. This hands-on archetype loves to DIY. Leave the Maven alone in a room and you never know what projects they'll walk out with. But when Mavens' projects start multiplying—let's call it octo-Maven mode because they have at least eight arms all doing different things at once—it's a distress signal. *S.O.S.! Maven overload! Deploy the backup generators!*

This is exactly why Mavens thrive when they work in partnership or with a team. Just because they *can* play every instrument doesn't mean they should attempt to be a one-person symphony. Mavens need to learn how to del-egate *before* they have to call for support in a moment of crisis.

From the very beginning of a mission, Mavens should get clear about what parts of the job they'll handle and which ones they'll hand off to a co-pilot. Caveat: Mavens are amazing talent scouts and friend collectors, but they must beware recruiting needy or narcissistic people who turn them into a sounding board or dump on them. Ma-vens should set guidelines and clarify roles as they build a team or social circle.

Even better, they could make the whole production pro-cess social and interactive. The more it feels like a party, the harder and faster the Maven will work!

Regular check-ins. It's not enough for Mavens to enlist other people. They need to check in regularly to ensure that everyone's aligned and moving toward the same target. Connecting to the team also helps Mavens feel supported in their own processes. Even if they're working independently, they like to know that they're not alone.

MAVEN CAREER CHALLENGES

Social distractions. Mavens might benefit from understanding a stress response called "tend and befriend," discovered by UCLA researcher Shelley E. Taylor in 2000. Taylor and her team found that "fight or flight" wasn't the only way that some people coped with anxiety. She observed that, when threatened, many animals and humans gather with a compatible social group or begin nurturing each other. This causes the brain to release the neurotransmitter oxytocin—AKA the bonding or cuddle hormone—which restored them to calm.

When Mavens start "wasting time" at the metaphorical watercooler, dropping everything to meet a friend or help someone in need, this may be a sign that they're in distress. So rather than slipping into small talk, Mavens should use their social breaks proactively, meeting up with helpful friends and sound advisors who can support them with problem-solving.

Messy workspace. Mavens can be shockingly messy when they're "in the zone." They'll pull open every drawer to find a tool—or just so they can see all of their supplies. They'll spread out in the middle of the floor, getting up midway to take over the nearest flat surface for another task. Before they have a chance to clean anything up, yikes! They get a five-minute reminder of a conference call that they forgot to review the documents for and are rushing off to their computer to prep, leaving the area in utter chaos . . . sometimes for days!

This mad scientist approach might be fine if the Maven has a private office, but even then, it can be quite unsightly for anyone who dares knock on the door. Plus, Mavens may waste precious time scrambling to find the tool they need. "Dammit, it was in that pile right under my desk just a few minutes ago!"

Regular cleanups are essential for the Maven, but so are periodic decluttering sessions. The Maven may not realize how many quick-grab items they've amassed, not to mention the mail they forgot to open and papers that need to be shredded. Clearing the space of junk has a magic of its own, freeing up stuck energy and making the Maven a magnet for opportunity again.

Group similar projects and tools together. Place them in the best area (near a well-lit window for filming and access to electrical outlets). Before long, voilà! A Maven multiverse is born—the amusement park and creation station that allows their wonderful ideas to blossom!

Indecision. Multi-passionate Mavens fear being pigeon-holed or limited if they pick one thing. As a result, they may sabotage their own progress by dropping balls—or even dropping out right before they're about to move to the next stage of the game. Mavens love the dopamine rush of anticipation much more than the victory rush of crossing the finish line (a phase beloved by achievement-driven Authorities). This probably explains why Mavens always need to have a few projects percolating at all times. They enjoy being fully immersed in the process, and they hate goodbyes!

Diana, a gifted healer, completed all the course requirements to become a professional acupuncturist. But when it was time to study for exams, she began questioning if this modality was really the right one for her to practice. She decided to take a little time off and took a job managing an organic food co-op. The people-centric environment stimulates Diana, who loves interacting with coworkers and customers alike—although the pay leaves a lot to be desired. It's been nearly a year and she still isn't sure she'll move ahead with acupuncture. Meantime, Diana's started a dog-walking side gig and recently dove back into another unfinished certification program for life coaching. "My friends are getting whiplash trying to keep up with me," jokes Diana, who admits that she's a "seasonal person" who tends to finish things in phases, punctuated by long breaks.

This tendency to change course might supply a steady stream of novelty, but it can short-circuit Mavens like Diana, who may quit "five minutes before the miracle" or just when the finish line is in sight. So why not just slide into homebase? Mavens may feel trapped by commitment, but in truth, they are restricting their options by not completing degrees, "forgetting" to show up for meetings, or leaving loose ends everywhere.

But here's the rub: their fear of being trapped or of failing is nothing compared to the inner guilt and shame the Maven may experience when dropping out before the final 5 percent is complete. Finishing what they start builds major confidence for the Maven. They just need a push!

Lack of focus. Mavens have a lot of projects in halfcompleted states, since they're easily pulled into every curiosity. Where to direct their energy when they're excited by so many things? Focus can be challenging. A germ of an idea turns into an instant empire with marketing plans, logos, and distribution channels spun from their imagination in a matter of milliseconds. Even if they have zero intention of starting that cannabis brownie truck business or buying land for an intentional micro-farming community, they'll spend two hours mapping the idea out anyway.

Maven Productivity Hacks

- Make it social and interactive. The more it feels like a party, the better

- Map big ideas into reality: a project management system is the Maven's best friend! (Learn to love the spreadsheet)

- Create quarterly focus projects: Mavens never have "just one thing," but might pick one of their passions as the top focal point for ninety days. They should give it 80 percent of their energy, and the other projects 20 percent for that window of time

- Contain, don't restrain: Mavens need to organize their growing stacks of projects for easy access when the mood hits—like a chef's prep stations or a science lab

- Delegate or bring in a co-pilot for the stuff they avoid; outsource when they get stuck for too long

- Build in "tinker time" and make a workshop where they can get messy

THE IDEAL MAVEN WORKSPACE

The Lab

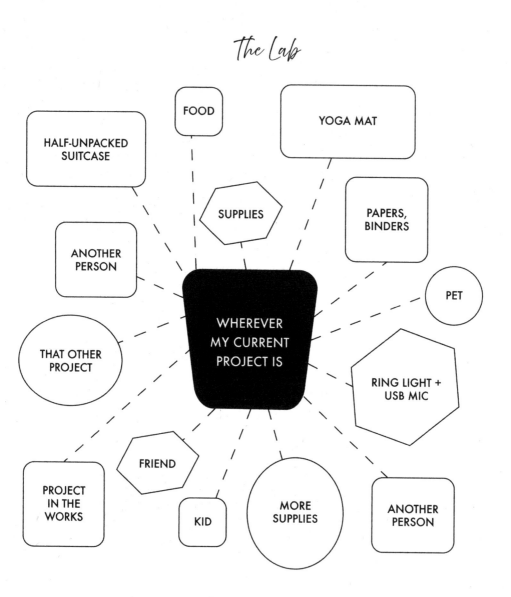

Maven Floor Plan

Like an octopus with tentacles that reach out from wherever the Maven is, or an atom with electrons swirling around in its outermost shell, the breadth of the multi-passionate Maven's workspace is ever-expanding. Creating "stations" for projects and bundling similar ones together can keep their genius from devolving into chaos.

Workspace Design for the Maven

Shelfies. Mavens are collectors whose treasures tell the story about who they are—and they love to bring their cherished items with them to work. For one thing, it just makes the Maven happy to be surrounded by favorite objects. But they also like to build personal rapport with their coworkers. These displays double as icebreakers and conversational warmups—perfect for friendly chit-chat before the Maven pivots over to shop talk.

Many times, we'll see Mavens with "shelfies" as their Zoom backdrops—artfully styled floating shelves with a pastiche of beloved curiosities: vintage cameras, neon signs with a cheeky mantra ("Game on" or "Bad Bitch"), potted plants, vacation souvenirs. Jill, a clutter coach and Maven, is famous for her color-coded bookshelf, the rainbow-bright backdrop she cheerfully greets her clients with when they meet for virtual sessions.

Stations for every project. Since their workspace location is dictated by their "project of the hour," Mavens tend to float between zones. They may thrive best in an open-floor plan with designated departments. This archetype should think like a prep cook at a restaurant or an herbalist at an apothecary. Where do they chop, mix, bake, cool? In this spirit, Mavens can make stations for their multi-step process.

Angelina is a Maven tech consultant, fiction writer, vegan blogger, and marathon runner. After learning about the concept of creating zones, she transformed the garage of her So-Cal home into a perfectly appointed Maven workspace. The large room has a desk area with dual monitors, a small kitchen with lighting and camera set up, and a workout area with weights and a treadmill. Throughout the day, she floats from one zone to the next until it's time to help kids with homework or prepare dinner.

Easy-access storage space. Mavens find space in unexpected places, so grab a closet, any closet! (It's officially an "office area" in Mavenspeak.) Cabinets, drawer sorters, and armoires can tame sensory overload. Label makers are great investments, so the Maven can go to town on semi-opaque plastic tubs and color-coded bins. From there, they can easily find a project without having everything out in plain sight.

Vertical storage is the Maven's friend too. We've seen many of them get clever, by stacking supplies in over-the-door shoe racks, on pegboards, and in covered bins. Mavens should allow just enough to peek out so they can find and grab what they need.

Quiet zones and people zones. Mavens tend to work in sprints, dividing their days between tasks requiring quiet concentration and interactive work that has them on the phone or Zoom, talking excitedly to their team. If the Maven shares a workspace with colleagues, it can be hard for them to find "just one place" to do all their work.

Mavens don't always realize how much their energy alone can fill a room. Troy, who handles customer service for a green energy start-up, will pace through the office when listening to a call. (Sitting still feels agonizing for him!) Although he's generally not speaking, coworkers can feel frissons of stress from Troy moving through the space. "They tell me I'm distracting them," he laments. "But I'm barely even making a sound!"

This is the "downside" of having such a magnetic aura. When Mavens do interact, they draw people to them, quickly turning the break room into a high-decibel party zone by inviting coworkers to chime in on a buzzy topic that's going viral on social media that day. It's all well and good if the zone is delineated for interactivity, but the Maven should take extra care to be considerate of quieter coworkers' need to zone out on breaks, too!

TEAM BUILDING

The Astrology Advantage for Team Building

I*AM GROUP DYNAMICS: BUILDING A TEAM THAT WORKS

Whether it's at work, in our personal relationships, or within a community, we all have a role to play. But how do we know which traits to lead with in which occasions—and when to bring the more expressive parts of our personalities?

So much anxiety stems from simply not knowing which face to put forward as you ease into an unfamiliar setting. Good news: your I*AM profile can help you get to know people without putting on a false front. Guided by this intel, you can be "socially appropriate" and authentic at once. And your relationships can move forward instead of going sideways.

When you understand the different personality types you can navigate group interactions and achieve collective goals, playing to everyone's strengths.

In this section, we'll explore how the I*AM archetypes collaborate and provide practical tips on how each type can use their qualities to build a harmonious and effective organization.

Astro-Ayurveda: Balance Your Group Dynamics

"Astro-Ayurveda," as we call it, involves consciously balancing for where you have either lack or excess. What happens when you have a lot (or only a few) of one I*AM type in your family, group, or organization? The internal culture will tip in a singular direction. The effect is like trying to steer a ship against the wind and tide, which keeps on pulling you in another direction. Frustrating!

Good news: There's something you can do about that. We know because we've worked with companies and teams of all sizes, helping them bring balance based on the spread of Innovators, Authorities, and Mavens in the house.

Balance Team Dynamics with I*AM

Groups with More	Need to Balance For
INNOVATORS	Dictators: too many captains, not enough teamwork
AUTHORITIES	Stubbornness: too many rules and processes, not enough flexibility
MAVENS	Overload: too many ideas, not enough follow-through
Groups with Fewer	Need to Balance For
INNOVATORS	Stagnation: lack of risk-taking, vision, and initiative
AUTHORITIES	Chaos: lack of structure, systems, and accountability
MAVENS	Irrelevance: lack of communication, creativity, and experimentation

BALANCING INNOVATOR ENERGY IN A GROUP

Innovator Majority: Peacock Pen

Do you ever feel like you're following the leader, even when no one's officially in charge? Chances are, you're in a group that has an Innovator majority. When there's an abundance of competitive and visionary Innovators in the group, it can sometimes feel like everyone is vying for attention or wants things done on their terms. Plans can pivot on a whim. While it's great to be nimble in today's world, you won't accomplish much if you abandon a project too soon—a temptation in this kind of crew. In Innovator-heavy settings, entitlement can easily get out of hand. You might find yourself in a conversation where one person is constantly interrupting, changing the subject, or dominating the discussion. If you're an Innovator, it's important to recognize that you may be contributing to this dynamic, and to practice active listening: a way of listening that builds connection through techniques such as eye contact, affirmative nods, and asking empathic questions to understand the other person's perspective, even if you don't agree with it. Share the spotlight and you'll prevent your democracy from turning into a dictatorship. If you're not an Innovator, push yourself to speak up and assert yourself in the conversation. Remember, everyone's voice deserves to be heard.

Signs and Symptoms of High Innovator Groups

- Everyone's leading but nobody's following

- A couple of "alphas" hold all the information, but nobody else knows what's going on

- Burnout from constant changes, team is stretched beyond capacity

- There's not enough time, money, or resources to make the idea truly viable

- Tendency to make decisions based on personal feelings or opinions rather than data or logic

- Overemphasis on image or appearance rather than substance and results

- Difficulty staying focused or following through on long-term goals

- Lack of attention to detail

- Resistance to feedback or differing perspectives

Balancing Remedies for High Innovator Groups

- **Encourage active listening.** Opinions run strong in high Innovator groups, which can create a chaotic, competitive environment. Create a structure where everyone shares and listens respectfully to each other, even when they have different perspectives. Set a time, pass a talking stick, make it fun. This will help to ensure that all ideas are considered, not just the ones that are the loudest or most persuasive. Hold quarterly brainstorming sessions (preferably off-site) to capitalize on Innovator creativity and allow everyone to share their blue-sky visions freely.

- **Provide structure.** While Innovators love to "wing it," a meeting agenda, daily check-ins, and a centralized plan (even if it's flexible) can save massive amounts of time. Having a clear structure or framework for decision-making and goal-setting can help keep the group on track and prevent it from becoming too scattered or unfocused.

- **Emphasize collaboration.** Bust up the "lone-ranger syndrome" and put people into small groups of two or three for projects. Encourage collaboration and teamwork by pairing people with different strengths and skill sets. Breaking into these task force crews can prevent one person from dominating the group—and will create the camaraderie that's often missing. Innovators need to learn how to pass the metaphorical ball!

- **Set clear expectations.** Where does the line get crossed and set off power struggles or rivalries? High Innovator groups may need clear expectations for behavior and participation. This can include guidelines for how to give feedback, how to handle conflict, and how to ensure that everyone's voice is heard.

- **Cultivate diverse perspectives.** Encourage the group to seek out and listen to diverse perspectives, including those that may not align with the group's dominant ideas or values. This can help to broaden the group's thinking and prevent it from becoming too insular.

Not Enough Innovators: Passion Shortage

Don't stop believing! Have you ever been in a group where nobody seems really passionate or enthusiastic? When your crew is low on Innovators, there can be a lack of vision. *Somebody* has to light the spark and take the risk—and Innovators are usually the first to volunteer. Without enough Innovators to keep everyone psyched about the "impossible dream," your crew could just go through the motions without getting invested in the outcome.

If you're in charge of the group, try to bring in someone who can inject excitement into the mix, like a motivational speaker or a coach. In your personal life, mix things up and try a new outing instead of just going to the same old spots. No matter what your title or status is, make a conscious effort to lead by example and bring your own passion and energy to the mix. Remember, enthusiasm is contagious.

Signs and Symptoms of Low Innovator Groups

- Quiet quitting is pervasive: people are going through the motions or waiting for permission and instructions because there's no vision or higher purpose to unify them

- You've fallen behind on technology and trends

- Difficulty generating excitement or motivation among group members

- People avoid taking risks or trying new things

- Lack of innovation and creative problem-solving

- Difficulty communicating ideas clearly

- The group gets bogged down in details and loses sight of the big picture

Balancing Remedies for Low Innovator Groups

- **Push the envelope.** Break through people's fear or resistance around experimenting. Encourage brainstorming sessions where everyone can share their ideas and opinions freely. This can help bring out the creativity and innovation of the group.

- **Bring in guests.** Outside perspectives are refreshing and set an example for new, trailblazing ways of thinking. Invite guest speakers or consultants who are knowledgeable in the area that the group is working on. Or, bring in someone who's an expert in something totally unrelated, like an art therapist or a laughter yoga teacher (yes, that's a thing), to lighten up the mood and get people out of their comfort zones.

- **Cultivate leadership.** Leading is a muscle! Create opportunities for team members to take on leadership roles and spearhead projects, and make sure to mentor them as they learn. Make it fun and add a spirit of friendly competition with prizes. This can help build confidence and allow team members to showcase their talents. Personality tests like Myers-Briggs, Enneagram, or this one (!) can help reluctant people feel more confidence developing their own signature style.

- **Try out trends.** What are the kids scrolling and swiping through today? Create a shared document, digital channel, or mood board for the team to jot down trending topics and think of ways you can incorporate them. Use social media and other team communication channels to stay up to date on current trends and topics related to the group's work. This can help spark new ideas and keep the group engaged.

- **Reward risk-taking.** Emphasize the importance of taking risks and trying new things. Encourage team members to step outside their comfort zones and experiment with different approaches to problem-solving. Use incentives to get them using those creative muscles!

BALANCING AUTHORITY ENERGY IN A GROUP

Authority Majority: Turf Wars

You know those situations when everyone seems to have a strong opinion—and a valid case for it—but nobody's willing to bend? In groups with an Authority majority, stubbornness can poison the culture. There can be a low tolerance for risk, which causes the group to plateau or depreciate, since you may not be willing to adapt as quickly as the world is changing. When there are too many Authorities in the group, it can feel like everyone is trying to be in charge. At the same time, a critical mass of rule-following Authorities can make the vibe *too* "play by the rules" and lead to a lack of initiative. People may argue over the best course of action, digging in their heels or taking credit for the group's success. Titles and hierarchies and side alliances can riddle this crew with more rivalries than the royal family. If you're an Authority, carve out time to explore new ideas. In personal settings, push yourselves to try one new thing a month. If you're not an Authority, focus on finding a solution that works for everyone.

Signs and Symptoms of High Authority Groups

- Resistance to change or new ideas

- Lack of diversity and creativity

- Overreliance on rules and procedures

- Lack of trust and collaboration

- Micromanagement and excessive control

- Difficulty adapting to new situations or challenges

- High turnover rate or low employee satisfaction at work

- Tendency to blame others for problems rather than taking ownership and finding solutions

Balancing Remedies for High Authority Groups

- **Flatten the toxic hierarchy.** Are jealousy and power-tripping tainting the team spirit? Develop shared policies and protocols, where everyone plays by the same rules. Get the C-suite out of their bubble and create ways that the leaders can learn from those lower on the command chain, perhaps pairing an executive with a junior member on a team. Reciprocity and goodwill may flow more naturally if this is a company-wide structure.

- **But give out titles, too.** Authorities like credentials and want to be rewarded for their contributions. Make the process of earning these more democratic to avoid a cutthroat culture. Monthly awards for milestones achievable by everyone could be posted by email or in any communal spaces.

- **Encourage transparency.** Make sure that everyone in the group feels comfortable expressing their ideas and opinions, regardless of their position or rank. Often, this happens in theory, but not practice. Ensure a safe space for sharing, to bring out the best in team members from all levels.

- **Promote collaboration and shared wins.** Foster an environment where people work together rather than compete against each other, to achieve shared goals. Authorities like to get (and take) credit, so it will be a balancing act. Name everyone individually on the teams who contributed to a win and thank them (gifts are always appreciated by Authorities!).

- **Delegate tasks and responsibilities.** Give people clear roles and responsibilities, and empower them to make decisions within their areas of expertise. Authorities need to feel proud of what they've done (and yes, to hear the praise for it!), so even the junior employees should be spotlighted when they do a job well from start to finish.

- **Provide regular feedback.** Offer constructive feedback and recognition to team members, both individually and as a group, to encourage growth and development. Authorities love to earn their shiny gold stars, but also want to know that they're growing and improving. Quarterly reviews and check-ins can help everyone feel confident in their progress or course-correct as needed.

- **Foster a culture of learning.** Encourage team members to continually learn and improve their skills, and provide opportunities for training and development. Hold off-site trainings and certifications. An educational expense or tuition reimbursement budget will be greatly valued by high Authority teams.

Not Enough Authorities: Camp Chaos

Have you ever been in a group where there doesn't seem to be anyone who's really taking charge or providing direction? Without enough Authorities, it can feel like there's no structure or organization. People may drift in different directions, or lack focus and clarity. If you're in charge of the group, try to establish clear goals and guidelines, and delegate tasks to others who can help keep things on track. It's kind of like a family where the parents disappear, and the kids have to figure out how to "adult" on their own. Once they realize there's no supervision or consequences, they're not likely to follow through on the responsibility part. Why eat vegetables when you can have candy and soda all day? In a workplace with too few Authorities, everyone could have really amazing ideas, but nobody has the willpower and grit to consistently roll up their sleeves, stay within budget, and hit deadlines. There are a lot of sprinters, but nobody's got the discipline for the long-distance marathon. At least, not without a cacophony of complaining!

Signs and Symptoms of Low Authority Groups

- Lack of direction or clear leadership

- Difficulty making decisions or taking action

- Tendency to avoid conflict or difficult conversations

- Group members avoid accountability or responsibility

- Frequent chaos or lack of structure

- Nobody feels confident enough or "authorized" to make a decision

- There's anarchy in the ranks and no clear policies or protocols

Balancing Remedies for Low Authority Groups

- **Delegate tasks.** Assign responsibilities to different members of the group to create a sense of structure and organization. Have regular checkpoints and small tasks that get marked "complete" to ensure things are done in the right order and on time. Fighting against employees getting overwhelmed will be an important initiative! Build their confidence and get-'er-done muscles with micro wins.

- **Establish clear goals and roles.** Define what the group is working toward and establish clear benchmarks for progress. Meet regularly, even daily, to go through the task list and see who needs support or where the project is drifting off course. Putting in corrective measures early will be key. Use project management tools to break things into granular action steps and deadlines.

- **Provide guidance.** Give clear, compassionate direction and feedback, and keep the tone positive and encouraging ("I know you've got this!" and "I'm here if you need to check in.").

- **Foster participation.** Inspire everyone to share their ideas and opinions, creating a culture of collaboration and inclusivity. A group mood board or a freestyle "open mic" channel on the shared team network can make things feel fun and less heavy.

- **Celebrate achievements.** Praise the successes of the group, whether small or large, to create a positive and motivating environment. Have a playful quarterly "paper plate awards" ceremony and give out commendments for creative and milestone-based accomplishments.

BALANCING MAVEN ENERGY IN A GROUP

Maven Majority: All Play, No Work

Attraction to distraction: incoming! You know when everyone seems to be always looking for the next fun thing to do, so it's hard to get anything done? When there are too many Mavens in the group, work easily takes a back seat to play. There's a strong attraction to distraction here! People are more interested in socializing than in getting the job done. If you're a Maven yourself, it's important to recognize that you may be contributing to this dynamic, and probably need to be more rigorous about time management and prioritization. If you're not a Maven, try to find ways to make work more enjoyable and engaging for the group, such as incorporating social events or team-building activities. Remember, a happy team is a productive team.

Signs and Symptoms of High Maven Groups

- Overreliance on buzz or hearsay without backing it up or checking the facts

- Analysis paralysis, and being overly cautious in decision-making

- Scattered in a million directions with everyone doing too much at once

- Lack of action or follow-through on ideas

- Mass distraction: nobody wants to sit down and actually do the work

Balancing Remedies for High Maven Groups

- **Prioritize.** A many-Mavens group can spiral out into too much of a good thing. Help the team prioritize tasks and projects so that they can focus on what is most important for the next designated block of time (month, quarter, year). Jot down all the other amazing ideas so they don't get lost. Revisit and refresh this list quarterly.

- **Delegate.** Mavens notoriously bite off more than they can chew, but too much juggling leads to dropped balls or burnout. Encourage group members to delegate tasks to one another and take on only what they can handle— which might require some support from the office Authorities to figure out.

- **Set boundaries.** Help the group establish clear boundaries and project parameters so that they don't get bogged down with too many projects or distractions. Regular check-ins can allow the Maven-heavy team to ask for support or pare down any tasks that their detailed brains are complexifying.

- **Minimize distractions.** Encourage the group to minimize distractions during work or focus sessions, such as silencing phones or closing unnecessary browser tabs. Create "zones" in the physical workspace like a quiet area, a shared library, a sketching spot, and a creativity corner. Let the team collaboratively design those.

- **Time management.** Teach the group time-management strategies so that they can make the most of their time and avoid overcommitting themselves. From setting a Pomodoro timer app to dance breaks to fun challenges, a high Maven group can't have too much playful reinforcement here.

- **Microdose.** Break big projects into granular, bite-sized actions so people get addicted to the buzz of getting things done. Micro wins add up to big victories—bonus points if there are drinks or a party at the finish line!

Not Enough Mavens: Stuck in a Rut

Is everyone around you mired in their ways, doing the same things over and over again with no new ideas or fresh perspectives? This can happen when there aren't enough Mavens in the mix. Mavens are the change agents who bring fresh ideas, trends, and the latest market buzz to the table. If you're working hard but not getting any traction, or your company is still doing the same thing it did fifteen years ago (e.g., making flyers instead of experimenting with social media trends), pour some Maven magic into the mix! Luckily, many Mavens are freelancers who like to wear a lot of hats, so you can bring them in for a short-term stint and get an infusion of fresh energy and experimental ideas. Mavens know what the kids are playing, watching, and buzzing about. Listen up!

Signs and Symptoms of Low Maven Groups

- Lack of creativity or innovation in problem-solving

- Resistance to change, risk-taking, or new ideas

- Difficulty adapting to new technology or trends

- Lack of curiosity or desire for learning

- Narrow-mindedness or inability to see things from different perspectives

- A lack of bonding, empathy, or emotional intelligence in the group

- Out of sync with culture, market, and current patterns—you're behind the curve instead of ahead of it

Balancing Remedies for Low Maven Groups

- **Encourage experimentation.** In low Maven groups, people may not be proactive about exploring new ideas. Break up the stagnant energy. Reward team members for trying out new ideas and approaches, even if they seem unconventional. Positive reinforcements like bonuses (gift cards are always appreciated), public praise, and other incentives can inspire the crew to take a risk.

- **Foster creativity.** Hold regular brainstorming and creative thinking sessions to generate new and innovative ideas. Snacks, prizes, and even some adult beverages will get people to loosen up and play. If your team is remote, send everyone a gift card to order from their local restaurant delivery service and dine together.

- **Seek diverse perspectives.** Cliques and competition can poison low Maven groups. Encourage members to seek out diverse perspectives and ideas from outside the group to broaden their understanding and inspire new ideas. Put unlikely pairs or trios of team members together on an initiative. Choose a volunteer or community initiative where they can team up for a day and get to know each other outside the office politics.

- **Provide resources.** Art supplies? Yes, please! Give members some right-brained tools (sketchpads, markers, crayons, colored pencils) to help them explore and develop their ideas in a nonlinear way. Host a journaling workshop with a creativity coach or a "lunch and learn" session.

- **Embrace change.** Be open to new ideas and perspectives and be willing to adapt your plans and strategies as needed. Cultivate an environment where people feel free to speak up when they think a process isn't working or could be improved. Make it a "listening party" (and once again, don't forget the snacks!).

- **Encourage collaboration and knowledge-sharing.** Mavens are communal, and when you don't have enough Mavens on the team, camaraderie must be actively fostered. Encourage team members to work together, share their expertise, and learn from each other.

- **Stay current.** Stay informed about the latest trends and developments in your industry or field and encourage team members to do the same. Share about the trends you find and make time to discuss them.

RELATIONSHIPS

The Astrology Advantage
in Relationships

Now let's bring the I*AM types together to make magic!

As astrologers, we've been fielding relationship questions for decades. People, it turns out, are truly confounded by each other, especially when they enter a new relationship. They want insight into their would-be or current partners: *Why do they talk, think, and act that way? What turns them on (or off) and makes them tick?* And (always) the big one: *Are we compatible?*

Our belief is that, while certain astrological matches can be smoother than others, "easy" doesn't necessarily equal "better." The person who lovingly challenges us most can bring us the gift of growth. In our opinion, human beings don't incarnate just to be stagnant or live blissfully unexamined lives. That said, we aren't here to suffer, either. Which begs another common relationship question that we hope this book can help elucidate: What is the purpose of relationships anyway?

As you'll soon find out, every I*AM type answers this differently. Sometimes, we can spell it out clearly: *I want to have three kids, raise them near my family, and homeschool them.* In other cases, it's a feeling-state we're after: *I just want to be with someone who never stops making me laugh and is strong enough to call me on my crap.*

Who you love and how you love is ultimately up to you. We're not here to make that choice for you. Our job as astrologers is to inform you how each of the three I*AM archetypes ticks, to arm you with quality intel so you can ask yourself: "Are these the traits I want in a partner? Will this be enough for me?"

So often, people are either doing the wrong thing with the right person . . . or the right thing with the wrong person. Love requires us to release control, which is the hardest thing for almost every human to do.

Our hope is that this section—really, this entire book—becomes your cosmic care-and-feeding manual, an operating guide to help you better understand yourself and the person you're with. If there's any part of life where an Astrology Advantage can help most, this is it.

THE I*AM OF RELATIONSHIPS

 The Innovator becomes **THE IDEALIST** with a core desire to unite as a power couple.

 The Authority becomes **THE ATTACHER** with a core desire to build a stable life together.

 The Maven becomes **THE MIRROR** with a core desire to find a lifelong playmate.

THE INNOVATOR IN LOVE: THE IDEALIST

Core Desire: To unite as a power couple

Relationship Strengths: Inspiring Partners

When in love, Innovators become idealists who see a grand vision for every relationship—and they'll do whatever it takes to make sure that unfolds. With their quest for novelty, Innovators make exciting mates! They're always cooking up fun ideas and adventures, guiding the relationship toward an inspiring future. As Innovators rise to success in their own lives, they encourage (and empower!) partners to do the same. Their ultimate vision is to be half of a purpose-driven power couple. Hey, why not? Innovators will put in the work to create a vibrant and exhilarating partnership.

Relationship Challenges: Hard to Pin Down

Innovators hold a high bar for relationships, but some days, their idealism gets exhausting, especially when partners just want to relax and be in the moment. The Innovator's go-go-go lifestyle can take them away from home a lot, causing their intimate connections to suffer from neglect or inconsistency. Autonomous Innovators can struggle with commitment, preferring to keep their options open because they don't want the responsibility of a relationship, or even because "someone better *could* come along." Breakups are equally difficult! Once they've invested in a partner's potential, the Innovator struggles to let go. Balancing their pursuit of personal growth while cultivating a deep bond with a partner can be a challenge for the Innovator.

What to Expect from the Innovator

- **Exploration.** The Innovator promises a relationship focused on growth that doesn't get stagnant.

- **Novelty.** The Innovator will teach you new ways of dating and relating that are forward-thinking and lure you out of your comfort zone.

- **Empowerment.** The Innovator sees your highest potential and will challenge you to become more than you thought you could be.

- **Support.** They'll roll up their sleeves and play "imagineer" as your partner, get into your schemes and dreams (when they're into something, they're into it).

- **Doing the work.** Even if that requires a few seasons of therapy, couples' workshops, and periods of separation here and there.

What to Not Expect from the Innovator

- **Consistency.** The Innovator can't promise to show up at every event or provide nonstop attention or doting, but they will be cheering you on from wherever they are!

- **Traditions.** Innovators are attracted to growth experiences and novelty more than repetition. Don't expect things to "always stay the same" or to get stuck in routines that you follow year in and out.

- **Enabling.** This type won't quietly accept things that don't align with their values. Innovators are problem-solvers and they won't stick their heads in the sand forever.

- **Coddling.** The Innovator needs you to hold your own. You may not be invited to be their 24/7 sidekick for every event. If you are, don't stress them out by sulking by the ceviche station or expecting them to check on you every few minutes! Sometimes, Innovators need to work the room alone without having to consider anyone else's needs.

Dating an Innovator

Attraction: Getting the Innovator's Attention

Innovators have a star quality and they love to be admired; however, they aren't looking for fawning fans. In relationships, Innovators become the idealists. They want to form a power couple with someone who, like them, stands out in a room full of people. Let them see you glancing in their direction once or twice, but don't stare. Make them wonder, *Am I imagining it, or is that person checking me out?*

No need to peacock! Excessive braggadocio is a turnoff to Innovators, who have a nose for poseurs and phonies. Instead, radiate a powerful, self-possessed presence with just a hint of swagger. Whether you're simmering with quiet intensity or engaging people in rapt conversation, you'll pique the Innovator's curiosity. Soon enough, they'll find an excuse to stand next to you, ask you a question, and see if you have the conversational chops to keep them enthralled.

It's fine if you walk up to the Innovator and confidently introduce yourself. Just have something interesting to say if you approach them, because this type's attention span is a moving target. Don't be surprised if their eyes drift over your shoulder to scan the room. A little rude? Yes, but don't let that discourage you! The Innovator may still be in "schmooze mode" and will be polite but apologetic. That's your cue to wait it out. Catch them at the end of the event when everyone's heading out the door . . . and invite them to the after-party!

Flirting with an Innovator

Smart equals sexy to most Innovators, and they love a captivating conversation. Your ability to hold their attention is a prerequisite. However, mere wit is not enough. Innovators need to feel utterly electrified in their bodies when your energy fields connect. Something about you must stop them in their tracks—it's a "feeling" they have, a profound and timeless recognition.

Despite all of this metaphysical mojo, the Innovator still must be wooed. Their preferred communication style rolls like a wave pattern from "socially informed" to "wise and witty." Innovators pride themselves on being ahead of the curve and in the know. Point out something ridiculous in the room and make them laugh as if the two of you are sharing an inside joke.

Just make sure your humor doesn't skew "bro" or "second-grade pigtail puller." Innovators are too sophisticated for dumb jokes. Silliness is tolerable, but immaturity is a turnoff. Be warned: never make your barbs at the Innovator's expense! They're hypersensitive about their performance and don't take kindly to being teased, especially about their insecurities.

Keep your gaze focused on the Innovator, no matter how many insanely gorgeous model-actor-servers trail through the party. Find out what they do for work and show deeper interest by asking smart, curious questions peppered with appreciative "wows."

Compliment the Innovator on their outfit or tell them that they look and smell amazing. Innovators are suckers for flattery as long as it's genuine! "Are you wearing Portrait of a Lady? It's such a sophisticated scent!" Ask them the meaning behind their tattoos or where they got a certain piece of jewelry they're wearing. Innovators work hard to cultivate a signature style, and swoon for anyone who takes time to notice.

Pepper humblebrags about what *you* do for a living throughout the conversation. Drop them in casually as a springboard from one of the Innovator's witty comments. "That reminds me of the time when I traveled to Asia for a global conference . . ." or "That's amazing! I've also won a prize for my writing." Get the Innovator thinking "power couple," and you've just 10x'd the odds of a number swap.

How Innovators Show They're Interested in You

Innovators tend to be obvious about their interest. They may just come out and say something along the lines of, "I find you fascinating and would love to get to know you better." If you meet at a gathering, they'll hover nearby or float back to you over and over again. By the time the event ends, you'll feel an insider's bond, as if the two of you share something that no one else in the room is privy to—a joke, an observation, a conversational thread.

Because their charts are made up of predominantly cardinal signs, leadership is in the Innovator's astrological DNA. In love, just like all other areas of life, they are not afraid to take charge. Invites start pouring in. "Want to check out this record release party with me?" Or, "Hey, I was going to take a walk to grab coffee, are you up for a stroll?"

If those casual encounters prove fun and enlivening, the Innovator will level it up by including you in a meaningful event, like a hangout with their treasured friend group or one of their own performances. Show up prepared to sparkle and win their squad over—all while paying adequate (and adoring!) attention to the Innovator.

First Moves: Wooing an Innovator

Wooing the Innovator is a delicate dance. You must show enough appreciation for them to feel admired and seen—but not so much that you trigger their "I'm going to lose my autonomy" alarm bells.

Innovator Scarlet, an interior designer, had a lively DM exchange with Micah, a digital marketer, about her favorite color palettes. When they decided to go off-app for a coffee date, Micah arrived bearing a bouquet of tulips in that very array of hues. Scarlet was both touched and taken aback by the thoughtful gesture. "I feel like a terrible person for saying this," she confesses, "but my avoidant attacher alarm bells went off. I felt pressured and I couldn't relax. We never had a second date."

Our advice? Keep things casual but also novel! Meet for a low-key hangout that gives you a chance to display your uncommon tastes to the Innovator. Did a hand-dipped ice cream shop debut a new set of flavors? Maybe there's a pop-up exhibit that's only in town for the weekend that you "must see!" Bring no gifts but pick up the tab or pay the entry fee, just because. Innovators are natural providers who abhor cheapness. When someone treats *them* for a change, the show of generosity is especially impactful.

Pro tip: have an end-time in mind, even if the Innovator suggests checking out a film or walking through a park after the first leg of the date. It's important for them to know that you have a full life. "I need to get up early for a shoot," or "Gotta get laundry done before the busy workweek kicks in."

The Innovator may be disappointed, dejected, even, but here's how to mitigate that: send a follow-up text when you get home telling them what a great time you had and "let's do it again soon!" Over the next couple days, shoot them a couple links to fascinating articles that circle back to conversations you had on your date.

Before the next weekend, ask the Innovator to meet up to "pick their brain" about something you're working on. Offer them your second ticket to a VIP event. (You were already going, but hey, if they're free, you'd love to have them join.) Soon enough, the Innovator may become your permanent plus-one.

Where to Go on Dates with an Innovator

- Hipster hangouts and in-the-know spots where stylish people convene

- Flea markets or thrifting: Innovators love to treasure hunt

- Food fairs, garden shows, anyplace where there's lots to try and talk about

- Walks through interesting neighborhoods that offer plenty of venues to discover

- Personal development workshops or spiritual events, like a new moon meditation circle or breathwork seminar

- Thought leader talks and town halls

- Road trips, nighttime bike rides, and urban hikes— as long as there's a specific destination to reach, like a sunset lookout or walkable bridge with stunning views

- Live shows that provide a few hours of solid entertainment: a concert, comedy, or theater performance

The Innovator in a Relationship

Why settle for a basic relationship when you can form a dynamic power couple? The Innovator becomes the idealist in affairs of the heart. Like everything else in their lives, Innovators view relationships as one of their ultimate creations—something magnificent to bring to life. They need to feel excited about a relationship's possibilities and potential!

Innovators are never desperate to be coupled—at least, not that they'd admit aloud. These people have far too many independent interests going on! Still, they do long for a companion who can hang with their lifelong learning adventures and creative quests. Innovators' autobiographies may contain stretches of singlehood, punctuated with long-term relationships that extended well past their prime. Developing good judgment can be a challenge for idealistic Innovators, whose "benefit of the doubt" policy can be a tad too generous.

"I'd rather be with no one than the wrong one," Franc, an Innovator, is famous for saying to friends. Three divorces later, no one questions him, but they respect his ability to remain friends with all his exes.

Another Innovator, Mara, has a well-stocked library of personal-growth books, many on relationship psychology and philosophy, and a CV of courses and workshops to match. She's fascinated by modern thought on how to craft an egalitarian union and hopes to design one of her own. While she hasn't yet achieved that legendary love story, Mara has gained plenty of wisdom from the patchwork of partners she's dated—all of them wildly different from each other. The only common denominator is Mara and the pedestal she temporarily hoisted each prospect onto while they auditioned for the role of lifemate.

Once the Innovator discovers their missing puzzle piece, the build begins! Innovators love to co-create with a partner, developing a tangible *something* that allows them both to shine. And while Innovators may hope for a happily ever after, they also understand that every relationship has a season, and if you can no longer grow as individuals together, there's simply no point.

The Innovator's astrology chart is made up primarily of status-conscious cardinal signs. How the relationship appears to the outside world *does* matter to this type. Not necessarily out of elitism, but rather because the Innovator longs for a relationship with a rich narrative. "We moved to Peru for three years where we lived among the locals and helped with reforestation work," or "We opened a sustainable furniture store selling the work of global artisans."

Innovators are natural providers and enjoy bringing their resources to a relationship, and shepherding its growth. Magnanimous as this trait may be, it can also prove problematic if the "scorecard" gets lopsided. While Innovators are eager to share their wealth, they may unwittingly set up a competitive dynamic, leaving their partners feeling obligated, intimidated, or overwhelmed. For this reason, it's important that Innovators regulate their generosity. They should also consistently acknowledge the ways their partners give to *them*—which may be offered in a totally different "love language" than their own.

Relationship hurdles don't deter the Innovator; in fact, they provide the magic ingredient for keeping an Innovator engaged—a challenge! When problems flare, the Innovator quickly rises up to "do the work." In record time, they'll compile a list of resources, from somatic couples' therapists to transformational workshops that double as weekend getaways. Whatever it takes to get the love back on track!

The pitfall? Hope springs eternal for the Innovator. (*There's gotta be another solution!*) The Innovator can become *so* intent on triaging a relationship crisis that they cling to it well beyond the expiration date. As difficult as it is for Innovators to begin relationships, it's at least a hundred times harder for them to exit, especially if they still see "potential."

Some heartbreaks are inevitable, but here's where the Innovator's future-forward mindset helps. Each relationship is a lesson to the Innovator; and the split, however painful, will be rebranded as a growth opportunity. Innovators get back on the horse and ride again, applying all those "in my next relationship, I'll do X" pledges they made during their recovery process. Shiny gold stars from Cupid, coming right up!

What Innovators Want from a Partner

While the Innovator is eager to be half of a power couple, they *don't* want to merge into a portmanteau. Losing themselves in a relationship is the Innovator's greatest fear. They value autonomy and want a partner who does the same. "You be great, and I'll be great, and together we'll shine with the light of a thousand suns!"

With their rich lives and varied interests, Innovators need a partner who will support their limitless expansion. And they'll provide the same in return, cheering their mate on through all their achievements and staying up late to help them design presentations or strategize solutions to a vexing professional hurdle.

That said, it's not uncommon for the partner of an Innovator to become a devoted force in the Innovator's empire. Since the Innovator's life is often organized around their career, they thrive with a mate who can contribute to their legacy. A partner who can elevate and amplify their mission will open a door that's wide enough for both people to walk through it.

The Innovator does not need a strict separation between their public and private life; in fact, having their mate engaged with their career is a total turn-on. Generally, they are thrilled to see a partner take charge of duties that they have no interest in tending to.

Aidan, an Innovator with a passion for vintage interiors, fell head over heels for Sam, a general contractor. This proved to be a clever move! Together they gut renovated her Craftsman home, then transformed an empty city plot into an urban farm with impressive crops of flowers and tomatoes that they sold to a fruit stand. "Sam literally made my real estate dreams come to life," Aidan marveled.

Odd couple alert! Innovators can be extremely particular about what attracts them, or they have a complex schedule (e.g., touring with a high-end circus) that doesn't allow for an "everyday" relationship. As a result, they can limit their dating pool and may end up with a polarizing figure or someone nobody would imagine them paired with. Innovators are also attracted to people who they suspect won't bore them, which might draw them to partners from very different backgrounds than their own—or, in some cases, whose boldfaced personalities become more problematic than entertaining after a while.

Sometimes it works out, as in the case of these famous Innovators: B-list actor Meghan Markle marrying the Prince of Wales, or A-list actor Julia Roberts marrying her cameraman, Danny Moder. Other times, it creates friction for the Innovator, as their chosen mate might not seamlessly fit into their friend group.

The truth? Innovators love people with grit and character. You're still grieving your divorce and haven't signed the papers yet? Your rocky childhood left you with the scars of intergenerational trauma and attachment issues? Deal-breakers for many folks, but not the Innovator.

This archetype lives in the future, not the past. "It's not where you've been, but it's about where you're going" could be their mantra. As long as your heart is open and your eye is on making a better life for yourself, you have the very *potential* that Innovators have been known to fall truly, madly, and deeply in love with.

The catch: you can lean on the Innovator, but you'd better be ready to return the favor. Because Innovators' lives can be a roller coaster of highs and lows, they need resilient partners who won't run in the opposite direction when one of their promising projects crashes to the ground.

To keep an Innovator around for the long haul, don't start dropping balls. The Innovator will invariably begin overfunctioning. They'll do it in an attempt to help you get back on your feet or to show you that whatever you're struggling with isn't really "that hard." But drag on the dependency for too long—or worse, drain the Innovator's hard-won resources—and you'll lose their respect, if not the entire relationship.

The bright side of a breakup with an Innovator? Since they're so focused on the future, they're unlikely to hang on to a grudge. Once the Innovator has processed the split, they just want to move ahead with life. They might even thank you for teaching them a treasured lesson and helping them become stronger, smarter, and savvier in the game of love.

Common Relationship Struggles for the Innovator

- Falling in love with a partner's potential instead of seeing them for who they are

- Being so proudly autonomous that they block a partner's support, then wind up feeling resentful and alone

- Giving too much, too soon ("I'll pay for it!") in their eagerness to make a partnership work—only to grow resentful when their gestures aren't reciprocated

- Taking charge instead of collaborating ("I'll just do it!"), leaving a partner feeling disempowered and de-incentivized to make an effort

- Setting up a power inequity by treating their partner like a personal assistant

- Choosing a partner based on their flexibility rather than compatibility (e.g., "I can do whatever I want and they don't complain.")

- Developing restlessness and FOMO when the relationship becomes "too secure," which can lead to sabotaging behaviors (emotional affairs, picking fights)

- Not balancing quality time with their many interests and leaving their partners feeling alone or neglected

- Being so fixated on the relationship's narrative and how it appears to others that they block authentic communication

How to Make It Last with an Innovator

- Stay engaged with the Innovator's passions and career; support their growth and success

- Keep growing and expanding your own success profile

- Invite the Innovator to be part of your successes too— not as a fan but as an irreplaceable advisor

- Keep them in the loop! Come to them first when you need anything and everything, even if they just help you find the right resource. Do not confide in someone else behind their back.

- Be committed to building and growing a shared empire

- Go on adventures with them, from work travel to bucket-list trips. Help the Innovator plan these, or better yet, bring the idea to them and get them excited.

- Share spiritual and personal growth: metaphysics, plant medicine ceremonies, trekking through ancient ruins . . .

- Help Innovators get ready for major events. Advise on outfit choices, keep them on track with the clock, make them food so they eat before they have to be "on"

- Represent in public in a way that people admire— it reflects on the Innovator, too!

- Network together and help them break the ice (Innovators struggle with small talk); introduce them to people they should meet.

THE AUTHORITY IN LOVE: THE ATTACHER

Core Desire: To build a stable life together

Relationship Strengths: Loyal and Consistent

In love, Authorities are the attachers—steadfast, loyal partners who make the effort to create an enduring bond. Daily rituals are their relationship superglue—and creating these are the Authority's stock-in-trade. They'll go out of their way to do "the little things" to make a partner feel secure. With their traditional approach to romance, there will be no shortage of memorable milestones to cherish. Relationships deepen and grow richer over time for these nostalgic souls.

Relationship Challenges: Stuck on Security

Devoted Authorities are reliable, but what happens when a partner wants to go off script? The natural pivots that arise in relationships can be hard for the change-averse Authority, spinning up conflict with their mates and even causing partners to act out and "rebel." At times, the Authority's focus on structure and responsibility can make the relationship feel more like work than play. Perfectionists who are especially hard on themselves, Authorities struggle with vulnerability. Their measured emotional expression may interfere with intimacy.

What to Expect from the Authority

- **Routine.** The Authority will be the steady drumbeat that keeps you both anchored through your days.

- **Tradition.** They'll regale you with rich stories of their family history, befriend your parents, and inspire you to deepen the connection to your own roots. Holidays are never sweeter than when celebrated with the Authority.

- **Thoughtfulness.** The observant Authority studies your rhythms, learning your timing as well as your tastes. They'll pick out figure-flattering clothes in your favorite colors, play soothing music when you're stressed, and have comfort food waiting when you come home from an exhausting day.

- **Strategy.** Authorities live in the past, carefully cataloging best and worst moves. They're always ready to craft a sensible battle plan to make the relationship—or their partner's life—flourish.

- **Showing up.** Got an important event? Family obligation? The Authority will be there, dressed to impress!

What to Not Expect from the Authority

- **Spontaneity.** The Authority prefers to plan in advance and gets thrown off when unprepared (i.e., not properly outfitted for the occasion or informed about the circumstances). A last-minute "adventure" could spiral into a major couple's fight.

- **Levity.** While Authorities have wicked senses of humor, they are worry-prone and tend to take life seriously.

- **Vulnerability.** Authorities stand on ceremony and aren't quick to drop their guard, even when a storm is brewing below their composed exterior.

- **Speed.** Anything worth having is worth working (and waiting!) for in the world of the cautious, methodical Authority.

- **Leniency.** The Authorities have a few hard-core deal-breakers that they announce upfront in relationships. Violate and they *will* drop you cold—no matter how much they like you as a person. Sorry!

Dating an Authority

Attraction: Getting the Authority's Attention

To get the Authority's attention, you must be the prize they long to win. The person in the room that "everyone" (or everyone who matters to the Authority) wants to be with. It's a high bar, we're not going to lie. But if you're the type who likes to be put on a pedestal, date an Authority!

The Authority's mate is their prized possession. Yes, we said "possession," although conscientious Authorities work hard to *not* be possessive. There's always a "my" before the Authority speaks of you. "*My* husband. *My* partner. *My* twin flame." As such, they want to swell with pride when they attach your name to theirs.

Jennifer, a music aficionada and Authority, waited two decades to marry "my dream guy," Shane. In their twenties, Jennifer worked in a record store, secretly swooning every time Shane rolled in to check out the vinyl, skateboard tucked under his arm. They reunited in their forties, after both had kids and divorces, and are currently living happily ever after. Jennifer gets adorably starry-eyed when she talks about Shane, whom she also calls "my silver fox."

Important distinction: the Authority is drawn to a trophy, but *not* vapid arm candy. Strong values matter to these traditional types and you need to stand for something of substance if you want to attract them. They might even find you on social media because they read your poetry or were interested in the specific type of coaching you offer. One Authority we know made a $25,000 donation to his now-wife's charity as a "first move"! It's fine to be a little bit of a diva around the Authority, in a non-obnoxious way. If you know your worth, the Authority is likely to see it too.

Flirting with an Authority

A distinct air of formality is required when flirting with an Authority. These "take it slow" types chafe at any gesture that's remotely lewd and crude. (Note: do not send nudes unless they are expressly requested by the Authority.)

Subtle signals, on the other hand, get the old-fashioned Authority hot under the collar. And said collar may as well be spun from the finest Victorian lace. Cheeky modesty is a flirtatious virtue with these types, as if you were transported to a prim, bygone era when direct talk of sexual attraction was strictly verboten.

Bring on the innuendoes and suggestive remarks that would cause fans to flutter. ("My dear sir, I cannot imagine what you might mean!") Flash the Authority a little smile, innocently brush their hand. Lean in, then lean back, keep them wondering if they have a shot with you or not. This aspirational archetype wants to earn your devotion. Make it too easy or rush through this phase and the Authority might pull back. They need a long courtship to assess your partnership potential, so keep building this subtle tension and let them control the pace.

How Authorities Show They're Interested in You

Authorities signal their interest with peacocking moves that can be misread as competition and even arrogance. You may feel like they're trying to one-up you, but nothing could be further from the truth! Authorities only pursue people they respect. The goal is merely to prove that they are in *your* league, fit for the job of your "one and only."

Authorities look for common ground, then flaunt their deep subject matter knowledge in an effort to engage you. They begin to use phrases like "the best" or "the most authentic" to describe anything from reality shows to high-end cocktail bars to show off their superior taste, hoping you'll be impressed.

Do you have similar musical preferences? You'll notice the Authority name-dropping rare artists in the genre, sending you links to recorded studio sessions that never made it to a commercial album, but are, naturally, the *ultimate* mix of the song you both love.

If you respond positively to the Authority's deluge of data, next comes the formal courtship phase. Authorities love to plan an incredible date. Don't take it personally if they schedule this a week or two out. They want to prepare accordingly for maximum impact: outfit, grooming, timing, reservations, tickets, GPS directions.

Even if you're only meeting for tea (selectively distinct from a basic coffee date), there's nothing spontaneous about the invitation. When the Authority plans in advance, it's a clear bet that *you* are the thing they're looking forward to the most.

Physically, Authorities are sensual and tactile. They're grazers, but they're absolutely *not* gropers. An Authority will put a guiding hand on your back to steer you to the VIP table they reserved, the one with the ultimate sunset dinner view. At a symphony performance, they may let their leg oh so gently rest against yours (then not!) during the adagio movement. Creating frissons of "will they or won't they?" excitement are the early steps in the Authority's dance of attraction.

First Moves: Wooing an Authority

Don't work too hard to impress the Authority, but do show off your impeccable tastes. When you meet for a date, dress up, be groomed, and emit an air of sophistication. The Authority loves when people stare at you with admiration and a touch of envy as you float through any room. They *will* remember the entrance you make and possibly recount it for decades to come.

Don't worry—it's a two-way street. The sensual Authority puts in effort to impress, from their sartorial flair to the custom-blended scent they dabbed on. Authorities love to treat their dates and may show up with a special card or a bouquet of peonies. Be vocally appreciative of all these gestures. That's enough to make the Authority swoon . . . at first. If they're particularly generous, say, springing for a luxurious meal or theater tickets, follow up with an appropriate thank-you, from a handwritten card to a small gift sent in the mail. That may seem like overkill, but Authorities will appreciate the effort.

Authorities love to talk—not so much about people, but more about history, the arts, culture, sometimes politics. They are interested in finding a partner who shares their values and can speak intelligently on meaningful topics. Demonstrate that and you may be the "keeper" they've been hoping to find.

Where to Go on Dates with an Authority

- Architectural tours or walks through neighborhoods with historical buildings. Leave time for the Authority to read all the plaques!

- A sweet little tea shop that specializes in a loose leaf selection brewed in pretty china or a French bakery with world-class almond croissants—Authorities love a sophisticated upgrade from coffee and muffins.

- Shopping dates! Wander through a high-end department store or a bespoke boutique zone where the Authority might even buy you something as a surprise.

- Highbrow cultural activities that the Authority can

dress up for, like the theater or opera. Concerts and music festivals are fun too, if the Authority is a devoted fan of the headlining artist. (They probably have the merch to prove it!)

- Charity galas and fundraiser events that support things that matter to the Authority, like finding a cure for breast cancer or building an after-school arts center for youth.

- Spa date! Authorities love to pamper themselves, so settle down together for mani-pedis or slip into your bathing suits for a sauna and steam.

- Ceremonial gatherings that are steeped in a tradition—drum circles, sound baths, even a religious service if you share faiths.

- Picnics in the park: fill that basket with gourmet treats and bring poetry to read aloud.

The Authority in a Relationship

The Authority becomes an attacher in affairs of the heart. These traditional types are searching for commitment with a capital *C*, and they carry a long list of criteria for their potential "forever partner." The dating process can be anxiety-inducing for these serious souls, who thrive in a state of certainty. Once they get to "real relationship" status, the Authority heaves a huge sigh of relief.

Not surprisingly, it takes many Authorities years to find their missing puzzle piece. They'd rather wait than settle, nonetheless! Like everything else in their lives, Authorities view relationships as priceless investments. They're simply unwilling to add anything but a blue-chip, high-performing "asset" to the portfolio of their life.

Does that sound heavy? It absolutely is. Even when "casually" dating, the Authority screens each candidate as if they were being interviewed for an executive position. The Authority wants a long-term, rock-steady partner to build a stable, loving life with. Although they *do* need some heart-racing quixotic moments in the courtship phase, the Authority is more interested in a "runner's high" than a romantic rush. After a period of effortful exertion (i.e., getting to know you and slowly building a bond), they become euphoric, similar to the endorphins that flood a runner thirty to forty minutes into their trek.

As partners, Authorities are fiercely loyal and devoted—and yes, a bit possessive, too. The Authority hoists their mate onto a pedestal, singing a true love's praises to everyone in earshot, as if they were hired publicity. Relationships, to the Authority, are like a fortress, buffering them against the cruel environment beyond their front door. "It's you and me against the world, babe," we've heard one Authority say to his wife on many an occasion. Indeed the two of them are fierce contenders in a game of doubles tennis and in the real estate empire they've built during their twenty-year marriage.

At home, Authorities find comfort in routine. They live to create special, "just the two of us" rituals with a partner. Here's where their romantic sides shine! They'll quietly study their partner's habits and behaviors, learning everything about how they move through their days. Then, they'll figure out how to make those routines even more pleasurable, efficient, and beneficial.

Andrew, a somatic therapist and an Authority, noticed that his hot-blooded hubby, Simon, a Maven, had a string of serene days once they began their mornings together on their backyard deck. Over the weeks that followed, Andrew began enhancing the ritual. First, he upgraded their plastic chairs to a cushioned patio set and brought out a portable speaker to pipe in meditative music. A couple months later, he suggested they try matcha instead of coffee, after reading that green tea provided a more sustained energy than the java jitters. They now have special mugs, playlists, plants, and crystals in the outdoor space. Life together, Andrew reports, is "a thousand times more peaceful." Authority mission accomplished!

A downside of the Authority's rock-steady romantic style? Relationships can hit a plateau if they don't mix it up every now and then. While Authorities appreciate predictability, they can be inflexible, even rigid. This can make them difficult to travel with and a buzzkill on spontaneous adventures. They want to map out the sights and restaurants, buy advance tickets, and book reservations to make the experience truly meaningful. But sometimes, the best moments happen when people just go with the flow.

Togetherness is something the Authority cherishes, whether collaborating on dinner or enjoying parallel play—they read a book while their partner is crafting. The nostalgic Authority's time zone is the past. They want to fill albums with tender memories and sentimental moments. They like to share their personal history and, in turn, learn their partner's customs.

While the Authority has a domain they rule over—"I'll manage the finances, you handle our social schedule"—they are egalitarian partners. Country music luminaries Garth Brooks and Trisha Yearwood were married for seventeen years when Yearwood attempted to surprise her husband, an Aquarius Authority, by having her last name officially changed to his. Brooks declined the paperwork, saying, "Tradition doesn't count here. What counts is when you have two celebrities, don't have one swallow the other."

Fair enough! But to illustrate the Authority's tendency to put a partner on a pedestal, Brooks added, "I'd be fine changing my name to Yearwood."

Though Authorities will show you every page of their family albums, they don't feel the need to be open books in all areas of their relationships. "A little bit of mystery keeps things intriguing," advises Sheryl, an Authority who has never shared a bathroom with her wife of fourteen years.

We know several Authorities who prefer to work through emotional issues with best friends or their therapist rather than "burden" a partner. That way, they can bring their best selves to their relationships, or so their logic goes.

We must warn Authorities against using this buttoned-up strategy in excess. Trying to keep up appearances is a surefire intimacy blocker. The Authority's partner is likely to pick up on this controlling energy after a while. They might even become self-conscious or fearful about making a "wrong move" that offends the Authority. And if they're fine with the Authority keeping them at arm's length? That may be a red flag unto itself. The Authority might question what secrets their partner could be keeping from them.

Most detrimental of all, this maneuvering can block a partner's ability to contribute to the Authority's happiness. Perfectionism is the Achilles' heel for many Authorities, who are hardest on themselves beyond anyone! But if they're able to relax and be vulnerable, Authorities will learn that a caring partner can be a safe harbor, a place where they can finally just . . . be.

Breakups can be particularly devastating for Authorities. These are the attachers, after all, and they don't enter relationships with the intention of ever letting go. They may hold on to relics for years, which can become a block to moving on.

Dev, an Authority who was married at twenty-six, then divorced at twenty-nine, was nearly forty when he realized that he couldn't shake the feeling of lifelong duty to his ex. He worked with a feng shui consultant who quickly spotted Dev's wedding band placed on his bedroom dresser, an attachment to vows that he couldn't seem to break.

Upon the consultant's advisement—and with some emotional support from his friends—Dev did a release ceremony for the band and sold it to a jeweler. Within a matter of months, he met Shani, the lovely owner of a local gift shop (one he'd passed for years but never entered). After a long dry spell, Dev invited Shani on a dinner date, and things have been going well ever since.

What Authorities Want from a Partner

Want to spend your life with an Authority? The vetting process begins with a battery of tests. Authorities only trust people who prove out over time and perform well in many different scenarios (meeting friends and family, going on vacation, cohabitating, etc.).

Make no mistake: the Authority has a checklist! And they are conducting interviews for long-term "hires." Candidates must comply with their nonnegotiable values or it simply won't be a fit. If you're the type who pays rent late so you can splurge on a celebrity's makeup drop, you could quickly be relegated to the Authority's friend zone. Authorities have a low risk tolerance and simply cannot bet on someone who is flaky, inconsistent, or in any way a long shot.

Can't make the cut? With a sincerely heavy heart—and if you've been out a few times, a classy parting gift—the Authority will announce their intention to move in another direction.

You might think that sounds hard-core. But if you tick all of the Authority's boxes, you'll also get quite the prize: a loyal, generous, and devoted mate whose interest in you only deepens with each passing day.

Since the Authority values reliability and stability, demonstrating these qualities will build their trust. Prove it by being consistent, dependable, and responsible—both in your own life and while interacting with the Authority.

History lessons are important to Authorities. They expect partners to take an interest in their background and make an effort to honor family heritage and customs. (Don't worry, they'll be just as keen to learn where you came from!) Holidays are sacrosanct to the Authority, and they love an elaborate ritual or menu.

If they come from a close family, Authorities often seek a mate who will slot right into their clan. Will you don the ironic Christmas sweater for the annual family photo? Learn to prepare the pizza crust their great-grandfather hand-rolled in his Neapolitan *cucina*? These things matter mightily, for the Authority wants to carry on these traditions with a partner, recording every moment for posterity.

Authorities are generous mates. They shower their partners with compliments, helpful acts of service, home-cooked meals, and sweet gifts. Authorities view these gestures as relationship superglue; it's how they seal the bond. Partners should *never* stop appreciating the Authority—with glowing reviews, affection, and loyalty. But when it comes to returning the favor, it's better to save up for a meaningful (and expensive) gift, like a signature piece of jewelry or VIP concert tickets. Give the Authority something they can wear every day or gush about to friends, or best of all, reminisce about forever.

In relationships, the Authority's favorite word is "we." They look for partners who share their urge to merge. "We eat family dinner at seven every night" or "We're voting progressive in the local election." A mercurial partner who changes course regularly—or worse, fails to include the Authority in fundamental decisions—will threaten the Authority's sense of security.

That said, their partners may never know! Authorities can struggle with showing their emotions—especially if that means feeling vulnerable or "out of control." A partner who provokes the Authority or pushes them to open up against their will could soon be shown the door.

If the Authority shares a personal struggle with a partner, they don't want advice! (Warning: this can feel hypocritical since the Authority tends to be liberal with their own unsolicited guidance.) What the Authority needs is a safe, comforting, and above all, judgment-free space. Partners of Authorities should learn to provide a "cone of silence," where they simply listen, nod, gaze sympathetically, and offer hugs. When gifted with that sort of support, Authorities will generally talk themselves into their own solution. But they'll remember how much better they felt sharing tender emotions with their mate. Over time, they will reveal more and more.

Common Relationship Struggles for the Authority

- Anxious attachment is real for Authorities, who struggle with the uncertainty of dating. Quickly, they want to know if the relationship has long-term potential. They may put pressure on a serious love interest because they want to lock things down.

- Routine-bound Authorities get set in their ways, so relationships can get stagnant over time. They need to open themselves up to novelty and be a bit more flexible around planning.

- In their desire to put their best foot forward, Authorities may resist vulnerability and remain too mysterious or controlled, blockading intimacy in the process.

- This type can be closed-minded and judgmental about their mate's differing opinions.

- Authorities may become rigid about timelines and schedules, raising an impossible bar for partners who are "punished" for being fifteen minutes late or need to cancel a plan at the last minute due to work.

- Old-fashioned Authorities may try to fit a partner into *their* agenda and life plan, rather than seeing the relationship as a co-created vision.

How to Make It Last with an Authority

- Create traditions together and honor them on a regular cycle.

- Celebrate any and every anniversary (our first kiss, our first real date, the first time we said "I love you").

- Reminisce regularly and surprise the Authority with all the sentimental objects you've saved over time. Bonus if you create a scrapbook or album.

- Get a pet together, whom you can nurture and coo about. This will get the Authority to soften up and share more tender emotions.

- Be open and supportive of the Authority's family. Share in traditions, go to all the events and holidays, and make yourself "one of them."

- Invite the Authority to play a significant role with your family; make them feel as if you've adopted them in

- Don't disrupt their quiet time when they are reading, relaxing, or concentrating on work

- Let them have their domain to rule over, be it cooking elaborate Sunday-night dinners or tending to the rose garden out back.

- Don't invade their privacy! Like it or not, Authorities may never share certain emotions or grooming habits with their partners. They'll feel humiliated if you pry. So not worth it!

- Be their steady, well-dressed plus-one for every important gala, graduation ceremony, fundraiser, etc.

- Keep the house pristine, as the Authority defines it, and abide by their shelving systems. Everything has a place, so please don't relocate their equipment and tools!

THE MAVEN IN LOVE: THE MIRROR

Core Desire: To find a lifelong playmate

Relationship Strengths: Lifelong Playmates

In relationships, the Maven becomes the mirror, seeking a soul twin and a best friend who can reflect their best parts back to them. They love to cheer their partners on, helping them glimpse their own greatness. Mavens bring excitement, expansiveness, and fun to their relationships, constantly seeking novelty and youthfulness. With their favorite co-conspirator as their chosen plus-one, Mavens create inside jokes, playful traditions, and even friendly competitions. These social butterflies thrive on communication. They love to swap stories and share their thoughts and experiences. With their fast-moving minds and quick wit, Mavens value partners who engage them intellectually and socially.

Relationship Challenges: Energy Bomb

While Mavens excel at bringing joy and excitement to their relationships, they can also be easily thrown off by minor provocations. They may struggle with emotional regulation and need space to unload their thoughts and frustrations regularly. Mavens' constant stream of chatter and need for interactivity can sometimes overwhelm their partners, highlighting the importance of having a strong support system outside of the relationship. Finding a balance between their desire for novelty and stability can be a challenge, and partners must set clear boundaries and consequences without falling into a parental role.

What to Expect from the Maven

- **Playfulness.** Fun-loving Mavens will reconnect you to your inner child, inviting you on wacky adventures and nonstop field trips.

- **Social stimulation.** Get out of your head and out of the house! Mavens know just how to keep things exciting, whether it's a daily lunch date or an afterwork picnic and softball game with their friends.

- **Freshness.** No need for a relationship to ever get stale. Mavens stay up on the latest modalities for fostering strong communication and intimacy. They'll make sure you try new ways of connecting, both in and out of the bedroom.

- **Communication.** Mavens will listen to you gush or vent! They'll help you talk through solutions. And they'll actually remember what you told them when you need a friendly reminder.

- **Inspiration.** Get ready for a never-ending stream of interesting and newsworthy events to talk and gossip about. Mavens are eternally hip with a finger on the pulse of pop culture.

- **Spontaneity.** Mavens live in the present and can pull a magic moment out of thin air. Two tickets for the food festival? Hot-air balloon rides? Coming right up!

- **Details.** Clever, curious Mavens love to organize the finer points of any plan. Bring them the schedule and outline, and they'll fill in all the juicy things that make it fun.

- **Craftiness.** Don't know how to fix a broken appliance or decorate your living room? Odds are the Maven has a solution for you!

What to Not Expect from the Maven

- **Calm.** Excitable Mavens are emotive and expressive. When they're lit up about a project or idea (which is often), they'll buzz around your shared space, making messes, and talking to anyone within earshot.

- **Consistent follow-through.** Mavens mean well when they make promises, but keeping their word can be a slippery slope. While they can be ruthlessly punctual in some cases, it's easy for them to get distracted and operate on their own timeline, or simply get too backed up with projects and requests to juggle it all. "Tomorrow" could mean three months from now.

- **Commitment.** Savvy Mavens know that it's their prerogative to change their minds and they aren't always keen on committing to plans. If they buy the tickets, they're coming, but otherwise, it's 50/50. They need to see how they'll feel when the moment rolls around. Save them a seat, but plan to drive separately.

- **Planned romance.** Mavens tend to be more spur-of-the-moment with their affections, which can irritate a partner who loves the pomp and circumstance of a special occasion. It's not that Mavens aren't sentimental, but they can turn any moment into a memory just by appreciating their surroundings and, of course, your company. That said, when Mavens *do* plan an outing for two or a birthday celebration, it will be epic!

- **100 percent devotion.** Monogamy is tough for the mercurial Maven, but that's not to say they can't be faithful. However, you might want to brace yourself for choppy periods. The Maven might have an emotional affair, texting a coworker or engaging in flirtatious energy with a neighbor. These "not so innocent" moments can shake their partner's trust and erode the relationship.

Dating a Maven

Attraction: Getting the Maven's Attention

Bright, bubbly Mavens steal the spotlight without trying. But guess what? They aren't actually trying to put on a show. Their lilting stream of chatter is like an offering, an open invitation—and maybe a search beam—meant to call in kindred spirits!

Want to get a Maven to notice you? Just jump in. Literally. Butt in to their conversations and start peppering them with questions. Tease them gently—or bluntly if they're being obnoxious! They love it! Most Mavens possess thick skin and the ability to laugh at themselves, if not be the actual punch line of their own colorful recaps. ("And then, the bouncer literally pulled me into the DJ booth and made me sit there for fifteen minutes to calm down . . .")

Go ahead and match the Maven's energy. Recount a hilarious story from your own archives. Mavens won't mind if you exaggerate or embellish for theatrical flair; in fact, they'll love it. A little shock value is often what it takes to get them to stop, drop, and listen.

If the Maven is waxing philosophical, find a way to build on whatever hypothesis they're spinning. It's probably brilliant, but a bit esoteric. Encourage the Maven to "say a little more about that." You might even catch them off guard by adding a thought-provoking perspective to the discussion.

Mavens are used to being the smartest, funniest, and most entertaining people in the room. But that's a lonely place to be! If you can make a Maven laugh or listen, you've definitely got them intrigued. With Mavens, relating is like a fun round of tennis. Appreciate their wild tales and witty wordplays—then be sure to return the serve!

Flirting with a Maven

Mischievous Mavens are never not flirting. These keen observers pick up on people's traits quickly and know how to mirror body language to put others at ease. They crack dad jokes that should be followed by a gong-crash sound effect because they're that bad. But that's the point: Mavens want you to loosen up. They manage to tease you in a way that makes you feel exposed yet not offended. This is their gift!

All they need from you is an appreciative audience. Laugh at their corny lines. They're being ironic! Match them with your own ba-dom-bomp humor and engage them in clever banter. Nothing turns a Maven on more than a sparkle in your eye. Dan, a Maven who works in TV, can turn any conversation into a campy show tune and loves nothing more than a woman who catches his drift and begins making up silly lyrics with him.

How Mavens Show They're Interested in You

It's pretty obvious when a Maven is into you. If you're at a party, they stop scanning the room and start engaging in conversation with you alone. They ask for your number, then use it with the utility of a common household object: regularly and all throughout the day. You probably won't mind! Not when that steady stream of hilarious texts, memes, videos, and news stories keeps you LOL-ing past your bedtime.

If a Maven pays attention to you, you can assume that, at the very least, they find you attractive. This archetype has shiny-object syndrome. They aren't going to waste time on anyone who doesn't sparkle.

However, we must add this caveat: just because the Maven is into you, doesn't mean that you're the sole apple of their eye. These multidimensional creatures are capable of swooning for about five people at once. There's a strong possibility they're copying and pasting the same GIF they just sent you into a few other threads.

Understand this: it's not that the Maven believes the grass is greener elsewhere. It's just that those other pastures look pretty cool, too. If you're the experimental type, the two of you might even roam around those fields together one day.

First Moves: Wooing a Maven

Mavens love to communicate! Draw them into fun and lively text threads and discussions and don't hold back! If you're connecting with the Maven, it's better to send twenty texts in a night than disappear for an hour because you don't want to seem "desperate." Mavens *want* someone who will banter with them. Engage the Maven with current events or jokes, or even with gossip or venting.

Important note: do *not* nag, pressure, or scold the Maven in any way. One whiff of controlling or parental energy in the early phases will turn your Maven into a ghost.

When you're talking, these four magic words can do wonders to keep a Maven engaged: *How was your day?* Send it by text, audio note, call and ask them before bed . . . whatever!

That may sound too basic to actually work, but stay with us here. Mavens know how to connect instantly with anyone and everyone. But rarely do those sparks evolve beyond a passing exchange, which, after a while, can bum a Maven out. Show up for the Maven, express consistent interest and care. Pop the "How was your day?" question. You'll become a priceless gem in the jewel box of the Maven's heart.

Then, put on your listening ears! Before long, the Maven will start unpacking chapters from their personal history. You'll know the names of their childhood BFFs, their favorite professors, and every one of their "psycho" exes.

Warning: Mavens tend to repeat the same long stories, sparing no detail. Don't feel rude about interrupting them here and there. They *do* want to hear about you, too! The thing is, Mavens don't need many prompts before they start sharing... and sharing... and sharing some more. Sometimes they forget that others aren't as free-flowing as they are.

When you're out with a Maven, be high energy, fun, and spontaneous. Mavens rule the present, and they love to "be here now." They get excited by shiny things, pointing them out with joy and amazement. So show enthusiasm for the Maven's discoveries. We recommend clearing a few hours in your calendar for a Maven date, if not the whole day!

Rob and Lisette, both Mavens, met over donuts and cappuccinos one spring Saturday in New York, intending to part ways after an hour. But they had so much fun chatting that they decided to walk around the neighborhood "for a little while longer." They checked out an outdoor sculpture installation, tried on vintage clothes, stopped for drinks at a biergarten, then hopped on bikes to ride over the Brooklyn Bridge. By the time they made it to the famous pizza spot near the bridge's base, it was long past dinnertime and they were both totally smitten.

If you're hoping to have the Maven all to yourself, steel your nerves. Do your very best to *not* take their mercurial attention span personally. Keep showing up for the fun events they invite you to, sparkling wit intact. Draw the Maven's interest with engaging conversation and spontaneous invites to the cool events you're attending. Becoming the Maven's best friend is the fastest way to get the nonplatonic benefits.

Where to Go on Dates with a Maven

- Get a bite together, somewhere lively and unique, like an empanada food truck or a brunch spot that's famous for serving breakfast sandwiches on donuts. Mavens love to try interesting food!

- Order coffees to go, then stroll around the Maven's favorite part of town, dropping in to record shops, looking at unique housewares, and maybe picking up ingredients from an outdoor farmer's market to turn into a home-cooked dinner together. Show the Maven that you know how to be spontaneous.

- Restless Mavens love to make things by hand. Take an interactive workshop together—glass blowing, Mexican cooking, tarot 101—or go to a paint 'n' sip.

- Get sporty together in a two-player game: squash, tennis, salsa dancing, canoeing.

- Take a road trip with a clear destination but a loose itinerary and plenty of time for random stops when the Maven spots a saltwater taffy factory, a barn full of antique treasures, or a petting zoo.

- Snag tickets to a comedy club or a top comedian's touring show. Mavens love to laugh together!

- Go camping (or glamping!). Frolicking in the forest brings out the best in the Maven, who feels most alive in the wide-open outdoors. Get ready to make some nature crafts and hunt for edible berries and medicinal herbs.

The Maven in a Relationship

For Mavens, companionship needs to have all the bells and whistles. They don't just want a warm body or a comforting presence. They need a dynamic, interactive partner who wants to engage in life full-throttle, cheering each other on and experiencing the adventure of every moment together.

Eternally youthful Mavens need their relationships to feel exciting, expansive, and fun. "Forget about growing old together," says Maven Shaun with a wink. "I want to stay *young* together. Otherwise, what's the point?"

Because their nature is to mirror a partner, Mavens need tons of interactivity in relationships. For this I*AM type, a "fairy-tale romance" is a fascinating conversation that lasts for hours, not princess-cut diamond rings or bent knees (though they'll happily take that, too).

Most Mavens possess a devilish sense of humor. They'll play practical jokes on their partners, tease them mercilessly (but with enough love to stay out of trouble for it), and build a catalog of inside jokes that may or may not cause someone to pee their pants with laughter.

Essentially, Mavens "gamify" their relationships. It's how they keep the challenge and excitement going that holds their interest. Mavens know that familiarity can easily breed contempt, so before that happens, they'll change up the itinerary. Daily routines become competitions and bets with hilarious prizes (not to mention playful punishments for the loser!).

When Phaedra, a Maven, moved in to an LA bungalow with their girlfriend Haley, they could already feel their feet growing cold. To mitigate this, they homed in on the full-sun backyard patio, then challenged Haley to a tomato-growing contest. They would each nurture a plant through the summer, counting each orb on the vine. Whoever had the most ripe fruit between August and September would get an entire month off from doing dishes, a chore they both hated. The plan was a hit (Phaedra won), and since then, the two have entertained themselves with everything from bake-offs to scavenger hunts.

Silly fun like this can become a tradition in the Maven's relationship—and it won't stop at that. There will be nicknames, matching outfits, costume parties, play wrestling, and lots of snack food that the Maven may have enjoyed (or been denied!) as a kid. Birthdays will have games, prizes, chocolate fondue, and/or signature drinks.

Alas, it's not all fun and games in the life—or relationship—of a Maven. As quick as they are to respond to playful energy, they are equally thrown off by the slightest provocation. A manager's "unfair critique," the rude cashier at Whole Foods, a parent who side-eyed the Maven at school pickup . . . when an infraction like this plucks the Maven's outrage sensors, welcome to Vent City.

Mavens need to unload regularly. Rant, even! And relationships are the safe zone where they can unleash without worrying that they'll tarnish their front-facing reputation as the rollicking life of the party. Holding space for the Maven's verbal processing is an essential qualifier. Remember, the Maven is the mirror. They'll be your sounding board and you'll be theirs.

Even when they're just musing about whatever's in their line of vision, Mavens need a lot of communication in relationships. The trouble? Their constant stream of chatter can be overwhelming if they expect their partners to be their audience every single time. It's best if Mavens have a long roster of friends to call when a partner can't drop everything on demand (even if the Maven will do that for their loved ones). Outside support—from friends, coaches, therapists, mastermind groups, healing circles—can be the saving grace of a Maven's relationship.

Modulation and moderation are skills that will take Mavens far.

They must learn to give a partner a chance to catch up. If possible, Mavens could dial it down a notch now and then for the sake of coming together.

Relationships don't have to follow a traditional script for the Maven; in fact, it's better if they don't! While there are plenty of monogamous Mavens out there, this archetype is the most likely to have an unconventional arrangement in a long-term bond, such as living in separate spaces, having an open marriage, or occasionally inviting a "third" into their bed. Experimenting can give Mavens the dopamine rush they're forever chasing (but also the crash if they veer too far into impulsive terrain).

Although most Mavens may claim they don't get jealous, that's generally an oversight. When partners pull away—often due to the Maven's insistence that they need personal space—it can create the very slingshot effect that revs up the Maven's attraction again.

It's easy for the Maven to take a mate for granted if their partnership becomes too ho-hum. Yet, once the daily routine they've grown so accustomed to is gone, the Maven may feel utterly lost. These mirrors rely on relationships not simply for affirmation, but often to confirm their own existence. If a Maven screams into the void and nobody hears it, did that scream even happen?

Alas, it may take the Maven losing a truly loving partner (or two) before they realize how important the little things can be! "Don't know what you've got 'til it's gone" can be the Maven's theme song until they develop a capacity to *not* flee or meander during the slower seasons of their relationships.

What Mavens Want from a Partner

Rule number one: don't be boring! Playful, mercurial Mavens need a lot of variety in order to stay interested in you. It makes sense: their astrological charts are primarily made up of planets in mutable signs, the most fluctuating energies of the zodiac. The more layers you have, the more likely you are to connect with the multifaceted dimensions of the Maven.

In relationships, Mavens need partners who can keep up with their constantly changing interests and who share their passion for learning and exploring new ideas. Mavens are attracted to people who are open-minded and curious, and who can engage in long, philosophical discourses. Janelle, a musical Maven, loves to sing but often loses patience when composing backing tracks for her lyrics. Luckily, her partner Scott picks up the baton, finishing Janelle's half-done songs and playing studio engineer when she's ready to record.

Mavens are sparkly people who generally have no shortage of admirers. Since they can afford to be picky, they tend to hold out for someone who engages them intellectually *and* socially. The person with the best entertainment calendar is most likely to win the restless Maven's long-term focus. If they can picture a lifetime of fabulous adventures—film festivals, VIP concert seats, weekends in wine country, RV trips—you might just get them to believe in the concept of happily ever after.

Raquel, a stylish Maven-about-town, was regularly invited to the best parties and openings as part of her job in fashion PR. She met Fred, a hotel investor, during a sunset DJ set and he invited her to fly to Barcelona that weekend where he would comp her a suite (her own) in their luxe, newly opened property in exchange for helping the brand get a few media placements. Raquel knew there was no way she'd turn that invite down! "It's always been my dream to travel the world with the love of my life," she confided. "I could envision that with Fred, so I figured I might as well go see if he was The One."

The truth is, Mavens fall in (and out) of love quickly. They get smitten by strangers who laugh at their jokes, hang on their words, or tell the Maven they're brilliant. (Mavens usually are.) Part of being with these mirrors means accepting that the Maven is in love with their own reflection . . . the one they see in your eyes.

Sometimes, however, Mavens can't tell the difference between love and infatuation. Our Maven friend Tonya is forever in whirlwind relationships that go from first date to bent-knee proposal at lightning speed. A few years ago, she even got engaged on an airplane flight! Tonya admits she wasn't sure whether it was true love or just the thrill of the moment that had her say "yes." While that relationship (and many others) didn't ultimately make it to the altar, Tonya and her former mile-high fiancé remain best friends who still enjoy those, er, no-strings benefits from time to time, too.

There's nothing wrong with enjoying a few peak Maven moments. Just make sure you're as "in like" with your Maven as you profess to be in love with them. Genuine interest can't be faked. And doe-eyed flattery only gets one so far. Mavens need their mates to authentically adore and admire them—and tell them why. Words of affirmation are 100 percent the Maven's love language!

Mavens are quick to react emotionally and can be easily overwhelmed, which is why they need partners who can help ground them and provide a sense of stability. They thrive in relationships that are built on a strong foundation of trust, and where they feel free to express themselves without fear of judgment. The trouble is, the Maven's insatiable attraction to risk, novelty, and even danger can leave *their* partners feeling wildly insecure.

There's another issue that Mavens don't always see. Despite their intense yearning for connection, Mavens can also be quite independent and don't like feeling being tied down or constrained. They value freedom and need partners who respect that and can give them space when they need it.

Be warned, however, that Mavens are rebellious in relationships, and like to test a partner's limits. Oh, how they can test their mates! Get ready to put your foot down. Once you're comfortably past the honeymoon phase, unwavering boundaries are a must when with a Maven.

Don't like when the Maven interrupts you while you're on a Zoom with your boss? Not fond of their penchant for staying out with drinking buddies past a respectable weeknight hour? The Maven may try to convince you that you're "making a big deal out of nothing," but they know when they're out of line. There's a saboteur in many a Maven; a teen-spirited renegade who will be owned by no one. The Maven's partner must learn to be firm without falling into a parental dynamic. Playing "mean Mommy" or "evil Daddy" gives the Maven more excuses to act like a child, a lose-lose for all.

Without losing your temper, you must clearly state to the Maven, "This behavior does not work for me." When you explain why, ask the Maven to reflect your words back to you, so you're sure they understand. This mirroring technique actually works wonders with Mavens when there's a lack of parity.

If the Maven continues to be a repeat offender, add a consequence. "If you continue to interrupt me when I'm working, I will put a lock on my home office door."

Important note! Do not suggest a consequence that you are unwilling to make good on. Charming Mavens know how to wriggle out of "trouble," and run all over folks. But they respect people who walk their talk, even if it means sending the Maven to the time-out chair to think about their behavior.

Although it flies in the face of convention, Mavens like it when their partners make them feel just a teensy bit unsure. The best way to keep a Maven is to show that you *can* leave them. In a way, this is the Maven's gift to their partner. You'll never slack off and turn into a complacent sloth. The Maven treasures a partner who remains a shiny object, a self-possessed prize they can chase into the sunset years.

Common Relationship Struggles for the Maven

- **Focus.** Giving a partner full focus can be challenging for the distractible Maven, whose attention is pulled and scattered by their 1,001 projects and friends. They may inadvertently leave a mate feeling neglected or low-priority.

- **Drama.** As lighthearted as Mavens can be, they take minor infractions personally. A wrong look or forgetful comment from a partner can spin them out and make them lose sight of all the good things in the relationship.

- **Defensiveness.** While teasing is fine for the Maven, they tend to be thin-skinned when it comes to any criticism that feels like a performance review. When the Maven gets defensive, it can be excruciatingly difficult for their partners to resolve some of the most basic conflicts.

- **Rebelliousness.** Mavens' rebellious streaks can create instability in the relationship, stirring up a parent-child dynamic. When the Maven feels "in trouble" they act out further, making this a bottomless pit of drama.

- **Wandering eyes.** Commitment is especially challenging for the variety-loving Maven, who may suffer from grass-is-greener syndrome when a relationship starts to get serious. Mavens should stay alert for their avoidant attachment behaviors to creep in, like idealizing an ex or starting a flirtation that teeters close to the edge of an emotional (or other sort of) affair.

- **Exhausting demands.** Mavens externalize—analyzing, processing, venting, talking through solutions. They may lean too heavily on a partner to be their sounding board or therapist, which can strain dynamics.

- **Complexifying.** Keep it simple? Not here! Mavens are complexifiers who love details. As a result, they may create systems that are meant to be helpful but are too hard for their partners to keep up with. "Wait, *how the hell* do I use this remote control now?"

How To Make It Last with a Maven

- **Don't fence them in.** Mavens need to feel free, so if you want to keep them in your court, give them an extra-long leash. If they can spend at least part of the day pretending to have zero obligation to anyone else, they are unlikely to stray; in fact, they'll probably talk about how great you are to all the strangers they're chatting up.

- **Don't react to their moods!** Mavens can ride emotional waves like championship surfers, but if you try to keep up, you'll get pulled into their undertow. Hold space while they vent—if they want advice, they'll ask for it.

- **Establish deal-breakers.** Have firm, no-nonsense boundaries about your deal-breakers. Your Maven will test you regularly until you show them that you mean business.

- **Have a life.** Stay immersed in your own life and passions and never make the Maven the center of your world. Not only is that too much pressure for the Maven, but they'll quickly become bored of you if you don't bring fun and entertainment to the table.

- **Keep them on their toes.** Charming Mavens can get cocky in relationships, treating a partner like the president of their fan club. The best way to keep them is to show them that you can leave them . . . in a nonthreatening way, if possible!

- **Admire them.** Use words of affirmation to glow and crow about the Maven's superior intellect, insanely creative ideas, and all-around brilliance. Give these compliments to the Maven directly or to a group of people while the Maven's standing beside you.

- **Leave room for reflection.** Expect indecision, buffer against indiscretions. There *will* be moments when the Maven questions your relationship, and they generally come at the worst possible times—moments before your vow renewal, when visiting your parents for the first time. While this is sure to trigger self-protectiveness, try not to shut down or lash out. The Maven questions everything! It's part of their analytical nature.

- **Get support.** Mavens may periodically confess to an attraction to someone else. If you have the steely nerves to hear their fantasies, that may be enough to dissipate the drama. But it could also be the clarion call to see a couples therapist—which is always helpful for the verbal Maven!

Which I*AM Are You?

Calculate your I*AM Type at
https://astrostyle.com/iam

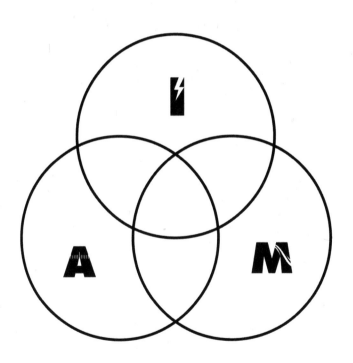

COMPATIBILITY

Compatibility: I*AM Matcher

I*AM COMPATIBILITY: HOW THE 3 TYPES GET ALONG WITH EACH OTHER

"Are we compatible?" Ask any astrologer and they'll tell you that it's one of the most common questions they hear. We understand why! When two people choose to blend their energies, it's hard to predict how the "cocktail" will turn out. Uncertainty is scary business, especially since a relationship gone awry has the power to disrupt every stable part of one's life.

And of course, there's the magic, the moments when everything just flows. It's human nature to romanticize; to hope that a peak soulmate experience can be reached.

Through our decades of counseling people about love, we've never come across a conflict-free relationship. We're pretty sure that they don't exist. Which is why we use a totally different measuring stick for compatibility. Rather than delivering a black-or-white answer ("You're perfectly matched" or "You're totally wrong for each other"), we prefer to lay out where you'll click and where you'll clash.

To carry on the mixology metaphor: Where will you swirl together like top-shelf gin and vermouth? And where are the two of you like beer and vodka—better kept apart?

Understanding how the three I*AM archetypes blend—for better and for worse—is a great way to *create* compatibility instead of hoping it just happens. Below are our best recipes for success, whether you're dating someone of the same archetype or branching out into the wild unknown of someone quite different from you.

Innovator + Innovator = Rewrite the Script

What works well. As two independent thinkers, Innovators understand each other's need for freedom and sovereignty. They may be comfortable with a more nontraditional relationship structure, where each partner has their own space and pursuits. They may even opt to live separately, or spend chunks of time apart, focusing on quality over quantity. At their best, two Innovators will inspire each other to pursue their own passions and continue growing as individuals.

What needs work. Who's the boss here? The risk of two Innovators in a relationship is that they can both be set in their ways. They want things done to their exacting specifications, which can lead to power struggles and a lack of compromise. Sharing space can be especially tough, as both Innovators spread out with projects and can be fussy about floor plans. Communication may also be an issue, as each Innovator may be more interested in sharing their own ideas than listening to their partner's. When two Innovators don't have enough common ground, they may drift apart. Consciously fostering a collaboration, like a passion project or even a joint entrepreneurial venture, can support this couple in retaining intimacy and connection. Start that business together or work to plan a big event. Two Innovators can easily mix business and pleasure.

Innovator + Authority = Domination Duo

What works well. Bringing dreams to life! Together, the Innovator and Authority make a dynamic team that churns out impressive accomplishments. The Authority is happy to play project manager, providing the structure and follow-through on the Innovator's big ideas. Meanwhile the Innovator inspires the Authority with their creativity and vision. The Authority's flair for precise planning can complement the Innovator's tendency to prioritize possibilities over practical details. When the Innovator and Authority play to their unique strengths, this can be a "dreams come true" power pair who design a magical and enviable life—without drowning in debt or putting on a show.

What needs work. Tug-of-war! The conservative Authority and the renegade Innovator may approach life with such different philosophies that they never get past the starting gate. Will either of them compromise . . . just an inch? Their differing approaches can be a source of friction. The Authority may prefer to stick to time-tested routines, while the Innovator wants to be spontaneous and experimental. This can lead to clashes in communication and execution of plans. For example, the Authority loves to plot things out far in advance, and the Innovator is hesitant to commit ("I don't know if I'll be in the mood for a concert eight months from now, okay?"). Their best bet is to find a middle ground—for example, book the vacations early but make dinner reservations on the fly—and they can circumvent this chronic conflict.

Innovator + Maven = Creation Station

What works well. When these two have a shared project or mission, the Innovator and Maven can make quite a dynamic duo. Both love the feeling of limitless possibilities. Bringing their "impossible" ideas to life can be the glue that keeps this relationship humming. The Maven helps the Innovator hash out their lofty concepts, listening attentively and providing savvy feedback. Meanwhile, the Innovator encourages the scattered Maven to move from talk to action, and might even share the Maven's ideas with their list of well-connected contacts. Still, there may be a lack of practical planning on both of these types' behalf. Ideas quickly balloon over budget and expected timeline, as both the Innovator and Maven lean toward overconfidence. This duo may want to pull in an Authority to act as advisor, sounding board, or project manager before leaping to implement their grand DIY schemes.

What needs work. The Maven and the Innovator are both outspoken and opinionated. They may get into fierce debates or outright defy each other. For example, if this duo has different parenting styles, they're more likely to polarize than develop a unified approach. The Innovator can act controlling and distant in a conflict, hurting the Maven, who tends to be more physically demonstrative. Hugging it out would solve everything for the Maven, but the Innovator's bruised ego turns them icy and superior. Both Innovators and Mavens have sharp tongues and can eviscerate each other in a fight. This duo can also fall into the trap of playing therapist for each other, only to end up frustrated when they can't solve each other's problems. Their million projects can also make it hard to stay in sync, since both of these types are constantly juggling. The Maven's need for attention and stimulation may clash with the Innovator's tendency to zone out into their latest obsession or make plans that don't include the more communal Maven.

Authority + Authority = Grow or Plateau

What works well. A relationship between two Authorities can provide stability, security, and certainty. Both people are comfortable in a traditional relationship structure. They prioritize practical details like finances and long-term planning. When it's time to buy a home or upgrade to a new vehicle, there's a good chance they'll have the funds earmarked, if not in their own special savings account. This is the relationship that should come with two rocking chairs and a cute porch, since Authorities love the idea of growing old together—and might even act like an old married couple while still in the prime of their youth. Stability is sexy to Authorities. Hey, we're not here to judge!

What needs work. With these two pragmatic souls steering the ship, the relationship can become humdrum and fall into a rut of regularity. Both Authorities need to make an effort to keep things fresh and exciting, so they don't lose intimacy when the inevitable plateau hits. They should try something new regularly that stretches them both out of their comfort zones—learning a language then traveling to that region, taking salsa or snowboarding lessons—to avoid becoming too set in their ways. The benefits of consciously cultivating a "growth mindset" are many for this duo. Two Authorities may develop the myopic belief that their cautious moves guarantee security. While mitigating against risk might make them better prepared, chaos happens. If they learn to embrace a little bit of it, they'll be better prepared for life's curveballs, like that leaking roof that needs replacing or company layoffs that leave one of them out of work.

Authority + Maven = Mixed Maturity

What works well. An Authority and a Maven can be a dynamic pair if they play to their strengths instead of polarizing into their many differences. The Authority can provide structure and set the plan, while the Maven can add innovation and creativity. The Maven's willingness to take risks and try new things can be exciting for the Authority, while the Authority's practicality can balance out the Maven's impulsiveness. Mavens struggle to prioritize, but the Authority helps them cut through the overwhelm and make a clear decision.

What needs work. Oh, behave! When the impish Maven and the stern Authority get together, there's a risk of falling into a parent-child dynamic. So not sexy! The Authority may play the part of the buzzkill and the Maven feels like they need to constantly seek permission. While that might free the Maven from thinking about those pesky details of adulting, it can eventually leave them feeling infantilized. Meanwhile, the Authority's in a "be careful what you wish for" bind: they have all the control but none of the fun! The Maven's need for attention and excitement may also clash with the Authority's preference for routine and stability. When the Maven forgets to pay a bill or has a few too many drinks at the party, the loyal Authority has to be the grown-up again. Loneliness can set in for the Maven if the Authority prioritizes work and responsibilities over shared playtime, or refuses to break their rigid schedule for a spontaneous adventure. Cancel the damn meeting, Authority . . . just this once?

Maven + Maven = Endless Carnival

What works well. Welcome to the fun factory! A relationship between two Mavens is never boring or quiet. This passionate pair loves exploring new ideas and experiences together. They'll talk and talk and talk . . . and talk some more. In fact, their "how we fell in love" story might involve a bottomless conversation or a dance party that stretched until dawn, followed by brunch, a power nap, and a day of adventures. ("And then she suggested we buy two train tickets and just get off at a random stop . . . and I said, why not?") Keeping this "new relationship energy" alive is the secret sauce to a Maven-Maven bond, so here's to their eternal honeymoon. Even so, restlessness can kick in. Some Maven duos may be open to unconventional relationship structures to whet their appetites for variety. No matter what, Mavens do best with lots and lots of communication. These couples (or throuples or whatever configuration the communal Maven chooses) should prepare for a lot of negotiation as they decide on the best commitment structure for all.

What needs work. With two spontaneous Mavens, there's a risk of getting swept up in unrealistic schemes or failing to plan for practical life responsibilities. Debt can balloon, bills are forgotten, or their *carpe diem* dreams crash harder than the 1929 stock market. Both partners may need to work on grounding themselves and balancing their creativity and excitement with a dose of reality. While Mavens' ultra-communicative powers can help them talk through any problem, there's a risk of getting caught in analysis paralysis. The good news? When their systematic sides kick in, Maven pairs can make powerful problem-solvers who know how to face a challenge with a spirit of adventure and playfulness.

Which I*AM Are You?

Calculate your I*AM Type at
https:// astrostyle.com/iam

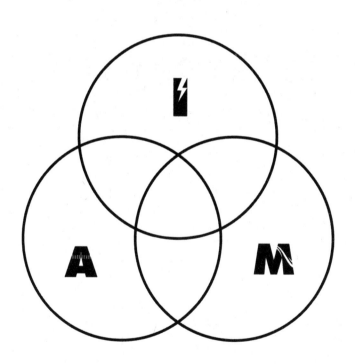

EVERYDAY LIFE

The Astrology Advantage
in Everyday Life

What does off-duty life look like for each I*AM archetype? All three have very different takes on downtime. Self-care rituals look like appointments and luxuriating chill time to the Authority, while the restless Maven needs a journal (stat!) to download the crush of thoughts that flood them when they have a rare moment alone. Innovator breaks happen on a whim—they'll immerse themselves in productivity for hours, then suddenly get a wild hair to go grab some Indian food or meditate in a botanical garden.

There are healthy habits each archetype can cultivate to remain balanced and flourishing—some that easily fall off the radar without conscious effort. (PSA for all the Innovators out there who forget to eat breakfast until it's practically noon!)

We didn't forget style! Dressing up can be an art form for each I*AM, a way to signal their inner truth without having to say a word. Innovators love to create a signature color palette, while Authorities trend toward sophisticated neutrals. Mavens give themselves shameless access to the entire spectrum. Why choose a pop of color when you can literally be a rainbow?

Our hope for you is that this section acts like a permission slip to RELAX. In our harried world, off-duty time is treated like a luxury rather than the necessity it is. We invite you to gain the Astrology Advantage and replenish your tanks with premium-grade, planetary fuel!

The I*AMs Off Duty

The Innovator needs

Unstructured Flow Time

The Authority needs

Unapologetic Pampering

The Maven needs

Space to Process Thoughts and Feelings

PERSONAL STYLE FOR EVERY I*AM

Style is subjective. What one person considers haute couture could elicit a citation from someone else's inner fashion police officer. Nevertheless, we've noticed strong similarities when it comes to the colors, eras, and silhouettes each I*AM type trends toward.

Social media has made us all walking representatives of our own personal brands. So why not send an accurate signal out into the universe? When you want to get noticed, it certainly helps to feel confident. Cultivating an authentic sense of style—one that declares *It's me!*—can boost momentum and get us out into the world, mingling and making magic.

I*AM Style

Innovators *prize originality*
and set the fashion curve

Authorities *spin the classics*
with a luxe twist

Mavens love to *play with trends*
across all eras

Innovator: Personal Style

Colors

Surprising combinations of colors, pulled together from every part of the spectrum.

Design Ethos

Fashion Haus. The Innovator's style evolves with the seasons based on their era or muse of the moment. Even when pulling from historical periods (Edwardian collars! '60s mod minidresses!), they'll add a personal twist.

Location Inspiration

Avant-garde cities and insider destinations where artists and creators commune: Paris, Marrakech, Bali, Mexico, Melbourne, Portland, Brooklyn, Dubai, Rio, Lisbon, Johannesburg, Tel Aviv, Greek Islands

Innovators don't follow fashion, they inform it! These trendsetting originals are at least a season ahead of the rest of the world. They're the street-style superstars who wind up on designers' mood boards (and later, their runways) for their fresh and daring "lewks." *Vogue* editor in chief, Anna Wintour, whose withering glares can crush the dreams of a fashion hopeful, was born with seven Innovator planets!

Stylish trailblazers, Innovators get a kick out of defying the rules of the so-called fashion experts. Picture Innovator Britney Spears in her plaid schoolgirl mini and white knee socks, or Beyoncé's iconic sequined leotards, which other performers simply cannot fill with the same aplomb.

Innovators don't care what the color of the year is! They've already created their own statement palette and it's probably nothing you'd find on the traditional retailer's racks. Salmon and lilac, with gold! Or caramel brown with neon pink! The Innovator thinks way outside the eight-color box of Crayolas and selects striking and unexpected combos from the entire spectrum.

Because originality ranks high on their list of "musts," Innovators prefer to shop small boutiques, go thrifting, even have clothes custom-designed for them by talented friends. Beyoncé hit the Innovator jackpot with talented fashion designer Tina Knowles as a mom and skilled seamstress Agnèz Deréon Beyincé as a grandmother.

Spontaneous Innovators never *really* know what direction the day can lead them in. Plans to go straight home and chill can quickly be rerouted when an invitation to dinner or karaoke comes in. Dressing in layers is a wise move for the Innovator, who should always keep an evening wrap or a pair of nice shoes on hand. An "everything bag" that isn't *so* big that it elicits chiropractic adjustments is a solid accessory for the Innovator.

Constraining clothes and heavy makeup may be fine for events and photo shoots, but Innovators are anything but high maintenance when they're off duty. Colorful sneakers and cute athleisure are a fixture of every Innovator's closet. They'll also incorporate their vacation clothes into their everyday wardrobe. Resortwear caftans, bikini tops, flowy pants, and billowy tunics should *not* be confined to the beach!

Authority: Personal Style

Colors

Classic and chic. May use one strong color, like burgundy or mustard, balanced by a neutral palette of browns, grays, blushes, and creams.

Design Ethos

Curated Classics. Sophisticated authorities spin the classics, reaching for timeless silhouettes and pieces that are both comfortable and chic. They may add whimsical or statement touches sparingly, often through their accessories.

Location Inspiration

Bright lights, midsize city! The Authority loves stately places where they can dress up, see "high design," and dine at great restaurants. Solid and more conventional cities like Austin, San Francisco, Nashville, Charleston, Savannah, London, Sydney, Chicago, Montreal, Dublin, Amsterdam, and Mexico City suit the Authority's more measured tastes.

Who wants to dress for dinner? [Authority raises hand.] Fashion is an *experience* for the nostalgic Authority, an opportunity to elevate any occasion into a formal affair. Want to make an Authority an offer they can't refuse? Invite them to an event with a code for attire, baking the whole primping process into the invitation.

Authorities live in the past, which means the preamble is at least as important as the actual occasion they are dressing up for. Appointments will be made: blowout, lashes, waxing, nails. Friends will be sent three carefully assembled looks from the Authority's closet to vote on.

Whether they're heading to Burning Man or a cousin's wedding, the Authority thrills at any opportunity to debut the killer pieces they've been collecting—from sample sales, estate sales, consignment shops, and trunk shows. These sophisticates know how to spot a timeless score that *appreciates* in value should they ever decide to re-release it into the resale wild. Take them to the Goodwill and they'll be the ones to find an original Chanel among the rumpled racks. Authority Megan Fox has turned her pinup looks into a red carpet art form. We hear it takes her hours to transform into a vintage bombshell and we bet she loves every minute of the process.

Everyday wear for the Authority is more subdued. These elegant souls lean toward "polished and relaxed" in flowy linen, organic cotton, and in-the-know brands by respected designers. Even their jeans and sneakers are meticulously chosen. In case you were wondering *who on earth* would spend $198 on a "basic-ass T-shirt," may we introduce you to the Authority? (It's Alexander Wang. From a limited-edition drop. No-brainer.) It's also an investment in the Authority's confidence. When they look expensive, they feel expensive, and that's when they attract the elite people and opportunities they want.

Getting dressed for the day can cause the Authority anxiety. They want to be appropriate but not invisible. Authorities may have some version of a uniform that they can easily slip on when they need to run out of the house. Why is the Authority wearing a blazer in the organic produce aisle (in the middle of summer, no less) or teetering on heeled sandals at the neighborhood pool? Because they're out in public, darling, and they need to represent!

Colors

Bright, eye-popping, and trendy; the entire rainbow!

Design Ethos

Playful and Youthful. Mavens pull inspiration from pop culture: multiple eras, street style, record album and book covers, retro kitsch

Location Inspiration

Flashing lights, up all night! Maven meccas have so many people to meet and things to do: New York (Times Square), Seoul, Tokyo, Rio de Janeiro, Detroit, Greece, Los Angeles, Rome, Barcelona, Tulum

Random-ass hodgepodge or perfect pastiche? Fashion is in the eye of the beholder, but one thing's for sure: Mavens serve their "audience" a lot to look at! And talk about, too, which is exactly the point. Clothes are conversation pieces for Mavens, a chance to locate kindred spirits in a crowd. They want you to ask them about their Virgo constellation necklace or come running up to them to gush that they just saw the indie band whose concert merch the Maven is rocking. *Ask me about my outfit*, the Maven's T-shirt might as well say.

Many of our Maven besties are known around town (and social media) for a signature accessory. Maven Angelina turns heads at tech conferences with the yellow hibiscus she tucks behind her ear. AJ's fuchsia-and-purple short 'do makes her instantly recognizable around her Detroit neighborhood. Amy's heavy metal tees are always a standout at PTA meetings. Mark's rose-gold grill is as charming as it is disarming when he flashes customers a light-reflecting grin while working on their cars.

As "gathered" and "wabi-sabi" as the Maven's wardrobe is, they can tie it together by choosing a pop of color. Some Mavens will wear all black but dye their hair an unusual hue for a head-turning contrast. Sarah Jessica Parker, who has seven Maven planets, was perfectly suited to pull off her *Sex and the City* character Carrie Bradshaw's tutu skirts, tank tops, and Manolos.

One Maven we know has made her mark on social media by splashing Barbie pink across every post, posing at pink boutique hotels among racks of pink dresses in pink wallpapered rooms and anywhere else she happens to find a blush-colored backdrop. She also manages to rock stripper heels with biker shorts and vintage tops by, you guessed it, matching their tones of pink.

Clashing might be the point for some Mavens, though! Kelvyn, who calls himself "an ironic dresser," can be counted on to show up with polka dots, plaid, and houndstooth in a single outfit. He knows he's a screaming eyesore. He also knows people will stop to give him fist bumps—and in many cases, their phone numbers!

SELF-CARE FOR EVERY I*AM

What exactly *is* self-care? This umbrella term spans everything from an annual physical exam to a relaxing cosmetic facial at the spa to taking a personal day off from work. Perhaps the only common thread among its iterations is the goal: to nurture ourselves so that we can operate as fully functioning beings in an increasingly demanding world.

In this section, we offer a "planetary prescription" to each I*AM archetype. What do you need during your sacred "me time"? Where might you stumble when it comes to self-care? What healthy habits are the best ones to cultivate so you can honor the temple of your body, mind, and spirit?

I*AM Self-Care at a Glance

Innovators need to learn how to
slow down and *be in their bodies*

Authorities need to *recharge*
at regular intervals throughout the day

Mavens need to *unplug*
from social stimulation, information, and devices

Innovator: Self-Care

Because Innovators are so consumed by their thoughts, they easily forget to pay attention to cues from their bodies. A morning news headline can pull them into a rabbit hole, eliciting an email chain that turns into a Zoom huddle. Before the Innovator knows it, the clock strikes noon and their only sustenance has been swigs from their giant mug of coffee.

The truth is, Innovators resist being embodied. Gravity slows them down, forces them to abide by the laws of the physical universe. They notice the sore muscles they were able to ignore while furiously typing their manifestos. It's only when their bodies send them strong signals—often in the form of a sharp pain, extreme fatigue, or a favorite pair of jeans that won't zip—that the Innovator decides it's time to make a lifestyle change.

Then, just like everything else in their lives, they tackle self-care with gusto. (They're more likely to call it a "self-improvement mission.") Results-driven Innovators want to see a change quickly and are notably impatient with the process. They'll sign up for a twenty-one-day challenge at their yoga studio, do a seven-day cleanse or reset, and order a new set of kettlebells or resistance bands.

Innovators stick to the program faithfully for a while, until the inevitable interruption arrives to throw them off their routine: travel, a work project, weather changes. This is why we recommend that Innovators think of their self-care habits in terms of "sprints" or "seasons." With their changeable lives, they may have to pivot self-care modalities. For example, Innovators might work from home for three months, which enables them to become Peloton devotees with a weekly acupuncture schedule. Then, they take a contract job and join the yoga studio in the adjacent building. Getting hung up on the "what" of self-care is a pitfall for Innovators. The point of the exercise is not the exercise modality itself but that the Innovator is doing something daily to take care of their body—stretching, ten-minute cardio, walking home from work, it all counts!

Me-Time for the Innovator

Innovators guard their "me time" like a mother elephant protecting her newborn calf. Some may even accuse them of being self-absorbed, which isn't altogether untrue. The Innovator literally needs to step away from people in order to process all the information and ideas they've soaked up.

Unstructured flow time is a must. The Innovator needs to lose track of the clock while doing something creative or physical. That could be gardening, reading a how-to book, going for a walk while listening to podcasts, or floating between the salt sauna and the cold plunge at a Korean spa. The point is that no one is watching over them or controlling their agenda. The Innovator gets to experience absolute freedom to do what they feel like for a set period of time.

Our sister Leora, also an Innovator, serves a long roster of clients as a Family Constellations therapist. To stay in balance between focused sessions of helping people unpack generational trauma, she reserves an hour for self-care in the morning. Some days she'll pull a goddess card and journal, other times she'll dance or simply meditate. It's all about what she's feeling called to on that particular day.

Morning exercise. To avoid getting lost in their heads all day, Innovators should start their morning with a walk, a workout, or some sort of movement. This can help activate their hunger so they don't skip breakfast, the day's most important meal.

Eating at regular intervals (and not too late). Achievement-oriented Innovators have "one more thing" syndrome and may try to stack in an extra task before giving themselves a much-needed break. By the time they actually stop working, they're not only hangry, but their bodies are desperate for fuel, upping the odds they'll reach for quick-burning carbs and sugar instead of the protein and veggies that will actually sustain them.

Box breathing. Innovators feel ungrounded regularly, but this quick breathing technique can help them slow spinning thoughts and connect with the present moment. Here's how it works: breathe in for four counts, hold breath for four counts, breath out for four counts, hold breath for four counts. Repeat four times. Box breathing also activates the parasympathetic nervous system, which helps us "rest and digest."

Prepping food in advance. Because Innovators throw themselves into whatever they're doing, we recommend they apply that zeal to meal prep, treating it like a project that they do once or twice a week. For example, the Innovator might choose two dishes to cook in batches, like a large lasagna or a stew. They can portion out the leftovers in smaller containers to enjoy for meals throughout the week. The French technique of mise en place, which translates loosely into "gathering," was made for Innovators. Essentially, this involves cutting up all the ingredients ahead of time so that they can easily be used for a recipe, like a chopped salad or a smoothie.

Best Vacations for the Innovator

When Innovators travel, they want to experience something novel and uplifting, a true departure from anything they can find close to home. (Otherwise, what's the point of spending all that time and money?) The ideal trip will be a dopamine-boosting getaway, filled with ultimate discoveries and memories they can pull up when life back at the ranch starts to feel too rote. "We found the best gumbo in NOLA!" or "I scored an appointment with one of Portland's most incredible tattoo artists for my first ink."

Some form of shopping is likely to be a daily ritual on the Innovator vacation; a chance to treasure hunt. When our own Innovator father brought us to his childhood home of Israel for the first time, there were daily runs to the produce stands for salad ingredients, bakeries that specialized in *bourekas* for breakfast, and a truly memorable trek through Jerusalem's Old City, where Jewish and Arab vendors alike sold textiles, spices, and sacred objects we'd be hard-pressed to find back home in Detroit, Michigan.

A loose agenda is advised, but we don't recommend the Innovator travel without *some* sort of itinerary. Otherwise their spontaneity can cause them to miss the best destinations in the area. Although they may grumble about waking up early or leaving their favorite pool lounger, they'll quickly perk up once they get on the road to a new destination.

Of all the archetypes, Authorities are the most consistent with self-care. It's not simply because they are routine-driven. Authorities' charts are made up of sensual fixed signs, making them particularly conscious of how their bodies are feeling. Many Authorities we know have elaborate morning and evening rituals.

Sharing a bathroom with an Authority requires complex scheduling—and it truly is best for these types to have a bathroom of their own. The Authority cannot be rushed through their exfoliating scrub, rose quartz *gua sha*, and makeup application! This is what sets them up to be centered all day.

Authorities love their appointments, with healers and glam squad alike. Getting away from home base and all their responsibilities is part of their relaxation process. Among the practitioners our Authority friends employ are "my lash lady," a ketamine therapist, a twin flame coach, "the best colon hydrotherapist in the Pacific Northwest," a naturopath who also does craniosacral massage, a laser esthetician, colorist . . . shall we go on?

Authorities hold these appointments sacrosanct and will not cancel unless there's a true state of emergency. We recommend supporting the Authority in your life with a weekly treat like this. The calming effect will pay dividends, boosting the Authority's mood and overall perspective on life.

Me-Time for the Authority

We'd never call an Authority lazy, but when it comes to their "me time," this type can lounge like a rainbow-hued iguana on a hot rock in the Yucatán. Many Authorities we know have a favorite chair or sofa that they've commandeered for their relaxation time. There, they'll spread out their books, oracle cards, herbal tinctures, water bottle, and snacks within arm's reach so they don't have to move far (if at all) to grab what they need while in flow state.

Sensual souls, they're probably playing soft background music while a candle with complex notes wafts its sophisticated fragrance into the room. Long baths will never get old for the Authority, who may bring crystals into the tub with them to soak up the important salts and softening powders they've already added to the water.

Pampering rituals are another Authority favorite when they have the luxury of solo time. Along with their fancy creams and face masks, reserved Authorities relish the chance to indulge in their "secret single behaviors" when alone. This term, which originated on a *Sex and the City* episode, refers to habits one might be too embarrassed to do in the company of others—plucking chin hairs, putting frosting on Doritos, anything the Authority would never admit to aloud!

Healthy Habits for the Authority to Develop

Daily stretching exercises. Authorities often have jobs that require them to sit at a desk or stand on their feet for long hours. Stretching can help them stay limber and avoid muscle issues later in life.

Join a fitness studio close to work. Authorities are hardworking, but more than the other archetypes, they need breaks throughout the day. Choosing a gym near their job helps them incorporate fitness into their busy days like a "Thirty-Minute Power HIIT" at noon or a favorite 5 p.m. dance-cardio class they can do twice a week before heading home for dinner with the fam.

Standing desks and medicine balls. Authorities who work in offices benefit from working at a back-saving standing desk or sitting on a medicine ball to work their core (and other fast-twitch) muscles, all while humming along productively.

Training for charity 5K or marathon. Since Authorities are deeply connected to their personal values, they're often motivated by exercise that has a dual purpose of raising funds for an important cause like breast cancer research or a community literacy program. Having an end goal to work toward is a bonus, as it allows the Authority to track their progress and look back on how far they've come with each passing week.

Best Vacations for the Authority

The first order of business for an Authority vacation? Catching up on their rest! No matter whether they're tent camping or splurging on a five-star resort, Authorities need a chance to unwind. They may have already planned the downtime, pre-booking a massage and spa services for the first day of the trip, then easing into the sightseeing and social components on the days to follow.

Authorities prefer a longer stay for that very reason. They hate to be rushed into action before acclimating to their new environment. Since they often bring a suitcase full of creature comforts, they also want to unpack and turn the space into their home away from home. As they absorb the culture of their new environment, they want to try "the best" of what the area offers, bringing home souvenirs and glorious stories to share with their people back at base.

Cultural activities are often a highlight for the Authority's trip. They'll take a commuter flight to see a favorite performer's live show in a sister city or a museum exhibit that was sold out for six months in advance. (The Authority doesn't mind patiently waiting.)

Family travel is another favorite for these nostalgic souls. They'll bring friends back to their hometown to see all the sites they've regaled them about over dinners or fly to a nephew's destination wedding. If the Authority isn't close to their own relatives, they'll create a "chosen family," and plan vacations around time together with these cherished friends.

Maven: Self-Care

Want to know what a Maven's self-care habits are? Look at their five closest friends. If they roll with a burgers-and-IPA crew, they might forget that "whatever's on tap" is probably not going to count as daily hydration. On the other hand, Mavens who huddle with health-conscious types are likely to meet friends for yoga and vegan brunch.

For this reason, Mavens should go out of their way to befriend people who take quality care of themselves—physically, emotionally, and mentally. If no one in the Maven's circle has a therapist or understands the quantum power of crystal meditations under a new moon, the Maven can (and should) connect to supportive online communities.

Mavens love to learn about new healing modalities. These early adopters are often the first ones to sign up for a wellness retreat, order a five-day microbiome reset, or record themselves for TikTok doing a fourteen-day dance challenge. They might go through yoga teacher training "just for the experience." One sporty Maven we know did just that as part of her physical therapy *and* to "save money on classes." The baseline certification requirement of two hundred hours didn't deter her. Interactivity is the name of the game, even when *self*-care is involved!

Me-Time for the Maven

Since Mavens process their feelings externally, they often rely on their sounding boards—close friends, family, therapists—to help them get centered. Spending time alone can feel empty for Mavens . . . until they discover the power of journaling. Freely writing their feelings can uncork a whole world of discovery and magic for the Maven. As pages fill, the Maven can process a childhood trauma and start sketching ideas for a social media campaign—all in the same morning.

The technique of automatic writing can get the journaling party started when Mavens feel stuck. The steps are simple: The Maven poses a question to themselves like, "Where should I go on summer vacation?" Then, they allow their hand to move across the page. An answer invariably appears, and it may come from further afield than the Maven's logical mind would expect.

One Maven we know likes to "audio journal," as he calls it. He'll get in his car at sunrise and go for a long drive and hit record on his phone as he essentially talks to himself. Before he tucks in to bed he'll play back to his own words, half of which he swears "seem to be coming from my spirit guides."

Any such practice gets the Maven into a sacred dialogue with themselves, an experience that feels divine and affirming, particularly for Mavens who struggle with loneliness or isolation. This type of me-time teaches the Maven to be their own best friend.

Healthy Habits for the Maven to Develop

Power down before bed. Mavens tend to keep their mobile devices near, often bringing tablets and phones into bed with them. Trouble is, these gadgets emit blue light, which can disturb sleep. Since winding down is already challenging for the curious Maven, we recommend they unplug and read a paperback or listen to music an hour (or more) before bed.

Let friends and family know your "do not disturb" hours. Mavens are the on-call friends who like to be available for a pep talk or an "OMG I can't believe this happened to me!" update. Yet at some point, giving people twenty-four-hour access can interfere with self-care. Mavens may need to let friends know, "After ten p.m. I prefer to only be contacted in case of an emergency."

Media time-outs. Savvy Mavens like to be up on the latest news, social media buzz, and celebrity gossip, but too many alerts can spin up their anxiety. We recommend that the Maven turn off notifications during certain hours so they aren't always waiting for a ping to interrupt their peace.

Keep healthy snacks on hand. Simultasking Mavens have their hands in many pots and burn through energy quickly. To avoid grabbing fast food or candy, they should keep "clean fuel" in easy reach, like raw almonds, protein bars, and fresh fruit.

Daily meditation to quiet the mind. Mavens have busy minds that can cause them to spiral if they don't take time-outs. Starting the day with a ten-minute meditation can be an absolute lifesaver, helping Mavens with focus and concentration, allowing them to prioritize their daily tasks instead of dive-bombing right in.

Best Vacations for the Maven

People are the Maven's raison d'etre, and when traveling, they want to be around friendly, fascinating folks who might just become their BFFs . . . at least while the Maven's in town. (Don't be surprised if a Maven hits you up a couple years later when they visit your neck of the woods again!)

Mavens love to research, so before they leave home, they've already scouted out the best place to get hand-dipped cones, see live music, and book five-star massages for an insanely good price. But that doesn't mean they'll stick to a rigid itinerary. Curious souls, Mavens love to be immersed in a totally foreign culture. They'll quickly scout out the authentic eating spots, invite-only parties, and local beaches with sunset drum circles. Spontaneous detours are often the memories Mavens buzz about the most. "We were just walking along the pier and these really cool women invited us to go sailing around the isles with them!"

Flexible, easygoing companions are as important to the Maven getaway as a portable charger. Mavens love to lose track of time wandering through colorful shopping districts and tourist hot spots, too. And they'll no doubt drain their batteries as they compose artistic photos and snap endless selfies.

HOME

The Astrology Advantage
at Home

DESIGN YOUR HOME WITH I*AM

If home is a sanctuary, why does its promise of restoration and relaxation so often elude us? Maybe it's the clutter we accumulate. The feng shui of the furniture. The tension with relatives and roommates. The stress we bring home from the office.

Or maybe we're designing according to an interior decorator's specs rather than our own cosmic rhythms. That open-plan loft that looked so chic in your favorite shelter mag may thwart rather than support what your I*AM archetype needs.

On the other hand, a home that's designed using the Astrology Advantage is optimized for the style of safety and serenity that your I*AM archetype requires. It bolsters home-based productivity, from preparing family meals to developing a kitchen-table business to hosting lively gatherings. It's a haven of health in every way.

We must warn you: your ideal specs are not always instantly compatible with those who share your address. If your home is a mix of I*AM archetypes, you'll confront design challenges.

For the Authority and Innovator who's encountered the dreaded

Maven Mess (why exactly *do* they need twenty-seven different moisturizers, all out on the bathroom counter?) . . . and for the Authority and Maven whose dining room tables have been commandeered by an Innovator's project du jour when they just want to have a family meal . . . and for the Innovator and Maven who chafe at the Authority's matchy-matchy decor demands (what is this, a museum?) . . . this part is for you.

In this chapter you'll learn the requirements of each I*AM personality so you can collaborate on common areas and find ways to respect one another's unique needs from a home. Home is everyone's castle—or ideally, it should be! How each I*AM type sets up their space can go a long way to support their recharge time. We've included a comprehensive floor plan to help every I*AM do just that.

And if you live alone, the Astrology Advantage helps you design your lair as a space where you can fully be yourself, in a style that supports your needs best.

THE I*AM ARCHETYPES AT HOME

The Innovator at Home: The Commuter

Incoming! Outgoing! The Innovator home can be like a "hub city" airport or main commuter train station where the many lines of their time traveling life cross. In some seasons of life, they're barely even there. When they are, beware the "solopreneur sprawl" of their many projects-in-progress.

The Authority at Home: The Monarch

Home is the Authority's castle, and they're in command of it. This I*AM type wants a secure, soothing lair that feels safe from the volatile outside world. Home is the one place Authorities can relax and be themselves! In theory, anyway. Once decorating begins, this type can be fussy about fixtures and furniture. They may need a reminder that this is a sanctuary, not a showroom.

The Maven at Home: The Host

Open-door policy! Maven homes are multipurpose venues and welcoming spaces. You never know who's coming to dinner (which is probably best served buffet-style). The Maven's household is a gathering ground to entertain friends and family for impromptu game nights, movies, and crafts. It's also a lab for the Maven's many hobbies that periodically spill into any unoccupied surface and space.

THE INNOVATOR HOME

If there's a homeowner saying a "good house is never done," we'd bet money there's an Innovator buzzing around under its roof. These futurizers are early adopters of trends, from greening their homes with living walls to installing smart gadgets and solar panels. As long as the maintenance isn't *too* complicated (they have no time to be slowed down by a zillion dials), an Innovator will give it a go.

You can learn a lot about an Innovator in your life by stepping into their home. Travel relics, framed prints from an avant-garde artist, and quirky mid-century pieces all coexist in overlapping styles and eras.

Rare is the Innovator who signs a mortgage on the first space they occupy as an adult. These achievement-oriented souls want to try out different living spaces. (High-ceilinged loft! Spanish Revival bungalow! Tiny house!) Their mission? To find the best fit.

Eventually, the Innovator *will* settle in to a home sweet home. But a space has to have enough visual interest, variety, and DIY potential to make it worth the commitment.

And—location, location, location! Ideally, the Innovator's address is within walking distance to a modern hub with a food scene and access to cultural hot spots.

Despite the fact that most of his friends have left the city, Alan, a perpetually cool Gen X Innovator who works as a sound engineer, "will never leave" his third-floor walk-up in the West Village of New York City. The proximity to lectures, shows, and galleries would be enough reason, but Alan is also a foodie. He loves having Michelin-starred restaurant choices steps outside the brownstone he calls home.

The Innovator Design Ethos

The Innovator moves through the world with purpose, collecting artifacts and accolades along the way. Their home might be part showroom and part vision board. It's a place to display their unique taste, an aspirational canvas with objects that exude the energy of originality and possibility.

Creating a home is very much a hands-on project for the Innovator. They love to be involved in the interior design, decorating, landscaping, even construction. Finding the right contractor can take some time.

Because their ideas can fall so far outside the scope of what's familiar, Innovators may struggle to get others on board or in budget for the build—even when detailed sketches are involved.

At best, the Innovator home looks like an eclectic and uber-chic gallery; at worst, it's a non-cohesive and inconsistent space. Why *can't* an amethyst pillar weave together with a mid-century credenza and tiki art? Gathered decor styles that are so beloved on Pinterest fit right in to an Innovator's home. Who wants to build a biophilic garden staircase? [Innovator raises hand.]

The Innovator Home: Floor Plan

Author Virginia Woolf evangelized the merits of "a room of one's own." For Innovators, you'd better upgrade that to *rooms* (yes, plural).

The expansive Innovator never feels fully settled in just one part of their home. Whether they're floating from kitchen to sofa to bed, or rearranging the furniture for the zillionth time, they cannot be contained to a single area.

When the busy Innovator is on a mission, any flat surface (or seat!) can become a pop-up workspace. "It just has to feel inspiring," explains Sam, a life coach and WFH Innovator.

"My bedroom has a south-facing window that floods the room with sunlight during the day," Sam continues. "I know you're not technically *supposed* to work where you sleep, but the warmth on my face keeps me from slipping into the winter blues. Since spring, I've relocated to the sofa where I get a stunning view of the front garden."

The dreaded "Innovator sprawl" can become problematic for roomies *and* for general functionality. Their books, papers, and supplies can creep into every common space. Dining areas, shelves, and bedside tables groan with the weight of the Innovator's accumulations. At some point, Innovators might want to rent a small office or storage space, or buy furniture with cleverly hidden drawers.

Since Innovators strive for excellence in all that they do, even prepping a lunchtime salad can mean taking over the entire kitchen. (What, you thought those dressing ingredients were going to mix themselves?) Immersion blenders, cast-iron pans, and fancy knives come out before a single leaf of lettuce hits the bowl.

A savvy workaround to combat the Innovator sprawl? Place a dedicated surface in each of the Innovator's favorite areas. True, most homes don't have a credenza desk in the family room. But on the plus side, this may increase the likelihood that the Innovator hangs out for movie night—even if he's copying and pasting files while everyone's taking in the flick.

Homes that cater to Innovators may feature:

- Stylish and visually appealing interiors that reflect their unique tastes and preferences

- Dedicated surfaces for work and projects in all their favorite rooms

- Outdoor spaces like patios, decks, or gardens for socializing and showcasing their flair for design

- Thoughtfully curated decor, artwork, and objects that reflect their appreciation for aesthetics

- At least one spacious area that exclusively belongs to them, with ample sunlight and air. Trespassers will be prosecuted in the court of cosmic law!

The Innovator as a Host

When the Innovator decides to host, it is an *Event* with a capital *E*. Why have a basic house party when you can add a costume theme (Island

Luau! Alice in Wonderland!) or rent a karaoke machine? Signature cocktails will be served, obviously.

Warning: the pre-party setup can turn into a stress-fest quickly. Innovators love to create an experience for guests, but the "how" of their vision can be hard to put into words. It may seem faster for the Innovator to just "do it myself" than deliver complex directions for programming the outdoor speaker system or pick out the just-right mix of plant-based hors d'oeuvres.

Alas, their visionary idealism can get them into trouble because (as the Innovator often discovers too late) decorating, cooking, serving, cleaning, and being a sparkling font of wit and wisdom is too much for one human to handle. Yet the Innovator's pride and overconfidence will get them into a few messes before they learn.

Pro tip for Innovators: hire some high-level hosting help like a cater-waiter, a chef, or a bartender. No budget? Enlist a couple of BFFs to help co-host and take ownership of various duties. If hosting at home is too much, Innovators might make a big group reservation at a bar or restaurant and tell everyone to meet them there. It will be a lot calmer and far less distracting—and the Innovator hopefully won't need to micromanage a professional staff. No guarantees they won't, though, especially if food and drinks take too long to be refreshed.

Sharing Space with an Innovator

"You never relax!" is a statement Innovators hear often from the people under their roof. Relatives and roommates fervently wish the Innovator would just sit still and calmly commune with them. It happens, but rarely. Generally, the Innovator's busy brain wants to be occupied—not to zone out, even if they know a little downtime would be good for their health.

The Innovator's "inspired" energy might light up an office, but at home, it can make others nervous, disrupting everyone's ability to unwind. With their strong self-focus, Innovators can become domestic dictators, disregarding how much square footage—not to mention emotional space—they take up with their puttering, zhuzhing, and mercurial moods.

One Innovator we know got serious flack from her family when she turned the dining room into a podcasting studio. She dashed out the door for an evening networking event without cleaning up, rendering it impossible for anyone to eat their meal on the table. (For the record, this was a repeat offense.)

Innovators must be careful not to treat housemates like annoying obstacles instead of sovereign beings with equal claims to this turf. For example, just because they're seized with the vision that the flat-screen TV *must* go on the opposite wall doesn't mean their roomie should turn off the NBA playoffs so they can do it *right now*.

Tips for Authorities and Mavens Living with an Innovator

Are you an Authority or Maven who shares space with an Innovator? Here are some tips for cohabitating in (relative) peace. First, accept that you can't make an Innovator sit still. To get quality time with your Innovator, join their project task force! Make a fun dinner together from their *New York Times*–reviewed cookbook, or work on a household project, like building a raised garden or installing a subway-tile backsplash.

The restless Innovator has a hard time giving other people undivided attention, especially when they're "off duty." They tend to reserve their total focus for projects more than conversations. So as rude or confounding as it may seem, the Innovator can actually focus on others more when they're cleaning, doodling, crocheting, or doing something with their hands.

There's a method to this seeming madness, it turns out. Research shows that working with one's hands puts the brain into a relaxed, "offline" state. When your Innovator roomie picks up an adult coloring book or spreads out the sixty-five-piece flatware to polish, *that's* when you want to pull them aside for deep talks and bonding. Tell the Innovator that long personal story and you'll have a captivated audience (as well as shiny utensils for the next holiday dinner).

THE AUTHORITY HOME

Who's afraid of the big bad wolf? Not the Authority, because they build their homes from solid bricks, creating a haven for themselves and everyone they love. Natural providers, Authorities function best from a well-stocked base camp where resources are in easy reach—both for using *and* sharing. The classic Boy Scout motto, "Be Prepared," could be borrowed as a nesting mantra for the Authority.

Even if they're roaming the world for a spell, Authorities pack travel-sized versions of their favorite essentials, from cleaning products to votives that smell like the hand-poured candle they burn at home. One Authority we know traveled through South America for six months with a complete portable kitchen (including a single propane burner, chef's knife, coffee boiler, and cutting board) efficiently packed in his suitcase!

Once the Authority commits to a permanent address, deep research begins. Buying a house may involve a lengthy period of construction or renovation. From comparing prices to sourcing raw materials, they treat every inch of their home like an investment. The traditional Authority likes to plant deep roots. Even as a renter, they scout for solid pieces that can one day move seamlessly into their forever home.

But first things first. The linear Authority likes to start at the beginning—the very foundation—and work from there. Function first, frills second! Before placing a single item in the space, the Authority checks the floor plan and square footage. Ideally, they get their hands on the architectural blueprints and learn everything they can about the plumbing, heating, and electrical wiring.

The Authority Design Ethos

There's no place like an Authority home, which can feel cozy and enveloping, as nostalgic as a Norman Rockwell painting, a portal to a simpler era. Authorities tend to like timeless items of quiet quality, with a few head-turning flourishes that pop against a classic backdrop. Oversized sofas, farm tables, marble countertops—these are all investment pieces, some of which the Authority envisions passing down to future generations.

Contractors will be hired to get the floors and windows and trim just so. An array of fabric and paint swatches are considered to design a cohesive decor scheme. (Modern farmhouse? Antique cottagecore? Scandinavian sleek?) If there was ever a type that would relish consulting an interior designer, it's the Authority.

If the budget doesn't allow for a specialist, the Authority will become an expert on whatever is required to pull off the finished look they demand. Although family members may grumble through the whole process ("It's just a stove! Who cares if it has a removable griddle?"), once the masterpiece is finished, they'll be forced to admit it was worth the Authority's fastidious fuss.

While you may gasp at what Authorities plunk down for a posh living room set, when you calculate the cost-per-use, the Authority's love of lasting value makes the purchase seem downright frugal. Twenty Christmas celebrations later, people will still cherish the sustaining familiarity of the Authority's home.

The Authority Home: Floor Plan

Authorities do best with well-defined zones that don't spill into each other. They need the freedom of a rumpled, toy-strewn family room just as much as the ability to serve a traditional holiday meal around a perfectly appointed dining table with cloth napkins and fancy flatware.

Our number one recommendation for any Authority home? Lots

of doors. Even if their tastes skew modern, an open-plan loft or studio apartment could become their biggest regret. (To the Authority who fantasizes about saving gobs of money by living in a "tiny house," allow us to caution against that, too.)

These same guidelines apply to the work-from-home Authority. Their very real need to unwind after working hours will be challenged if their desk and computer are close to the comfy seating area where they devour books, crochet throw blankets, or binge a TV series. Authorities appreciate homes that exude stability, comfort, and a sense of security.

Homes that cater to Authorities may feature:

- Well-organized and structured layouts that have all the traditional features: a master bedroom, a dining room, a great eat-in kitchen, a garage or defined parking spot

- Home offices or dedicated workspaces that align with their professional roles

- Strong foundations and sturdy construction—this home might stay in the family for generations

- Ample storage space

- Guest bedrooms and family-friendly entertaining areas so they can host multiple generations in style

- Energy-efficient features to align with their frugal budgets and interest in sustainability

The Authority as a Host

You probably won't be surprised to hear that Martha Stewart is an Authority. This archetype prefers to host in the style of a chic boutique hotel. Think: rolled towels, guest soaps, linen spray on the bedding.

Even if visitors don't care about the stack of unwashed breakfast dishes or the worn-out pillows, the Authority *does*. The pressure they place upon themselves could make the concierge of a five-star hotel break out in a sweat.

Consummate planners, Authorities prefer plenty of advance notice and firm date RSVPs so they can "set the space." But for moments when family or friends show up unannounced, they'll be stocked up on supplies. And if someone needs a place to crash? Most Authorities don't have the heart to turn a friend away once they've entered their cozy quarters.

Holidays at the Authority's place are the stuff memories are made of. They'll put a leaf or three in the dining table, set up stations for cookie decorating or crafts, and let the Pinterest-worthy moments begin. Whether they lay out a "casual" brunch buffet or serve a multi-course meal, there's likely a well-planned and cohesive theme—and a shopping list somewhere on their phone to make sure no supply or side dish is forgotten.

Of course, the pressure of hosting can be more than some Authorities can bear. "If I can't do it right, I'd rather not do it at all" is a policy that Marcos, an Authority with a degree from the French Culinary Institute, lives by. Most of his closest friends have been treated to a perfectly plated, seven-course birthday dinner at least once. (His cauliflower cream soup is legendary!) But he's thrown in the red-ticking towel on preparing any more holiday feasts. "Those are too many special requests for me to handle at once on a day off!"

Luckily, the Authority is usually a consummate *guest*, too. They'll bring a thoughtful host gift or a lovingly prepared dish from their own kitchen.

Sharing Space with an Authority

Two words: house rules! The Authority's love of policy and protocol can be stifling at times, but in the right doses, it makes cohabitation work. If you live with an Authority, prepare to negotiate quiet hours, study hours, visitor hours . . . and stick to the agreement.

Authorities are not actually trying to be controlling, although it may seem so. Routines anchor this anxiety-prone type. It probably took them a good many years to figure out that eating dinner any later than 7 p.m. also meant tossing and turning for half the night.

People may grumble and take the Authority's vigilance for granted—until they go away for a week, and they find themselves flailing without the Authority's stabilizing rituals! Those regular mealtimes, movie nights, Sunday pancake breakfasts . . . wait, who's gonna be in charge of these? The Authority's structure and consistency make a house feel like a home.

Those who share space with an Authority can't help but feel more anchored, shielded from the uncertainty of the world "out there." But the Authority must make sure their nest doesn't get *so* cozy that the birdies never want to fly . . . or so stifling that cabin fever strikes and tension builds under their roof.

Tips for Innovators and Mavens Living with an Authority

Pull your weight, even if the Authority doesn't ask you to do so. This capable archetype has it all under control, or at least, makes it look that way. The Authority might quietly corral the Maven's mess before guests drop by or clear the Innovator's sprawl from the dining room table before dinner each night. But they *are* keeping score.

To an Authority, actions speak louder than words. If you don't want resentment to build, let them know you love them and appreciate their A-plus (and yes, type A) care by returning it with equal consideration. Just don't phone it in, okay? Living with an Authority can feel like boot camp some days, but your downtime will be far sweeter in an uncluttered space.

And it's true that most Authorities like the dishes stacked and the pillows plumped, and the soaps lined up just so. "Well, if they need it done so perfectly, let them do it themselves!" one might huff. Wrong conclusion. Excellence is one of the Authority's love languages. Show that you care enough to do a job to the highest possible standard and you'll fill your Authority's tank up for weeks.

THE MAVEN HOME

Call it a creative studio, a bed-and-breakfast, family base camp—the Maven home is a high-traffic space. Social butterflies, Mavens need a space to hold court with their crew. Popping by for a casual afternoon visit on the Maven's deck can spill over into an impromptu barbecue, chatting around the firepit, a slumber party, and pancake breakfast.

Putter time is soothing for Mavens, who like to keep their minds and hands busy. You may find them macrame-ing an oversized wall hanging while streaming a movie with the family. Morning coffee rituals may include at least fifteen minutes of journaling or reading. (Please don't sit in the Maven's favorite nook!)

Many Mavens prefer interactivity to parallel play, so look out, roomies! The Maven may toss you an apron and lure you into the kitchen to prepare a feast. Friends of the Maven are treated to a steady stream of invites: game nights, crafting circles, vision-boarding parties, wine tastings. The more you get together (at *their* place!), the happier the Maven shall be.

To accommodate the spirit of spontaneity that Mavens love, things get moved around often. Modular furniture, nesting tables, and pullout sofas are ideal furnishings. Fussy pieces should be confined to select areas—or avoided altogether.

Even the most introverted Mavens will find a way to fill their space with the energy of other people, from books by their favorite authors to music streaming in from one of their many lovingly curated playlists. They love to be surrounded by culture and ideas!

The Maven Design Ethos

Playful, curious Mavens are collectors by nature and they have the display shelves to prove it! Friends of Mavens are used to joining them on treasure hunts through flea markets and Goodwills to scour for rare finds: Colorful Pyrex mixing bowls from the 1940s. Oil paintings and prints for a gallery wall. Unexpected objects that can be repurposed as planters (A child's cowboy boot? A set of silver gravy bowls? Why not!).

Maven decor can tread dangerously close to being kitschy, but that's by design! Their homes are conversation pieces, so if a visitor responds to a cheeky needlepoint (*My favorite thing to make for dinner is reservations*) or an ironic movie poster, they've done their job.

Olivia, a Maven creative director, has a passion for vintage Japanese action figures *and* all things Bauhaus—and she has the figurine shelves, tiered pendant lamps, and framed art prints to prove it. Sounds like *a lot,* no? Clever Olivia unifies her decor with her favorite trio of colors: saturated sunshine yellow, bright orange, and neon pink. The palette ripples throughout the rooms of her home, accenting her neutral furniture and complementing the lush green plants that are everywhere. (Oh yeah, she collects those, too.) Somehow, it all just works!

The Maven Home: Floor Plan

Mavens thrive in vibrant, social environments that allow them to shine and express their creativity. When lit up about their latest obsession (Sous vide cooking! Terrarium gardening! Encaustic wax painting!), they go whole hog with their hobby. Trouble is, Mavens tend to develop amnesia about the square footage of their space. Well, at least until the boxes of supplies start arriving. It's not uncommon for them to feel cramped at home, which we've heard several Maven friends readily admit is "my own damn fault."

Mea culpas aside, the dreaded Maven Mess can be highly problematic. When clutter gets out of control, it pulls their focus in a million directions and makes it impossible for Mavens to relax. Piles can piss off roommates and (worst-case scenario) become a hazard.

The solution to the Maven's "more is more" design ethos? Build upward. Savvy utility of vertical space is *the* key to serenity in a Maven home. Layers of floating shelves transform into works of art when arranged with stacks of color-coded books, plants, and miniature sculptures. Enclosed floor-to-ceiling cabinets are advised for housing the Maven's less aesthetically pleasing tools and supplies.

Hiring a closet organizer or space designer would be a wise investment for Mavens. When every object has a dedicated shelf or drawer—and the Maven commits to cleaning up at the end of each day—serenity is possible!

Homes that cater to Mavens may feature:

- Open-concept layouts with plenty of space for entertaining and hosting gatherings (hello, impromptu dance floor!)

- An unused area like a basement or garage that they can renovate into their own personal craft room and clubhouse

- Cozy and inviting spaces with comfortable seating and reading nooks for intellectual pursuits, journaling, and binge-watching their favorite series

- Libraries or study areas to accommodate their love for books, research, and learning

- Smart home technology, solar panels, and other gadgets that become fun talking points

- Game rooms, karaoke machines, VR headsets, and other playtime areas

- Giant walk-in closets with all of their outfits organized by color and season

The Maven as a Host

This is where the Maven shines! Their communal style and collaborative approach make them the ultimate entertainers. Hosting is the perfect opportunity for Mavens to show off their DIY skills with a creative charcuterie board or a hand-built home theater that they just rigged with surround sound. And let's not even get them started with a theme. Unleash a Maven and soon there will be costumes and historically reenacted scenes, with invites, decorations, and custom-printed tableware to match.

Holidays at Maison du Maven? Let the decorating begin! Hosting loved ones is a Maven specialty, and if the Maven is a parent, they'll take great pride in being the preferred hangout for all their children's friends. (They've got the swag to prove it!) Video game and karaoke consoles. Hot tubs and swimming pools. Ping-Pong tables, yards with volleyball nets. Tiki bars and barbecue pits.

Did someone say toast? Mavens can make excellent MCs, as their witty (though not always G-rated) commentary warms up the crowd, provided they don't shock people with too much candor. The best part about hosting for Mavens is that it gives them a chance to play matchmaker. These superconnectors thrill at the opportunity to introduce their favorite people to each other, in the hopes of sparking synergies or making a love connection.

On the Maven's guest list? Bring a friend! Inclusive Mavens never met a stranger and have a flair for breaking the ice and putting newcomers at ease.

Sharing Space with a Maven

The Maven's best quality—swan-diving into every moment with child-like delight—can also be their most challenging. Living with a Maven is a merry-go-round ride of high moods and crashes. With their active minds and mouths, Mavens "process" situations verbally...on the phone or to anyone in earshot. When guests drop by, they tend to lose track of time, forcing housemates to play bad cop and end the party when they need to go to sleep.

These issues aside, Mavens are the kinetic energy of their households, the ones who get everyone rallied for a movie, game night, or celebration. When someone needs a thoughtful ear, Mavens will drop everything to listen raptly and counsel them back to center. And while the Maven's "look at me!" antics might brand them as attention-seeking or immature at times, they have no problem sharing the stage if others want to get silly too.

Tips for Innovators and Authorities Living with a Maven

Are you an Innovator or Authority living with a Maven? Grab a trash bag and call in the cranes—you may be helping them clean up a Maven Mess every season. Good news: once a Maven finds a method to their mayhem, they can become as obsessed with keeping order as they are with their other passions.

You can help the Maven create a system, but word to the wise— get their participation in the process. When Camilla, an Innovator, moved in with Ben, a Maven, his home "looked like a bomb went off in it," she confessed. When he went camping with the guys for a weekend, she decided to surprise him by creating a brilliant shelving solution for his project area. "Selfishly," Camilla admitted, "we had a loft and I hated seeing all his tools and supplies exploding everywhere."

Camilla fastidiously arranged Ben's tools and even brought in bins and organizers to keep the tiny screws from getting lost among a sea of nails. Alas, it was a thankless task. Not only was Ben furious that she had "mixed up all my things," but within a week the tools were scattered haphazardly around again.

Although this nearly led to a breakup, Camilla hung in there. When they moved, she insisted on a place with rooms so that Ben could have his cave and she wouldn't have to deal with his Maven Mess. Recently, she was surprised to see that Ben had organized some small hardware into the bins she bought him back in their loft-living days—this time, without her help.

FAMILY

The Astrology Advantage
for Family

Ah, family. They're the folks you're connected to by biology, but not always chemistry. There's no perfect science to explain how to coexist with your clan, but maybe that's not the point! Parents, siblings, and children can be our greatest spiritual teachers. Even (especially) when they test our patience.

In this section, you can bring the Astrology Advantage home by learning about the I*AM profile for parents and kids. How does an Innovator mom or dad deal with discipline compared to an Authority or Maven? Why do the same rules that get an Authority child to cooperate totally backfire with your little Innovator daydreamer or your Maven mini-me? You're about to find out—and hopefully heave a shoulder-dropping exhale of relief!

THE I*AM TYPES AS PARENTS

If only parenting came with instructions! Thanks to astrology, it does. Each of the I*AM types takes on the job of parenting with a signature style. And if there's any area of life where an astrology advantage is helpful, it's here. We won't belabor (pun intended) this preamble. Here's how your I*AM profile shapes your approach to raising kids.

I*AM Parenting Styles

The Innovator parent raises kids
to be **self-sufficient**

The Authority parent creates
security with structure and **routine**

The Maven parent knows how
to be their **kid's best friend** and **ally**

The Innovator Parent

Parenting reinvented! By now, we shouldn't be surprised to hear that Innovators do parenting the same way they do life: re-engineering it to suit their values and preferences. But despite valiant efforts, the job of raising kids is fundamentally at odds with the Innovator's essential desire to be free to come and go as they please.

The "parent trap" can shock the Innovator's system. No book can prepare them for the lack of glamour, the mind-numbing routines, the depth of a little one's dependency. Until the Innovator figures out how to hack this lofty assignment, parenting can mark some of the most overwhelming seasons of their lives.

As far as most Innovators are concerned, disrupting norms should start from birth. These parents consider it their duty to help their children find their purpose as early as possible. They have an idealistic desire to shield their kids from the traumas and tribulations of childhood, while still fostering a sense of independence. Whether that leads them to a preschool with a unique educational philosophy, nontoxic and gender-neutral toys, or communal living, the Innovator is anxious about making sure their kids are guided in all the right ways. They want their children to feel special, to have a competitive advantage, but also to cultivate a well-developed soul, and a life that reflects who they are as individuals.

A tall order? Yes! But for Innovators to stay engaged, parenting is best framed as a creative act, one the Innovator can leave their unique stamp on. And indeed, with mixed results but plenty of love, they will. Once Innovators have been through the wild experiment of raising a human, they can become some of the most helpful guides, offering savvy, keep-it-real advice to newer parents.

What's Great About the Innovator Parent

- Nurtures their kids' individuality and creativity

- Allows their kids to explore their identities and break the mold if they want

- Hip parents (and hipster parents) who kids know they can ask about anything, and in some cases, speak directly as "friends"

- Introduces their kids to cutting-edge ideas and cultural activities

- Teaches their kids to be competitive

Pitfalls for the Innovator Parent

- Can put pressure on their kids to be superstars—but kids then develop an entitled attitude, don't learn how to follow rules

- Can teach kids hacks and workarounds, but kids then don't learn to do the steps necessary to gaining mastery

- Casts a shadow where their kids can't just be kids

- May be too busy or consumed to put kids on a schedule, help them with homework, or drive them to activities. Struggles with creating consistency for their kids.

Innovator: Becoming a Parent for the First Time

Parenthood can be a shock to the Innovator's system. Not only does the cost of living spike with kids, but the restrictions to the Innovator's no-limits lifestyle might be the first time these libertine souls mold their lives totally around another person's needs. This archetype is not especially into structure, and the highly regimented schedule that parenting demands quickly overwhelms them.

"I had the best life in San Francisco for years, and I planned to stay there forever," recalls Anthony, the Innovator dad of an eight-year-old. "But when my son was born, it was a huge wake-up call."

Anthony's once-spacious loft apartment filled up with toys and diapers and playpens, and the open-concept floor plan made it impossible to find coveted personal space. Running to the coffee shop for a quick almond latte became an epic journey with a bulky stroller and a cranky toddler in tow. "Maybe it was the hypodermic needle on the playground . . . or when I found out that private nursery school costs as much as out-of-state college tuition," Anthony says. "But as much as it hurt my heart to leave, it was time to bounce." He moved to a nearby metropolitan area, but is saving up for a pied-à-terre in the city center, because "a part of me just can't do suburbia full-time."

Innovator Parenting Style

Innovator parents want their kids to be successful *and* happy—and above all, to be self-sufficient. If all goes according to plan, the Innovator's kids will grow up to be emotionally astute, financially literate, and independent thinkers who make an impact wherever they go. Innovators will encourage their children to enter contests and step into the spotlight, and to feel good about winning. Sure, they'll applaud a brown participation ribbon, but the Innovator parent will also push their kid to go for a blue one!

As much as they might value status and good grades, Innovator parents have little patience for the bureaucracy and politics of institutions. School—or, as one Innovator mom calls it, "the educational-industrial complex"—doesn't just mean textbooks and report cards to this parent. Innovators want to instill the spirit of lifelong learning in their kids, a "growth mindset" that sparks natural curiosity about the wider world.

Robin, a magazine stylist with eight Innovator placements, is the trailblazing mom of two multiracial teen daughters. When the girls were little, they attended public school in a progressive town, but Robin supplemented their education with her own artsy and hands-on lessons. She had a full beekeeping farm set up on her property and was the school's staunchest advocate for including girls in a STEM curriculum.

To combat the perils of American teenage-hood, Robin recently moved her family to Bali and enrolled her kids in a sustainable "educational village." With its bamboo and mud walls, solar panels, and biodiesel school bus, this exclusive but utopian campus sounds like many an Innovator parent's progressive dream.

Still, Robin laments that her twelve-year-old daughter "just wanted to straighten her hair and go to the mall" when they first arrived in Indonesia. On top of that, the school was rife with problematic politics, and fell far below the bar of Robin's idealistic hopes. There's no beating the pressures of adolescence—or an exact way to shield kids from life's realities—but the Innovator parent will try!

Parenting Sweet Spot for the Innovator

The glory days for many Innovator parents is when their children are between the ages of eight and eleven. Cognitive and critical-thinking abilities are developing. There can be thoughtful conversations between parent and child, and the Innovator can help steer their little one's journey while encouraging them to bravely express who they are.

For this reason, newborns and toddlers are usually *not* the Innovator's sweet spot. Young children's antics, however adorable, are mostly exhausting to the Innovator. Nothing disrupts the Innovator parent's flow state quite like chasing after an irrational two-year-old or the constant interruption of snack fetching, blowout diapers, or *Peppa Pig* obnoxiously oinking from the iPad.

Parenting Strengths of the Innovator

"What makes my child special?" The Innovator parent genuinely wants to know. And they'll devote at least eighteen years to helping their kids discover their innate gifts and talents. Once that special spark is identified, the Innovator parent will invest everything in cultivating it, whether that's letting their kids train for an Olympic-level sports championship, enrolling their child in advanced art programs, or homeschooling them while they run a thriving YouTube channel.

Innovator parents take more into account than their child's biological age. If a kid has an old soul, or displays a propensity beyond their years, the Innovator will steer them to college-level courses in high school. Similarly, if a child's development is less mature than the societally appointed standard, the Innovator parent will find support systems to help their kid catch up. Admittedly, this will be harder for the achievement-driven Innovator mom or dad. They may blame themselves for their children's struggles—a mistake since this often prevents them from getting their kids the outside support they need.

Sure, the Innovator may be busy with their own pursuits, but they'll do their best to blend their kids into their lifestyles—or hopefully have plenty of help! To wit: iconic former co-parents Brad Pitt and Angelina Jolie, both Innovators, whose six children traveled the world with them, a multinational family of global citizens during their golden era. We may never know what really happened on that fateful private jet trip . . . but with two Innovator parents, we'd bet it was an epic power struggle.

The Innovator parent will have second acts . . . and possibly third and fourth ones. Their own dreams may be delayed—or, more likely, squeezed in around soccer practice—but the Innovator rarely, if ever, snuffs out the flame of their own passion projects.

As Innovator kids ourselves, raised by two Innovator parents, there was never a dull moment in our childhood—or a free one! Piano lessons, ice skating and swimming lessons, Girl Scouts, Sunday school, art competitions, band and orchestra . . . we did it all, week after week. Our mom was usually late to pick us up from these activities, since they were interspersed with her own packed schedule. Still, her devotion to our personal enrichment never wavered.

When we were in high school, our mother found a way to stay involved in our lives, stepping in as PTA president, which she somehow pulled off while studying for a master's degree in social work. She green-lit our idea to produce a schoolwide talent show. With our mom's encouragement, we put on a massive event that resembled a late-1980s version of *America's Got Talent*. Students from all walks of life performed magic tricks, hip-hop routines, R&B solos, heavy-metal sets, comedy routines, and traditional cultural dances.

As devoted as Innovators are to their children's futures, these ambitious parents look forward to the day when they can be free again. Once all three daughters were off to college, our mom enrolled in a Jewish seminary at age fifty-two to pursue her lifelong dream of becoming a rabbi. She moved to New York City from Detroit for the four-year program. Our dad, who had a seasonal landscaping business, joined her in the Big Apple every winter, often accompanying her to class and student events. Only two Innovators could make this kind of relationship work!

Parenting Challenges for the Innovator

Innovators may spend much of their own lives worrying about the future. They'll move mountains to avoid living on someone else's terms—and to ensure they have the flexibility to be there during their children's most meaningful moments.

As utopian and pro-individuality as the Innovator parent claims to be, they can actually be surprisingly controlling and even overprotective. The Innovator parent may project their idealistic standards onto their kids, even in a well-intentioned way. The Innovator's chart is composed of competitive cardinal signs, after all. They want their kids to feel special and to stand out in the world.

Ironically, the Innovator can turn into a helicopter parent—the very thing they rail against—by pushing too hard to shape their kids' futures. Many Innovators have strong preferences about the kind of shoes they want their children to fill, not to mention wear. And this presents a parenting dilemma. After the Waldorf or Montessori tuition, the troves of non-gendered toys, what happens if the Innovator's child wants to be an accountant or a cheerleader or something totally "basic," as one Innovator puts it?

Some Innovators will come around to a place of acceptance (after going through a few of the stages of grief). Disappointment, even feelings of failure, can wash over this parent. Alas, that reaction can translate as disapproval to their kids, who may start acting out or under-performing in protest.

The friction for Innovator parents is between their own high standards and the time needed to actualize those. Innovators are idealistic parents who may struggle to consistently provide structure for their children. With their busy lifestyles and erratic calendars, the Innovator's work, projects, and personal interests are in constant competition with the demands of parenting. Yet many of them try to be super-parents and do it all: homework with the kids, taking conference calls from the soccer bleachers or gymnastics practice. Overachieving has its limits, but the Innovator will only sacrifice so much before feeling trapped. Call for backup!

Parenting Techniques for the Innovator

Parallel play. Learning the art of "parallel play" can be a life-saver for the Innovator mom or dad. It's relatively easy: Set up the child and a friend with an activity that will keep them occupied—and throw a tarp down if they're likely to make a mess. Then, slip off to the periphery with a laptop, book, or project du jour. The Innovator is still supervising, but gets to keep some of their precious attention span for adult-level interests (unless said Innovator actually likes water balloon fights or making homemade slime, which they probably don't).

Assemble a village. Pro tip to Innovators: find childcare if you can! Whether that's hiring a tutor or babysitter, getting help from trustworthy relatives, or doing a co-op style arrangement with other parents, letting go can be a sanity-saver. And yes, Innovators may need to screen the applicants before they feel comfortable handing off duties. While some Innovators will gladly welcome co-parents and co-pilots, they can be controlling about how their kids are raised (spy camera equipment was made for this parent).

Isabel, an Innovator mom, remembers walking to the playground to secretly observe a nanny that she suspected was slacking. "I saw my two-year-old climbing up the steps to the big kids' slide while the sitter was scrolling through her phone, totally checked out," recalls Isabel. "I never said anything to the babysitter, but I phased her out of the job because I was always worried about my daughter—and I couldn't focus on my work!"

Bottom line: if the kids are all right, the Innovator parent's all right. The challenge for the Innovator is to work on their trust issues while also finding a trustworthy enough co-parent or co-pilot to help raise the kids. Will there be messes and mistakes? Sure. But it's better to scrape Play-Doh off the wall than have to peel themselves off the bathroom floor from an existential "I don't even know who I am anymore!" crisis—which can happen if the Innovator parent gives up their whole identity for their children. The stay-at-home role is not suited for most Innovators!

Remember that the days are long, but the years are short. The dueling desires for five-star parenting and self-actualization can make the Innovator feel trapped and overwhelmed, especially when their children are young. But if they can make it through those younger years, they become great role models, always eager to inspire their kids to think big and pursue their dreams. Teachable moments: incoming!

Build in a buffer for "learning experiences." Slipping grades or a behavior infraction will send the Innovator parent into solution-seeking overdrive. And while their creative problem-solving efforts can get their children's futures back on track, they can also backfire. By taking all the responsibility on their own shoulders, these parents miss the chance to teach their kids a valuable lesson about maturity and responsibility. Taking the shame and self-blame out of a setback can help Innovator parents and their kids reframe "failures" as learning opportunities.

Admittedly, this will be hard for the achievement-driven Innovator mom or dad. In some cases, Innovators might encourage their kids to take shortcuts or use hacks to get ahead. Innovator parents would be wise to remember the saying "learn the rules before you break them." Otherwise, they can cheat their kids out of learning important life management skills.

The Authority Parent

Who's in charge? When an Authority is the parent, you probably don't even need to ask. In most cases, Authorities are the "head of household," its alpha commander and provider who's running all the things. Hey, it's a demanding job—and somebody's gotta do it! That said, Authorities can also be traditional, and that includes with their gender roles. Some Authority parents may be comfortably ensconced in a supporting role, deferring to the other parent's leadership. ("Go ask your mother" or "Your dad's in charge of allowances.")

No matter what the Authority's gender or distribution of household power may be, one thing is consistent: this parent likes to stay in one lane. Without firm expectations, the Authority can't fulfill their duties, much less measure their parenting performance accurately. (The kids aren't the only ones getting graded!)

Having clear parameters around their parenting role is crucial to the Authority. If they're in charge of meals, shopping, and school pickup, fine. If they're a single parent responsible for everything, that's fine too. Whoever's supporting the Authority (babysitters, daycare) will have a well-organized list of duties, and they'll be expected to perform them with excellence. Kris Jenner, the ultimate "momager," is an Authority who's turned each of her six Kardashian-Jenner kids into an empire unto themselves.

The Authority is the consummate planner and scheduler and will work hard to keep the family on track. These responsible parents value routine and structure—but they need support. If the Authority parent is driving the kids to Monday soccer practice, don't you dare dump Tuesday piano lesson pickup on them. For starters, they have plans. But worse, you're making them look (and feel) like bad parents. The Authority hates to be "set up" to fail and let their kids down. They want to give their best and keep their word.

Graduations, holidays, summer breaks: the Authority will host the barbecues, plan the vacations, and keep the traditions alive. If there's a bake sale or a fundraiser, there's probably an Authority nearby. The Authority steps in when nobody else steps up.

Thankless job or not, the dutiful Authority parent creates a backdrop of ease for their loved ones. It's only when the Authority's steady presence is *not* around that everyone notices! Dishes pile up, the bathroom's not cleaned, and chaos creeps in. Things fall apart without the Authority—and that can be a wake-up call for their families. Like the drummer or bassist in a band, the Authority may not get a lot of solos, but they faithfully keep the whole group in sync.

Authorities are not typically helicopter parents but more what pediatrician and author Dr. Kenneth Ginsburg dubbed "lighthouse parents," "stable beacons of light" that the child can always count on, no matter how far from the metaphorical shore they may go.

What's Great About the Authority Parent

- Dependable: holds a steady, safe space for kids

- Family glue, brings people together around traditions so kids get the legacy of their heritage

- Instills values in their kids

- Teaches kids boundaries by gently but firmly asserting (and repeating) the rules

- Build fortitude and persistence in their kids and prepare them for the real world

Pitfalls for the Authority Parent

- Pushes kids into academics, sports, or extracurriculars that aren't right for them in an effort to teach them not to quit

- Focuses more on achievement than self-expression. May teach kids that being good means getting approval or being polite and nice. Kid may develop an "employee mindset" or stay quiet when they need to speak up

- Kids may be sneaky or rebellious and "on their best behavior" around parents

- Attacher: overidentifies with the parent role, struggles with empty nest . . . may pull kids into the cozy home base and not let them fly.

Authority: Becoming a Parent for the First Time

Getting ready for parenthood is both exciting and daunting for the Authority. On the one hand, these consummate project managers love nothing more than a fresh opportunity to gain expertise. Prepping for baby is the kind of deep dive the high-achieving Authority loves. (And what is a parent, after all, if not the ultimate authority figure?)

The Authority parent will discern which books and experts are the best, likely following the ones recommended by their OB-GYN or a friend they deeply respect. Then, they'll craft a thoughtful birth plan. One Authority we know, terrified of being thrown off her strict work schedule, learned everything she could about sleep training and even proactively hired a "night nanny" for the first six months. "Turns out my kid slept solidly through the night, so I really overprepared," she recalls in hindsight. "It was expensive, but at least I had the peace of mind that, in case my son did wake up at three a.m., he would be taken care of immediately." Whatever works!

Authorities might do well to remember the saying that "the mother is born with the child." Even the best-laid plans can be disrupted by the mysteries of life, the fierce love of parenthood, and the unique personality that emerges as their child develops. If the Authority can let go a little, parenthood can connect them to a softer, more playful side of themselves.

Authority Parenting Style

Proud, self-sufficient, and steady, the Authority parent aims to be the rock in their children's lives. Providing is their priority, whether that's love, enriching experiences, financial support . . . or all of the above. They take the job of raising a child seriously, and maybe a little too seriously at times. Even when they act cool and unruffled, behind the scenes the Authority is making sure everything is in place. They want their kids to have the best possible childhood and to be fully prepared for their future as honest, upstanding citizens.

There are consequences for bad behavior in the Authority's home. The newer Authority parent believes that holding the line is more important than caving to their children's demands. Of course, there's always the chance that their kids will rebel or start sneaking around to get what they want. Finding the balance between firm and flexible is a line the Authority parent constantly walks.

The Authority's child might start work at an early age, from paper routes to scooping ice cream to babysitting the neighbor kids. Chores and good behavior will be required for the Authority's child to earn their treats or allowance. There are no handouts in the Authority's household, but there's plenty of praise and encouragement for a job well done.

Authority parents can be stoic, but don't let their stern demeanor fool you! These are some of the most nostalgic and sentimental souls on the planet. Authorities want to honor how precious and fleeting childhood is. They'll save their kids' report cards and drawings, and they'll get teary-eyed over handmade cards and gifts.

Still, rules are rules. Authorities might be even-keeled, but their kids know not to cross a certain line. This is the parent who has "the look" that can snap their misbehaving young ones into gear.

Stricter Authority parents may struggle to connect emotionally with their children and can even suppress their kids' individuality by setting the bar too high. It's more important, the Authority may believe, that their kids learn healthy boundaries, emotional self-regulation, and don't grow up to be entitled narcissists who expect everything handed to them. Authorities know that raising kids is a marathon, not a sprint. Even if their teenager slams the door and shouts "I hate you!" after being denied a curfew extension, the Authority is not here to bend the rules and lose the upper hand. They just keep showing up and try to model the behavior they want their kids to repeat.

Dan, an Authority from San Diego, took a job relocation in New York after his divorce. His ex-wife stayed in California with their three kids, who were firmly entrenched in their schools and sports. For others it would be a heartbreaking obstacle, but Dan didn't miss a beat. "No way was geography going to stop me from being a stable presence in my children's lives," Dan says emphatically.

Every Saturday night, Dan boarded a cross-continent flight to Southern California and settled in to a small condo he rented a mile from his old house. By Sunday morning, he was picking his kids up for breakfast and coaching his son's Little League baseball team at noon. Tuesday night, Dan headed back east and worked the next three days in the office. He talked to his kids before bed every night and was a regular presence in their lives.

The divorce was far less traumatic because of Dan's consistent Authority style. His kids knew what to expect, and since he always showed up for them, they quickly adapted to their new routine. Dan's son is now a rising baseball star, and during playoffs season, Dan has arranged to work remotely from San Diego so he can be at every practice and game.

Parenting Sweet Spot for the Authority

If the Authority excels at one parenting skill, it's structure. Even if they feel like a "hot mess" inside, that won't stop the Authority from being consistent with their boundaries, rules, and routines. While they may be called strict, Authorities know that clear "do's and don'ts" help their kids feel safe. The Authority's child never has to guess where they stand or what's expected of them. The rules are clear and simple, which in the best situations, leaves plenty of room for fun.

Parenting Strengths of the Authority

Authorities are values-driven parents. They teach their kids to be kind, say please, and write thank-you cards. While Authorities might occasionally micromanage their kids' lives (they like to call it "steering"), they also want to empower them. One Authority we know hired her ten-year-old to be her assistant when her Etsy shop got a deluge of orders. Authorities are patient teachers who specialize in breaking everything down into clear steps and sequences. They know how to simplify a complex task.

"My thirteen-year-old son recently took the train into New York City to see his grandma," says Rhonda, an Authority and native New Yorker now living in a suburb forty-five minutes away. "We programmed his GPS so he could walk from the train station to her apartment, and he found his way just fine!"

Authority parents are great at incrementally adding privileges (and yes, taking them away) as they test their children's maturity and capability. "It's like a recipe," says Authority Ana. "You add and subtract until you find the right amount for them."

Humble Authorities make raising kids look easy. In truth, it's their steady devotion that creates that flow. Their secret to success? They just don't overcomplicate things. Taking the path of least resistance, it turns out, works best more times than not. The pragmatic Authority knows to try that time-tested route first, before dabbling in the latest parenting fad.

Many Authorities have also mastered the art of "slow parenting." Because they separate work and personal time better than most, Authorities love to unplug and enjoy quality time with their kids. From family vacations to chaperoning Scout camp to daylong outings, Authorities make sure that shared time is special and memorable.

Parenting Challenges for the Authority

Pride can be a pitfall for the Authority parent. When life gets tumultuous, they want to shield their children from adult problems and stressors, a noble effort, in theory. However, by projecting the image that they've got it all together—even when they don't—Authorities are a little too good at fooling the outside world! Authorities fear that showing vulnerability will make them look weak, a threat to their role as admired and trusted leaders in their homes, families, and communities.

Taken too far, the Authority's extreme self-sufficiency and "I'll figure it out myself" approach can backfire. These parents might wait far too long before reaching out for help. By the time they do, the problem has compounded: illness, financial turmoil, relationship troubles. Ironically, the very thing the Authority hoped to avoid—exposing their kids to a messy breakdown—ends up happening exactly *because* the Authority didn't enlist support sooner.

While it's no small feat to get an Authority to send smoke signals, here's something this "type A" parent might want to consider: by hiding struggles from their children, they miss the opportunity for a teachable moment. Their children don't get to witness their parent's creative problem-solving abilities, and don't learn resilience by example.

Jacqueline, an Authority who's solo parenting her son, is an example of this sort of pride. "I never took a dime of child support and I certainly could have used it," she says. "It's not like my ex didn't have money. But I didn't want him to have control. I wanted to parent Jesse my way."

The other common parenting pitfall happens when the Authority hands too *much* power to another adult, either in an effort to be egalitarian, or because they're deferring to a more dominant partner. "My girlfriend moved in with us when my daughter Annie was ten," recalls Candace, a single mom and an Authority, "and it was a disaster. For years it was just me and Annie against the world. We had a groove and a routine. Then my partner came along and thought she could start disciplining my kid and making house rules. At first I let her, which was a mistake. The two of them clashed, and then I tried to mediate, and soon we were all fighting with each other! We broke up a couple months later. I still feel like I traumatized Annie from it. But I was lonely—I hadn't dated in over a decade and I made a choice out of desperation at that point."

Authorities thrive as parents when they speak up for their needs, rather than sacrificing. While it can take a few emotional breakdowns, the most successful Authority parents learn to build a family structure that has room for *their* humanity, too.

Parenting Techniques for the Authority

Make time for yourself. Sacrificing for the family might feel comfortable for humble, hardworking Authorities, but what message does that really send? The happiest Authorities are the ones who prioritize their needs on a regular basis. Note to Authorities: you're setting an example of a balanced life for your kids.

"My daughter started having anxiety and really freaking out about her grades and college admissions," recalls one

Authority. "I had to step back and look at where she learned it—and sadly, it was from me. I was always driving myself so hard to achieve, never giving myself any credit, and shrugging off compliments. That was a wake-up call. I had to change so she could."

Model healthy risk-taking. The Authority parent can stay in their lane a little too faithfully, talking about dreams but letting years slip by before they pursue them. If an Authority parent is too timid or law-abiding to bend the rules, their children may also grow up playing it safe instead of discovering their passions. It's better for the Authority's child to see their mom or dad "go for it" and fail, than never try at all.

Outsource some parts of parenting. Authorities want to prepare their kids for the competitive world out there. When they're in parenting mode, they're all in. They want their children to succeed, get better, learn all the valuable lessons. But even the long-suffering Authority's patience can run out, or their kids just need other role models for variety's sake. Sometimes, it's best to hand off those duties to a coach or tutor or mentor. Stepping out of the "in charge" role might actually improve their parent-child relationship, allowing the Authority to not always be the heavy-handed disciplinarian.

A safe space to speak. *Respect your elders. Mind your manners.* Sadly, not all adults are safe or trustworthy. If the Authority teaches their children to defer to someone's age, rank, or position, their children may not speak up or advocate for themselves when they feel endangered. The "obedience training" some Authority parents put their kids through can backfire. Remember: the idea is to keep kids out of trouble, not make them afraid they'll get in trouble by telling the truth. "My mom had strict policies about no sugar," says one Authority's grown daughter. "But all I did was sneak candy and soda whenever she wasn't looking. I probably wouldn't even have cared about it as much if she didn't make such a big deal out of it." Following the letter, rather than the spirit, of the law can be an Authority parent's pitfall.

The Maven Parent

Who's the kid here anyway? The eternally youthful Maven is a parent, teacher, and BFF in one. These multi-hyphenates have so much to share. Parenting is a chance to pass on their wide breadth of knowledge and dabble in new curiosities together. Mavens want to explore the world with their kids, glimpsing it all through curious and wonder-filled eyes.

Alas, kids are often moody and mercurial, and many don't live up to the Maven's idealistic hopes. When their children complain "I don't wanna!" and "Why are you dragging me here?" the Maven smiles and proceeds according to plan. There's a method to the Maven's madness. If a Maven parent signs you up for sports or summer camp or private lessons, you'd better believe you're going. Later in life, their children will appreciate these cherished memories and skills that gave them a career advantage.

One Maven dad was offered a friend's Florida condo in August, already the ickiest and most humid month there, during a heat wave. The family, which included a seven-year-old and two teens, protested, but he piled them into a car and drove down the East Coast from New Jersey to Boca Raton. And of course, the Maven was right. With a swimming pool right outside the sliding glass doors and the beach a block away, everyone had the time of their lives.

Mavens might *seem* like they're throwing caution to the wind, even being reckless risk-takers. In truth, they think about everything with the precision of an engineer. If you could see inside a Maven parent's brain, it would probably look like a diagram of interconnecting flow charts or the operating manual to a piece of heavy machinery. They have a plan, whether they can explain it or not!

What's Great About the Maven Parent

- Eternal playmate—the fun parent who takes their kids on field trips and cultural experiences. Our Maven grandfather took our mom and aunt out of school for a six-week European vacation when they were kids!

- Does projects with kids, gets in the sandbox, is not afraid to get their hands dirty too

- Encourages curiosity and experimentation

- Asks questions, teaches kids to do the thinking themselves

- Reads all the latest parenting books on everything from child psychology to nutrition

Pitfalls for the Maven Parent

- Helicopter parent: neurotic and worried about every fluctuation

- Overly involved in kids' day-to-day affairs, butts into their business, and overwhelms their children with intensity

- Can be the parent that embarrasses their children—posts all about the kid on social media

- Scattered and emotional—kids may feel they have to take care of their parents

- Complains and gossips; may say things like, "Ugh, I hate being a parent!" and hurt kid's feelings with their loose-lipped style

Maven: Becoming a Parent for the First Time

There's no such thing as "too much information" when the Maven prepares for their firstborn to arrive. These human sponges will read all the baby books, follow the Instagram child psychologists, and of course, document the highs and lows of their own pregnancy or adoption journey on video. Open the opinion polls! Home birth or hospital? Co-sleep or crib? Mavens will geek out over everything from organic baby food reviews to the best bassinets to the state-of-the-art stroller they scored secondhand or on a "freecycling" website.

The first-time-parent Maven might drive friends and family a little crazy with their intense preparing and obsessing over all the options. But communal Mavens want to share this life experience with their closest people. If ever there was an archetype to say "we're pregnant," it's this one! Doing this journey alone is *not* the way for Mavens. The Maven parent-to-be should check out the local birthing groups, parenting circles, and newborn classes, then find the one that fits their vibe best.

Maven Parenting Style

Interactive, hands on, and involved, Mavens see parenthood as an extension of their own childhood. If the Maven's parents were stern, having kids is a chance to do it better and make up for the shortcomings they experienced. And if the Maven had an idyllic childhood, well, here's a chance to share that with the next generation.

Mavens don't *mean* to be helicopter parents, but since they're a curious blend of neurotic and playful, they can be hard-core about instilling certain skills in their children. If that means being PTA president or school board chair, sign them up for the ballot. On some topics, Mavens can be overly didactic, corrective, and critical, and in other areas, stunningly permissive. One Maven we know sends her kids to private Catholic school but has no curfew for them on the weekend. Mixed message much? Well, yes . . . but the Maven contains multitudes, and reserves the right to change their mind without notice. Often, their supersized emotions will cast the deciding vote.

Alex, a Maven dad, was in foster care as a child. Every couple of years, he was shuffled between homes, never able to put down roots. Now he's "obsessively involved" with his son's sports, academics, and discipline because, as Alex puts it, "I always wished I had someone to guide me, so I'm going to make sure he does." You can find Alex in the front row, iPhone camera filming, at every school concert and basketball game.

A Maven couple we know, both tennis lovers, put all four of their children into racquet sport lessons from an early age. "We're a tennis family," these parents are known to say. ("We" and "us" are favorite pronouns of the Maven.) Indeed, their shelves are lined with trophies and medals, and their house is a regular party spot for every Wimbledon and US Open.

The Maven parent is a built-in superfan, but they'll also call their kids out for underperforming. Tact isn't their strong suit, but the Maven's harsh words are well-intentioned. When they know their kids can do better, they'll push them to reach beyond their perceived limits.

Of all the three archetypes, Mavens are most likely to be a best friend and parent. They'll bring their kids into the family business and teach them everything they know. The mom that comes to the music festival and fits right in with her kid's friends? Probably a Maven. "My twenty-five-year-old daughter and I went on a resort trip, and she picked a hotel where her favorite DJ would be playing," says Lisa, a Maven whose daughter is also her business partner. "I was twice as old as everyone there, but I didn't mind—I had a blast, and we danced our butts off until three a.m.!" While some eyebrows might rise skyward, this is who Lisa is at her core, and she has a close-knit mother-daughter bond to show for it.

Parenting Sweet Spot for the Maven

The hands-on Maven may complain that they have no time for themselves, but they wouldn't have it any other way. The early childhood years, which are the bane of many parents' existence, can be a favorite of the Maven adult. These uber-patient teachers get right into the toddler trenches, and no "threenager" tantrum or preschool meltdown will stop them. They love kids when they're most malleable.

There's a famous story in our family that when we first started crawling as babies, we crawled backward. (We're Innovators, after all, so why would we do it like everyone else?) Our grandfather, a Maven, got down on the floor to teach us how to crawl the "right" way.

His diligent efforts were in vain, but that didn't stop our grandpa from trying for quite a while. And he made up for lost time when we were older, showing us how to compose photographs and develop them in a darkroom, draw with proper perspective, ride bikes without training wheels, and so many other things. His own versatility (he was an engineer, an artist, and a writer) taught us not to pigeonhole ourselves in life either!

Parenting Strengths of the Maven

Creative solutions are the Maven's specialty. Although they may worry about, even catastrophize, the little things, when things really go off the rails, the Maven is usually the calm eye of the storm. This I*AM archetype can even thrive in chaos, which is an opportunity to pull out all the knowledge they've collected over the years.

Claudia, a Maven, enlisted an art therapist to accompany her son Jason to preschool. Jason had a speech delay but was able to express his feelings and thoughts through painting (with some impressive brushstrokes, we might add!). Jason began talking at age five but had lifelong sensory issues that were soothed by listening to classical music. Claudia bought season tickets to the symphony that year, and nearly a decade later, it's a regular ritual for them to bask in acoustic bliss, followed by a special lunch at Jason's favorite bistro.

Mavens love when their homes are bustling with visitors, and they've got the open-door policy to prove it. Château Maven is the neighborhood clubhouse and gathering place for prom pictures, sleepovers, and parties. The Maven parent might even take in a troubled teen or two, giving them shelter and guidance. There's always room for more under the communal Maven's roof, no matter how snug the quarters. These parents are happiest surrounded by the buzz of human activity.

And note to the kiddos: your eternally hip Maven mom or dad might actually give *you* cool points! Kim Kardashian and her oldest daughter, North West, both Mavens, amassed millions of followers on their shared TikTok account, Kim and North. The Maven's pop culture cred and playfulness can make them seem more like a sibling than a parent. We know several Mavens who've done psilocybin journeys with their young adult children (no judgment). "At least I was there to supervise, and I knew where the plant medicine came from," reasoned one of them.

Outgoing, no-filter Mavens are the adults that might embarrass their kids during their teen years. But that won't stop them from cheering loudly at the football games, posting every highlight on social media, even teasing their kids and their friends in a loving way. In the end, it works out because the Maven's ageless spirit is incredibly entertaining. Parent most likely to be turned into a meme: the Maven!

Parenting Challenges for the Maven

When is the Maven's involvement too much of a good thing? That's a blurry line for some Mavens. We're not calling the Maven neurotic but . . . their anxious attachment style can make it hard for their kids to cut the cord. Mavens aren't always the best at filtering their feelings. Whether they're stressing about bills or tree nut allergies or work-life juggles, their kids pick up on this angst and may develop nervous habits themselves.

Maven parents can swing from carefree to controlling. One day they're confiding in their kids like peers, talking openly about their personal lives (TMI, Mom and Dad!), or dressing in the same popular clothing brands as their children. Shared experiences are great, until the Maven's kids start to feel like the only adult in the room or develop a subconscious sense of guilt when they want to break free and individuate.

When this happens, the Maven may struggle with empty-nest syndrome, even as soon as the teenage years. While Mavens with young children might complain that they never have time for themselves, the other extreme can be just as challenging. Once the Maven's mini-me no longer wants to hang out like besties, an identity crisis could follow.

Parenting Techniques for the Maven

Gamify parenting. The playful Maven is not above an "incentive" to get chores, homework, and other don't-wannas done. Our friend Angelina gave "cash bonuses" for her kids to earn straight As and do their homework. From color-coded chore charts to pricey purchases, the Maven parent can be extravagant with their bribes.

Change the channel. Emotions blow up big and fast for Mavens. From sentimental sobs to bellowing rages, when a Maven loses their cool, it can be an alarming scene. The Maven needs their go-to outlets for blowing off steam: regular workouts, therapy, time with friends. Whatever it takes!

Let the kids individuate. Mavens are mirrors. Nothing thrills a Maven parent more than a child who's a "chip off the old block," or a "mini-me." At a certain point, the Maven parent needs to park the helicopter and let their kids choose their own flight path.

The Maven won't hide their disappointment when their child diverges too far from the yellow brick road laid out for them. But Maven parents might have to accept a heartbreak when their kid turns down the college swim team scholarship (all those years in the pool!) or opts to spend the summer backpacking with friends over the fancy family villa rental in Mallorca.

"My son refused to go to his eighth-grade graduation dance," says Darlene, a Maven. "I have to admit, I was bummed out. For starters, I was hoping to chaperone. But also, I never missed a dance when I was growing up, and I don't want him to lose the chance to make memories."

Darlene took a pause, talked to (many) friends, and recognized that her son, an Authority, was a very different child than she'd been. What mattered to her did not mean much to him. Luckily, Mavens are adaptable at the end of the day, and she was able to accept his choice.

Keep your own interests alive. About that nest? At a certain point, the Maven's baby birds will fly off and there *will* be feelings about it. If the Maven has organized their entire social life around their kid's hobbies and interests, the adjustment will be hard. Bethany, a Maven novelist friend, travels a few times a year to writing conferences and workshops. "I think it's healthy for my kids to grow up understanding that they'll be fine if Mommy's not there for a few days," she asserts. We very much agree!

THE I*AM TYPES AS CHILDREN

They say that kids don't come with instructions, but with the I*AM System, we beg to differ! Understanding whether a child is an Innovator, Authority, or Maven makes a huge difference in how parents and educators alike can support their development.

While adult role models, parents, and guardians can do their best to guide children, there's no "one size fits all" method to raise them successfully. What works for one kid in a family or classroom won't necessarily work for another—and once again, the Astrology Advantage can supply a rough template that helps you understand the "junior edition" of each I*AM archetype. By giving these impressionable souls a little more of what they need, including boundaries and structure, we can help them become happy, well-adjusted citizens when they're all grown up.

I*AM Kids: What They're Like

The Innovator Kid is a **wide-eyed trailblazer**
who **craves autonomy** and wants to do it **"my way."**

The Authority Kid likes to **learn the rules** and thrives on
positive feedback and **hard-earned praise.**

The Maven Kid loves **sharing** and **interaction**
and wants to know **"why"** about everything!

The Innovator Child

Learns through:
experience, experimentation, doing it "my way"

Encourage them to:
express their uniqueness, slow down, and read directions

Steer them away from:
hogging the spotlight, bossing other kids around

Traits of the Innovator Child

Bossypants. Who's in charge here anyway? The Innovator child will find a way to get what they want, no matter what you tell them. They're not so much devious as they are determined, though they're not above a little sneaking around. These kids know what they like and what they don't. The tricky part for parents of these headstrong kiddos is supporting the young Innovator's unfettered self-expression while also teaching them to respect rules and boundaries.

Negotiators. Want to create a miniature mutiny? Refuse to let your Innovator child quit gymnastics or piano lessons when they ask to, even if they have talent for it. "But you've invested so many years into this!" or "You're just one award away from a scholarship!" The Innovator child doesn't want to hear it.

It's a slippery slope for parents of Innovators to know when to hold or fold. On the one hand, parents can be easily bulldozed by this "boss baby," and it's up to you to provide guidance. Sometimes, it does make sense to push these impatient little ones to stay the course. Other times, bargaining becomes a tool that works as a litmus test with Innovator children. "If you quit the swim team, you have to replace it with another activity" is a good way of testing whether they're just trying to score some extra iPad hours or if they're genuinely not passionate about the activity.

Creatives. Innovator kids were born to break the mold! With their cardinal sign–heavy charts, they lead by example, playing and creating freely as if to show the rest of the kids, *See, you can do it too!* Parents of Innovators would do well to encourage their little one's uniqueness. Be warned, however, that this may result in lopsided report cards. Even as kids, Innovators are specialists, preferring to excel in one or two favorite subjects and paying little mind to the rest.

That was certainly the case for us! Art and reading came easily to us and we never met a tub of Play-Doh or a Little Golden Book we didn't like. Our dad, an Innovator like us, gave us some STEAM activities when he bought us a chemistry set and mini microscope, but it was never our favorite. We always had to study harder for science class, but that early encouragement got us through AP Chemistry and Physics. For best results, make learning fun and exploratory for the Innovator kid, and work with them one-on-one.

Learning Style: Innovator

The creative Innovator is happiest in a state of discovery, when everything is rich with potential and possibility. Spark their imaginations by showing them colorful examples of what's possible. Innovators are originals, but it helps anchor them when they can see what's already been done. This also gets the wheels turning. Then, step back and watch the Innovator do it their way, taking risks and breaking the mold.

Give the Innovator ample free rein and you won't have to work so hard to engage them. Let them use every single color in the paint set. Invite them to choose the book *they* want to write about for their report. Give them lots of supplies to play with. Experimentation is what motivates young Innovators to learn. Subjects with a lot of rules, like math, may require some other motivational tools, like a quarter (or digital coins for their favorite game) for every problem correctly solved. That way, the Innovator can think about what they'll explore *after* they get through the grunt work.

Definitely give them *some* sort of parameters; ideally written down so the Innovator can see where the red lines are that they don't want to cross. We've seen Innovator kids do the completely wrong homework assignment because they didn't have the page number in front of them when they started.

Innovator kids live in the future and struggle to slow down and take in directions. They get restless and impatient and just want to get it done. For this reason, it can help to teach them things one step at a time. *First, we'll find all the verbs in this paragraph, then we'll circle the nouns.*

One-on-one tutoring may be necessary, or at the very least, extra time with a helpful adult or older sibling when they do their homework. The dreamy Innovator can easily zone out in class and gets impatient having to follow the pace of the herd. A tutor or private lesson can ignite their interest and help the Innovator student discover that they're actually *good* at a subject they thought they hated. Turns out, they were just restless and bored.

The Authority Child

Learns through:
repetition, clear instructions, taking on responsibilities

Encourage them to:
share their toys, self-soothe, explore creativity, play!

Steer them away from:
comparing and despairing, taking everything personally
(sticks and stones)

Traits of the Authority Child

Pleasers. Because Authorities have an inborn need for rules and structure, they are often the ones branded the "good kids." They certainly know how to charm the grown-ups. Observant souls, Authorities figure out how to please their parents and teachers and get the praise they thrive on.

If you have a "perfect" Authority child, don't just write it off as a sweet relief. Your kid might be easy for you to parent, but hard on themselves. It's possible that they're behaving in this grown-up way because they don't feel 100 percent safe to make a mistake. In cases like this, adding more structure and routine to their days can help. Give the Authority a bedtime, regular mealtimes, and a nap if necessary.

Like every other kid out there, the Authority child has a mischievous streak. They're just sneakier about their rebellious moves. There may come a day when you're shocked by something your Authority kid did, even if the proof is staring you in the face.

Competitors. Authorities are the high achievers of the playground and may do whatever it takes to win—collecting the most charms, hurling a dodgeball mercilessly. Their in-it-to-win-it attitudes might earn them honor roll status, but parents of Authorities would be wise to encourage good sportsmanship in their little ones. Otherwise, Authority kids can get outright snobby, looking down on kids who don't perform the way they do in whatever area the Authority deems important—academics, style, sports, music. In worst-case scenarios, this might even show up as bullying.

Losing can be rough on these kids. They may fall into a "compare and despair" hole when someone else shines brighter than they do. Underneath it all, Authority kids struggle with overly high standards and perfectionism. They need lots of encouragement to play and make mistakes. Be sure to praise your Authority for their quirks, too, and steer them toward activities they don't have to be "the best" at.

Risk-avoiders. Authorities love comfort. As a result, they can be cautious, play-it-safe kids who get stuck in a rut. Many have fixed mindsets, getting stuck in "right or wrong" thinking and failing to experiment after they've learned one way of doing things. Encouraging risk-taking and a growth mindset would be a good plan for parents of Authorities; however, change can stir up anxiety for these little ones. Teach them techniques for self-soothing: hugging a teddy bear, taking three deep breaths, counting sheep—anything meditative will do.

Possessive. Mine! The Authority child is possessive—of their things, of their siblings, friends, parents, toys—you name it! As adorable as it is to have your Authority child organize a family movie night, they may have pre-designated seating for everyone so that they can be in close proximity to their favorite person of the moment.

Sharing is a mixed bag for these kids who aren't keen to let just any old playmate touch their precious toys. While parents might be embarrassed by their young Authority's refusal to allow a visiting kid to get close to their Barbie Dreamhouse, pushing the Authority to share on the spot is not advised. There's a good chance this kid has a reason for guarding their favorite toy like a state secret. These kids understand boundaries—at least, about their possessions.

As soon as you get a private moment with your kid, ask them to explain their logic. Then, help them understand the benefits of sharing. Next time they have a friend over, they might put their off-limits toys in a closet or somewhere else out of reach while placing shareables out for group playtime.

Learning Style: Authority

Lather, rinse, repeat: that's the trifecta when it comes to teaching the Authority basically anything. These systems-loving kids will catch on after a few tries, and once they do, they make it their mission to master their craft. Ophi's stepdaughter Clementine, who has eleven Authority placements, learned how to apply makeup as a teen, then parlayed her lessons into a thriving YouTube channel offering tutorials. After amassing over forty thousand subscribers by her senior year of high school, Clementine was regularly stopped on the street and sent enough merch to never *have* to spend a cent in Sephora. (Which didn't stop her from shopping there all the same.)

The structured Authority wants to know the beginning, middle, and end of an assignment. What's the ultimate goal? To captivate this little one's interest, paint an exciting picture of the reward at the end of the mission. Then, reverse engineer the process, checking off milestones along the way. Whether you're baking cookies or doing long division, explain the purpose of what they're about to learn.

Praise is a great motivator for Authorities who are the "shiny gold star" kids of the I*AM archetypes. They love hearing you brag about them to friends. "Phoebe was so amazing at swim practice today. You should have seen her on the high dive! So brave and graceful!"

These achievers also thrive when there's a prize at the end. Set firm expectations and watch them perform. "I need you to finish your homework by four thirty" then follow up with a reward. "When you do, you can have one of the cupcakes I baked and get thirty minutes of iPad time." Done deal!

The Maven Child

Learns through:

interactivity, travel, reading directions

Encourage them to:

get involved in groups, explore their sense of wonder,

ask before they touch

Steer them away from:

touching the hot stove, climbing on the roof, ignoring rules

Traits of the Maven Child

Team players. The playful Maven loves to connect and share. These kids thrive in group activities—provided, of course, they are actually into the extracurricular and not being forced to play along. One Maven we know was flunking out of every class his sophomore year because he was "basically just bored." Then, the cross-country coach saw him dashing down the hall and blew the whistle . . . to recruit him for the track team. Our friend wound up graduating with a not awful GPA and joining the Coast Guard, a huge 180!

For best results, get your Maven involved in clubs and sports when they're young. For one thing, these active kids need to burn off energy, so physical activity is always advised. But any sort of organized pursuit where their social skills shine will do the trick—Scouts, marching band, theater, chess club—whatever allows them to interact and create something in concert with other kids.

Side note: Maven kids can be *so* social that they fail to cultivate a strong sense of self. This can lead to feelings of emptiness and abandonment when they are left alone for more than a few minutes at a time. Encourage them to express their feelings through art or keeping a diary. There's nothing more powerful than a Maven who knows their own mind!

Baby Einsteins. Curious Mavens have a natural sense of wonder and discovery. They like to figure out how things work and may amaze you when you set them down with toys that capture their ingenious imaginations: Legos, chemistry sets, baking ingredients, electronic equipment. Even if they struggle to concentrate in class, hand them a set of directions and they'll pore over them, teaching you the steps to building the model.

Since Maven kids have a knack for finding a needle in a haystack, turn mundane activities into scavenger hunts. Reward them for their finds. Then, don't be surprised if they start making up contests for their peers to play along with.

Daredevils. "Hot stove, don't touch"? Those rules don't seem to apply to the young Maven (or the Maven at any age, come to think of it). Danger seems to lure these little ones in with a mysteriously magnetic force field. We know a Maven whose mother put him on a leash as a kid, just to keep him from climbing onto rooftops and pulling down clothing racks at every department store.

The Maven just wants to see what would happen if they tried. Maybe they're the one who can defy gravity and sprout a pair of wings as they leap from that tree branch. Yikes! There's no denying that it can be stressful to parent these kids.

While your young Maven may never stop making your heart drop in your chest, you can minimize potential issues. How? By explaining exactly what will happen if the Maven takes the risk. Be matter-of-fact; don't speak in a fearful tone. Just help the Maven understand the mechanics of gravity and how a fall might impact their bones and what a shame it would be to have a cast on all summer and not get to swim in the pool. Losing out on playtime is often enough to keep the Maven from risky moves.

Boundary issues. Where does "yours" begin and "ours" end? Most kids don't share quite the same way that generous Mavens do. Hurt feelings—and playground fights—can erupt when the young Maven assumes that everything in their line of sight is fair game. They have to learn not to put their hands in everything. These tactile kids may grab stuff, touch things that aren't theirs, even give hugs without asking. Permission and consent are things Mavens need to learn about early to prevent innocent mistakes.

Learning Style: Maven

Rule number one: your Maven kid is probably not going to be a traditional learner, so adjust your mindset right now. While there are plenty of Maven academics, the scholastic grading system is no reflection on the intelligence level of this kid. Fidgety Mavens hate to sit still and may be branded the troublemaker, class clown, or ADD kid in the traditional school environment. It's a shame, since their true talents are often not fostered as a result. If schools measured ingenuity and social intelligence, your little Maven would get straight As.

Mavens are like mini philosophers who do well learning by the student-teacher dialogue of the Socratic method—one that's certainly not popular in modern schools. Mavens don't just want to copy and paste the right answers. They're curious about why things are the way they are. Teachers may get frustrated by the Maven's habit of shooting a hand in the air every two minutes, but these kids truly want to grasp a concept. When they're allowed to ask a flurry of questions, they *will* have their lightbulb moment.

Play-based learning works wonders with little Mavens. Anything that can be gamified will capture their attention. Even better if it's interactive and the Maven can engage with other kids in the lesson, discussing, digesting, and celebrating a team victory.

Conclusion:

Making I*AM Part of Your Life

Hopefully after finishing this book, you have a deeper understanding of yourself and the people around you. With I*AM at your fingertips, you have a code for coexisting that you can tap into anytime.

You now have the Astrology Advantage—the ability to look at anyone's I*AM profile and understand their desires and motives. You can build healthier relationships and teams. You can set clear expectations and boundaries. You understand your own cosmic operating system, and if our wish is fulfilled, you feel more potent and powerful because of it.

Of course, we understand that no personality system will be 100 percent accurate for anyone, nor is it supposed to be. Archetypes, like characters in a novel or stage play, are meant to provide a teachable mirror. They jump-start the inner work and spark self-awareness, then they hand the keys to you. Just because you have the Astrology Advantage doesn't mean you have to use it. The choice is yours. (Contrary to what some think, astrology and free will are complementary, not opposite.)

As with anything, take the best and leave the rest. If you felt validated and "seen" by the I*AM System and this book, download those positive emotions and let them take root. If you learned a smarter and more self-affirming way to give feedback, manage time, dress for a date, or set up a vibrant environment—we'd love to hear your story.

Keep in touch with us at astrostyle.com/iam, where you'll find empowering resources to help you use the I*AM System and supplement this book. Thank you for letting us share our life's work with you. Go forth and thrive!

Ophira & Tali Edut
February 10, 2024
New York City

Acknowledgments

To our parents, Rabbi Dorit and Shimon Edut, who nurtured our Innovator spirits, encouraged every dream we've had, and taught us by example to live a life of creativity, appreciating both the heavens and the earth.

Heartfelt and eternal gratitude to our luminous literary agent Jackie Ashton (Pisces Authority) and our earth angel editor Ronnie Alvarado (Capricorn Innovator) for making this dream book into reality.